COLLECTED LEGAL PAPERS

BY

OLIVER WENDELL HOLMES

THE LAWBOOK EXCHANGE, LTD.

Clark, New Jersey

ISBN-13: 9781584776116 (hardcover)
ISBN-13: 9781616190620 (paperback)

Lawbook Exchange edition 2006, 2010

The quality of this reprint is equivalent to the quality of the original work.

THE LAWBOOK EXCHANGE, LTD.

33 Terminal Avenue
Clark, New Jersey 07066-1321

*Please see our website for a selection of our other publications
and fine facsimile reprints of classic works of legal history:*
www.lawbookexchange.com

Library of Congress Cataloging-in-Publication Data

Holmes, Oliver Wendell, 1841-1935.
  Collected legal papers / Oliver Wendell Holmes.
    v. cm.
  Originally published: New York : Harcourt, Brace and Howe, 1920.
  Includes bibliographical references.
  Contents: Early English equity -- The law, speech, 1885 -- The pro-
fession of the law : part of an address, 1886 -- On receiving the degree
of LLD : speech, 1886 -- The use of law schools : oration, 1886 --
Agency, 1891 -- Privilege, malice, and intent, 1894 -- Learning and
science : speech, 1895 -- Executors, 1895 -- The bar as a profession,
1896.
  ISBN 1-58477-611-0 (alk. paper)
  1. Law.   I. Title.
KF213.H6 2005
340--dc22

                                          2005027608

Printed in the United States of America on acid-free paper

COLLECTED
LEGAL PAPERS

BY

OLIVER WENDELL HOLMES

NEW YORK
HARCOURT, BRACE AND COMPANY

THE PLIMPTON PRESS
NORWOOD·MASS·U·S·A

CONTENTS

PREFACE

This collection has been made by the kindness of a friend, Mr. Harold J. Laski, and I owe him thanks for gathering these little fragments of my fleece that I have left upon the hedges of life. They are printed as they appeared and I have been unable to do more than run my eye over them, but I am glad to see them put together in a book, as they offer some views of law and life that I have not expressed elsewhere so fully. The place of original publication is given at the head of each paper, and I thank the several publishers for their assent to the reprint.

A later generation has carried on the work that I began nearly half a century ago, and it is a great pleasure to an old warrior who cannot expect to bear arms much longer, that the brilliant young soldiers still give him a place in their councils of war.

OLIVER WENDELL HOLMES

June 15, 1920
WASHINGTON, D.C.

EARLY ENGLISH EQUITY *

I. Uses

At the end of the reign of Henry V. the Court of Chancery was one of the established courts of the realm. I think we may assume that it had already borrowed the procedure of the Canon law, which had been developed into a perfected system at the beginning of the thirteenth century, at about the same time that the Chancellor became the most important member of the King's Council. It had the "Examination and oath of the parties according to the form of the civil law and the law of Holy Church in subversion of the common law."[1] It had the subpoena, which also it did not invent,[2] and it had a form of decree requiring personal obedience.[3]

* Law Quarterly Review, Vol. 1, p. 162. (1885.)

[1] Rot. Parl. 84 (3 Hen. V. pt. 2. 46, No. 23).

[2] See writ addressed to sheriff, Rot. Claus. 16 Hen. III. m. 2 dorso in 1 Royal Letters, Hen. III (Rolls ed.), 523. Proc. Privy Council (Nicholas) passim. Stat. 20 Ed. III, c. 5. The penalty was usually money, but might be life and limb; 1 Proc. Priv. Counc. (21 R. II. A.D. 1397). The citation of Rot. Parl. 14 Ed. III, in 1 Roll. Abr. 372, which misleads Spence (1 Eq. 338n.) and earlier and later writers, should be 14 Ed. IV. (6 Rot. Parl. 143), as pointed out already by Blackstone, 3 Comm. 52 n. We also find the writ *Quibusdam certis de causis,* a writ in the form of the subpoena except that it omitted the penalty; Palgrave, King's Council, pp. 131, 132, note X; Scaldewell v. Stormesworth, 1 Cal. Ch. 5.

[3] See Audeley v. Audeley, Rot. Claus. 40 Ed. III, *"sur peine de sys*

1

Down to the end of the same reign (Henry V.) there is no evidence of the Chancery having known or enforced any substantive doctrines different from those which were recognized in the other courts except two. One of them, a peculiar view of contract, has left no traces in modern law. But the other is the greatest contribution to the substantive law which has ever been set down to the credit of the Chancery. I refer to Uses, the parent of our modern trusts. I propose to discuss these two doctrines in a summary way as the first step toward answering the question of the part which Equity has played in the development of English law.

As a preliminary, I ought to state that I assume without discussion that the references to *aequitas* in Glanvill, Bracton, and some of the early statutes passed before the existence of a Chancery, have no bearing on that question.[4] I ought also to say that the matters of grace and favour which came before the Council and afterwards before the Chancellor do not appear to have been matters in which the substantive rules of the common law needed to be or

mill livres au paier au roy," cited Palg. King's Council, 67, 68; 2 Cal. Ch. x. See prayer in 3 Rot. Parl. 61 (2 R. II. 26). Imprisonment for contempt again is older than the Chancery, e.g. Mem. in Scacc. 27 (M. 22 Ed. I) in Maynard's Y. B., part 1.

[4] Glanvill, Prologus, Bracton, fol. 23b; *ib.* 3b, *"Aequitas quasi aequalitas."* Fleta, II. C. 55, § 9. Petition of Barons, C. 27 (A.D. 1258), in Annals of Burton (Rolls ed.), 443, and Stubbs, Select Charters, for remedy *ex aequitate juris* by writ of entry or otherwise. *Dictum de Kenilworth,* pr. (A.D. 1266) Stat. of Realm, 51 Hen. III, and Stubbs, Select Charters; Close Rolls of Hen. III, cited in Hardy, Int. to Close Rolls, xxviii. n. 5 (8vo. ed. p. III). So "right and equite," letter missive of Hen. V. to Chancellor, I Cal. Ch. xvi.

were modified by new principles, but were simply cases which, being for some reason without the juris-diction of the King's ordinary courts, either were brought within that jurisdiction by special order, or were adjudged directly by the Council or the Chan-cellor according to the principles of the ordinary courts.[5]

I agree with the late Mr. Adams[6] that the most

[5] Supervisory powers of Council over the Court, I. Gesta Hen. II. (Ben. Abbas, Rolls ed.), 207, 208; Assize of Northampton, §7, *ib.* 110; and in Stubbs, Select Charters. Jurisdiction of *Curia Regis* over pleas of land, not coming there as a matter of course, acquired by special order: "*Quod debeat vel dominus Rex velit in curia sua deduci*"; Glanv. I. C. 5. Jurisdiction of actions of contract *de gratia;* Bracton, fol. 100 a; Case referred by Chancellor to Curia Regis, 38 Ed. III., Hardy Int. to Close Rolls, xxix (8vo. ed. 113 n). Grants of jurisdiction *de gratia* in the form of Special Commissions of oyer and terminer complained of Palgr. King's Council, §§ 12, 13, pp. 27–33; Stat. Westm. ii (13 Ed. I), Ch. 29; 1 Rot. Parl. 290 (8 Ed. II. No. 8); Stat. Northampton (2 Ed. III.), C. 7; 2 Rot. Parl. 286, 38 Ed. III. 14, No. VI; 3 Rot. Parl. 161 (7 R. II. No. 43).

As to cases terminated before the Council, see Rot. Claus. 8 Ed. I. m. 6 dorso, in Ryley, Plac. Parl. 442, and in 2 Stubbs, Const. Hist. 263. n. 1; 2 Rot. Parl. 228 (25 Ed. III. No. 16; cf. No. 19). 3 Rot. Parl. 44 (3 R. II. No. 49) seems mistranslated by Parkes, Hist. Ct. of Ch. 39, 40. Matters at common law and of grace to be pursued before the Chancellor; Rot. Claus. 22 Ed. III. p. 2, m. 2 dorso, cited Hardy, Int. to Close Rolls, xxviii. (8vo. Ed. 110), and Parkes, Hist. Court of Ch. 35, 36 n. See Stat. 27 Ed. III. st. 1, C. 1; Stat. 36 Ed. III. st. 1, C. 9. All the reported cases in Chancery through Henry V., with the exceptions which have been mentioned, are trespasses, dis-seisins, and the like. And the want of remedy at law is generally due to maintenance and the power of the defendant, or in one instance to the technical inability of the plaintiff to sue the defendant (2 Cal. Ch. viii), not to the nature of the right invoked. The object of the repeated prayers of the Commons from Richard II. to Henry VI, directed against the Council and the Chancellor, was that common law cases should be tried in the regular courts, not that the ancient doctrine might prevail over a younger and rival system. See Adams, Equity, Introduction, xxxiii–xxxv.

[6] Adams, Equity, Introd. xxxv.

important contribution of the Chancery has been its (borrowed) procedure. But I wish to controvert the error that its substantive law is merely the product of the procedure. And, on the other hand, I wish to show that the Chancery, in its first establishment at least, did not appear as embodying the superior ethical standards of a comparatively modern state of society correcting the defects of a more archaic system. With these objects in view, I proceed to consider the two peculiar doctrines which I have mentioned.

First, as to Uses. The feoffee to uses of the early English law corresponds point by point to the salman of the early German law, as described by Beseler fifty years ago.[7] The salman, like the feoffee, was a person to whom land was transferred in order that he might make a conveyance according to his grantor's directions.[8] Most frequently the conveyance

---

[7] Beseler, Erbvertragen, I § 16, pp. 277 et seq., 283, 271.

[8] Beseler, I. §§ 15, 16; Heusler, Gewere, 478. Compare 2 Cal Ch. iii; 1 id. xviii. and passim. "Pernancy of profits, execution of estates, and defence of the land, are the three points of the trust" or use. Bacon, Reading on Stat. of Uses, Works (ed. Spedding), VII. p. 401; 1 Cruise, Dig. Title XI., Ch. 2, § 6; see Tit. XII., Ch. 1, § 3; Ch. 4, § 1. Some of the first feoffments to the use (ad opus) of another than the feoffee which I have found mentioned by that name seem to have been a means of conveying property to the cestui que use in his absence, very like the earliest employment of the salman. But as the conveyances are supposed to be made to servants of private persons (Bract. fol. 193 b) or officers of the king, it may be doubtful whether any inference can be drawn from them; 1 Royal Letters, Henry III. pp. 122, 420; cf. 421 (A.D. 1220, 1223). Compare Provisions of Oxford (Oath of guardians of king's castles) in Annals of Burton (Rolls ed.), 448, and Stubbs, Select Charters; it seems doubtful whether the expression ad opus was used at first in a technical sense, e.g. "castellum Dofris — ad opus meum te facturum," Eadmer (Rolls ed.), 7. "Ad

was to be made after the grantor's death, the grantor reserving the use of the land to himself during his life.[9] To meet the chance of the salman's death before the time for conveyance was over, it was common to employ more than one,[10] and persons of importance were selected for the office.[11] The essence of the relation was the *fiducia* or trust reposed in the *fidelis manus*,[12] who sometimes confirmed his obligation by an oath or covenant.[13]

This likeness between the salman and the feoffee to uses would be enough, without more, to satisfy me that the latter was the former transplanted. But there is a further and peculiar mark which, I think, must convince every one, irrespective of any general views as to the origin of the common law.

Beseler has shown that the executor of the early German will was simply a salman whose duty it

opus ejusdem mulieris," 2 Gesta Hen. II. (Ben. Abbas, Rolls ed.), 160, 161; Y. B. 3 Ed. III. 5 pl. 13; 2 Rot. Parl. 286 (38 Ed. III. 14 No. vi).

But as early as 22 Ass. pl. 72, fol. 101, in the case of a gift alleged to be fraudulent, we find the court inquiring who took the profits, and on the inquest answering that the donor did, Thorp declares that the gift only made the donee guardian of the chattels to the use of the donor. See further St. 7 R. II., Ch. 12.

[9] Beseler, I., § 16, pp. 277 *et seq.;* Heusler, supra. Nearly every feoffment mentioned in the Calendars of Proceedings in Chancery down to the end of Henry VI. is for the purpose of distribution, after death. I Cal. Ch. xxi, xxxv, xliii, liv, lv, lvi; 2 *id.,* iii, xix, xx, xxi, xxii, xxxiii, xxxvi, etc. Abbrev. Plac. 179, col. 2, Norht rot. 15 do.; *ib.* 272, H. 9 Ed. I., Suff. rot. 17. Fitz. Abr. *Subpena,* pl. 22, 23; Littleton, § 462.

[10] Beseler, I., p. 283; 2 Cal. Ch. iii.

[11] Beseler, I., p. 271.

[12] Beseler, I., p. 267: *"Fidei suae committens,"* *ib.* 286. Compare the references to good faith in all the bills in Cal. Ch.

[13] Beseler, I, pp. 265–267; 2 Cal. Ch. iii, xxviii; 1 *id.* lv.

was to see legacies and so forth paid if the heirs refused. The *heres institutus* being unknown, the
foreign law which introduced wills laid hold of the
native institution as a means of carrying them
into effect. Under the influence of the foreign law
an actual transfer of the property ceased to be required. It was enough that the testator designated
the executors and that they accepted the trust; and
thus it was that their appointment did not make the
will irrevocable, as a gift with actual delivery for
distribution after the donor's death would have
been.[14]

There can be no doubt of the identity of the continental executor and the officer of the same name
described by Glanvill; and thus the connection between the English and the German law is made certain. The executor described by Glanvill was not
a universal successor. Indeed, as I have shown in
my book on the Common Law, the executor had not
come to be so regarded, nor taken the place of the
heir in the King's courts even as late as Bracton.
To save space I do not copy Glanvill's words, but
it will be seen on reading that the function of the
executor was not to pay debts — that was the heir's
business,[15] but to cause to stand the reasonable division of the testator as against the heirs.[16] The mean-

---

[14] Beseler, Erbverträgen, I., pp. 284–288; Brunner in I Holtzendorff, Encyclop. (3rd ed.), 216; cf. Littleton, § 168, Hob. 348, Dyer,
314 pl., 97, Finch, Law 33.

[15] Glanv. VII., C. 8; see XIII. C. 15; Dial. de Scaccario, II., 18;
Regiam Majestatem, II., C. 39.

[16] Glanv. VII., C. 6–8.

ing of this function will be further explained when I come to deal with the rights of the *cestui que use*.[17]

The executor had already got his peculiar name in Glanvill's time, and it would rather seem that already it had ceased to be necessary for the testator to give him possession or seizin. But, however this may be, it is certain that when the testator's tenements were devisable by custom, the executor was put in possession either by the testator in his lifetime or else immediately after the testator's death. As late as Edward I. "it seemed to the court as to tenements in cities and boroughs which are left by will (*que legata sunt*) and concerning which there should be no proceeding in the King's Court, because it belongs to the ecclesiastical forum,[18] that first

---

[17] As to the functions of the executor in the time of Bracton, see The Common Law, 348, 349, and further, Bracton, fol. 407b, "*Et sicut dantur haeredibus contra debitores et non executoribus ita dantur actiones creditoribus contra haeredes et non contra executores.*" *Ibid.* fol. 98a, 101a, 113b; Stat. 3 Ed. I., Ch. 19. The change of the executor to universal sucessor upon the obvious analogy of the *haeres* was inevitable, and took place shortly after Bracton wrote. It was held that debt lay against and for executors; Y. B. 20 & 21 Ed. I, 374; 30 Ed. I., 238. See further, Stat. Westm. II. 13 Ed. I., C. 19, 23, (A.D. 1285); Fleta, II. C. 62, §§ 8–13; C. 70, § 5; and C. 57, §§ 13, 14, copying, but modifying, Bract. fol. 61a, b, 407b supra. As to covenant, see Y. B. 48 Ed. III., 1, 2, pl. 4. The heir ceased to be bound unless named; Fleta, II. C. 62, § 10; The Common Law, 348; cf. Fitz. Abr. *Dett*, pl. 139 (P. 13 Ed. III.). Finally, Doctor and Student, i. c. 19, *ad finem*, speaks of "the heir which in the law of England is called the executor." In early English, as in early German law, neither heir (Y. B. 32 & 33 Ed. I., 507, 508) nor executor was liable for the parol debts of ancestor or testator (Y. B. 22, Ed. I., 456; 41 Ed. III., 13, pl. 3; 11 Hen. VII. 26; 12 Hen. VIII. 11, pl. 3; Dr. and Stud. II, Ch. 24), because not knowing the facts they could not wage their law: Y. B. 22 Ed. I., 456; Laband, Vermogensrechtlichen Klagen, pp. 15, 16.

[18] Cf. Bract., fol. 407b.

after the death of the testator the will should be
proved before the ordinary, and the will having been
proved, the mayor and bailiffs of the city ought to
deliver seizin of the devised and devisable tenements
(*de tenementis legatis et que sunt legabilia*) to the
executors of the will saving the rights of every one."[19]
A little later the executor ceased to intervene at all,
and the devisees might enter directly, or if the heir
held them out, might have the writ *Ex gravi
querela*.[20]

If, as I think, it is sufficiently clear that in the
reign of Edward I. the distinction between an executor and a feoffee to uses was still in embryo, it is
unnecessary to search the English books for evidence
of the first stage when the testator transferred possession in his own lifetime. A case in 55 Henry III.
shows executors seized for the purpose of applying
the land to pious uses under a last will, and defending
their seizin in their official capacity, but does not disclose how they obtained possession.[21] A little earlier

[19] Abbr. Plac. 284, 285 (H. 19 Ed. I. Devon, rot. 51). Note the
likening of such tenements to chattels, Bract. 407b; 40 Ass. pl. 41; Co.
Lit. 111a.

[20] 39 Ass. pl. 6, fol. 232, 233, where there is no question of the
executor, but special custom determines whether the devisee shall enter,
be put in by the bailiff, or have the writ. In Littleton's time the
devisee's right of entry was general: § 167; Co. Lit. 111. As to the
writ, see 40 Ass. pl. 41. fol. 250; F. N. B. 198 L. *et seq;* Co. Lit. 111.
The only writ mentioned by Glanvill seems to be given to the executor, or if there is no executor to the propinqui; lib. VII., C. 6, 7. Of
course I am not speaking of cases where the executors were also the
devisees, although even in such cases there was a tendency to deny them
any estate, if there was a trust; 39 Ass. pl. 17; Litt. § 169.

[21] Abbrev. Plac. 179, col. 2; Norht, rot, 15 in dorso.

still Matthew Paris speaks of one who, being too weak to make a last will, makes a friend *expressorem et executorem*.[22] It is a little hard to distinguish between such a transaction and a feoffment to uses by a few words spoken on a death-bed, such as is recorded in the reign of Henry VI.[23] But the most striking evidence of the persistence of ancient custom was furnished by King Edward III. in person, who enfeoffed his executors, manifestly for the purpose of making such distribution after his death as he should direct; but because he declared no trust at the time, and did not give his directions until afterwards, the judges in Parliament declared that the executors were not bound, or, as it was then put, that there was no condition.[24]

Gifts *inter vivos* for distribution after death remained in use till later times.[25] And it may be accident, or it may be a reminiscence of ancient tradition, when, under Edward IV., the Court, in holding that executors cannot have account against one to whom the testator has given money to dispose of for the good of his soul, says that as to that money the donee is the executor.[26]

[22] 4 Matt. Paris, Chron. Maj. (Rolls ed.), 605, A.D. 1247.

[23] 1 Cal. Ch. xliii; S. C. Digby, Hist. Law of Real Prop. (2nd ed.) 301, 302. Cf Heusler, Gewere, 478, citing Meichelbeck (1 Hist. Fris. Pars instrumentaria), No. 300; "*Valida egritudine depressus traditionem in manus proximorum suorum posuit, eo modo, si ipse ea egritudine obisset, ut vice illius traditionem perfecissent.*"

[24] 3 Rot. Parl. 60, 61 (2R. II Nos. 25, 26).

[25] Babington v. Gull, I Cal. Ch. lvi, Mayhewe v. Gardener, 1 Cal. Ch. xcix, c.

[26] Y. B. 8 Ed. IV, 5, pl. 12. In Mayhewe v. Gardener, 1 Cal. Ch.

At all events, from an early date, if not in Glanvill's time, the necessity of a formal delivery of devised land to the executor was got rid of in England as Beseler says that it was on the Continent. The law of England did in general follow its continental original in requiring the two elements of *traditio* and *investitura* for a perfect conveyance.[27] But the Church complained of the secular courts for requiring a change of possession when there was a deed.[28]   And it was perhaps because wills belonged to the spiritual jurisdiction that the requirement was relaxed in the case of executors.   As has been shown above, in the reign of Edward I. possession was not delivered until after the testator's death, and in that of Edward III. it had ceased to be delivered to them at all.   Possibly, however, a trace of the fact that originally they took by conveyance may be found in the notion that executors take directly from the will even before probate, still repeated as a distinction between executors and administrators.[29]

It is now time to consider the position of the *cestui que use.* The situations of the feoffor or

---

xcix, c. the defendant, who has received all the property of a deceased person by gift in trust to pay debts, etc., was decreed to pay dilapidations for which the deceased was liable.

[27] Glanv. vii., Ch. 1, § 3; Annals of Burton (Rolls ed.), 421 (A.D. 1258); Bracton, fols. 38a, b, 39b, 169b, 194b, 213b, § 3, 214b; Abbr. Plac. 272 (H. 9 Ed. I), Suff. rot. 17; 1 Cal. Ch. liv, lv; Beseler, Erbverträgen, I. § 15, p. 261; § 16, pp. 277 *et seq.;* Heusler, Gewere, pp. 1, 2: Sohm. Ehschliessung, p. 82; Schulte, Lehrb. d. Deutsch. R.u. Rechtsgesch, § 148 (5th ed.), pp. 480 *et seq.*

[28] Annals of Burton (Rolls ed.), 421 (A.D. 1258).

[29] Graysbrook *v.* Fox, Plowd, 275, 280, 281.

donor and of the ultimate beneficiaries were different, and must be treated separately. First, as to the former. In England, as on the Continent, upon the usual feoffment to convey after the feoffor's death, the feoffor remained on the land and took the profits during his life. Feoffors to uses are commonly called pernors of profits in the earliest English statutes and are shown in possession by the earliest cases.[30] As Lord Bacon says in a passage cited above, pernancy of the profits was one of the three points of a use. It was the main point on the part of the feoffor, as to make an estate, or convey as directed, was the main duty on the side of the feoffee. But all the German authorities agree that the pernancy of the profits also made the *gewere*, or protected possession, of early German law.[31] And in this, as in other particulars, the English law gave proof of its origin. In our real actions the mode of alleging seizin was to allege a taking of the esplees or profits.[32]

If the remedies of the ancient popular courts had been preserved in England, it may be conjectured that a *cestui que use* in possession would have been

[30] Stat. 50 Ed. III., Ch. 6; 1 R. II.,Ch. 9 *ad fin.;* 2 R. II. Stat. 2, Ch. 3; 15 R. II., Ch. 5; 4 Hen. IV., Ch. 7; 11 Hen. VI., Ch. 3, 5; 1 Hen. VII., Ch. 1; 19 Hen. VII., Ch. 15; Rothenhale *v.* Wychingham, 2 Cal. Ch. 3. (Hen. V.); Y. B. 27 Hen. VIII. 8; Plowden, 352; Litt. §§ 462, 464; Co. Lit. 272b So 1 Cruise, Dig. Tit. 12, Ch. 4, § 9: "if the trustee be in the actual possession of the estate (which scarce ever happens)."

[31] Heusler, Gewere, 51, 52, 59; Brunner, Schwurgerichte, 169, 170; Laband Vermogensrechtlichen Klagen, 160; 1 Franken, Französ. Pfandrecht, 6.

[32] Jackson, Real Actions, 348 and passim. See Statutes last cited, and Stat. 32 Hen. VIII, Ch. 9, § 4.

protected by the common law.[33]   He was not, because at an early date the common law was cut down
to that portion of the ancient customs which was
enforced in the courts of the King.   The recogni-
tions (assizes), which were characteristic of the royal
tribunals, were only granted to persons who stood in
a feudal relation to the King,[34] and to create such
a relation by the tenure of land, something more was
needed than *de facto* possession or pernancy of
profits.   In course of time the fact that the new
system of remedies did not extend itself to all the
rights which were known to the old law became
equivalent to a denial of the existence of the rights
thus disregarded.   The meaning of the word "seizin"
was limited to possession protected by the assizes,[35]
and a possession which was not protected by them
was not protected at all.   It will be remembered,
however, that a series of statutes more and more
likened the pernancy of the profits to a legal estate
in respect of liability and power, until at last the
statute of Henry VIII. brought back uses to the
courts of common law.[36]

It is not necessary to consider whether the denial
of the assizes to a *cestui que use* in possession was
peremptory and universal from the beginning, because the feoffor had another protection in the covenants which, in England as on the Continent, it was

[33] Franken, Französ. Pfandr., 6.

[34] Heusler, Gewere, 126, 423, 424.

[35] Heusler, Gewere, 424.

[36] See Statutes before cited, p. 11 n. 30, and 1 R. III. Ch. 1; 27
Hen. VIII., Ch. 10.

usual for him to take.[37]   For a considerable time the
Anglo-Norman law adhered to the ancient Frankish
tradition in not distinguishing between contract and
title as a ground for specific recovery, and allowed
land to be recovered in an action of covenant, so that
it would seem that one way or another feoffors
were tolerably safe.[38]

But *cestuis que use* in remainder were strangers
both to the covenant and the possession.   There was
an obvious difficulty in finding a ground upon which
they could compel a conveyance.   The ultimate
beneficiaries seem to have been as helpless against
the salman in the popular courts on the Continent
as they were against the feoffee in the Curia Regis.
Under these circumstances the Church, which was
apt to be the beneficiary in question, lent its aid.
Heusler thinks that the early history of these gifts
shows that they were fostered by the spiritual power
in its own interest, and that they were established in

---

[37] E. g. Rothenhale *v.* Wychingham, 2 Cal. Ch. 3.

[38] The Common Law, 400. See further, Ll. Gul. I., Ch. 23;
Statutum Walliae, 12 Ed. I, *"Breve de conventione, per quod petuntur
aliquando mobilia, aliquando immobilia"*; *"Per breve de conventione
aliquando petitur liberum tenementum."* Fleta, II. Ch. 65, § 12; Y. B.
22 Ed. I., 494, 496, 598, 600; 18 Ed. II. (Maynard), 602, 603; Fitz.
Abr. *Covenant*, passim.   This effect of covenant was preserved in the
case of fines until a recent date; 2 Bl. Comm. 349, 350, and App. IV.,
§ 1.   As to a term of years, see Bract, fol. 220a, § 1; Y. B. 20 Ed. I.,
254; 47 Ed. III., 24 (cf. 38 Ed. III., 24); F. N. B. 145 M; Andrews'
Case, Cro. Eliz. 214; S. C. 2 Leon. 104; and as to chattels, see Y. B.
27 Hen. VIII., 16.   As to the later raising of uses by way of covenant,
see Y. B. 27 Hen. VIII, 16; Bro. Abr. *Feoffments al Uses*, pl. 16;
Dyer, 55 (3); *ib.* 96 (40); *ib.* 162 (48); Sharington *v.* Strotton, Plowd.
298, 309.

the face of a popular struggle to maintain the ancient rights of heirs in the family property, which was inalienable without their consent.[39]   In view of the effort which the Church kept up for so long a time to assert jurisdiction in all matters of *fidei laesio,* it would seem that a ground for its interference might have been found in the *fiducia* which, as has been said, was of the essence of the relation, and which we find referred to in the earliest bills printed in the Chancery Calendars.

This is conjecture.   But it seems clear that on some ground the original forum for devisees was the Ecclesiastical Court.   Glanvill states that it belongs to the ecclesiastical courts to pass on the reasonableness of testamentary dispositions,[40] and, while he shows that the executor had the King's writ against the heir, gives no hint of any similar right of legatees or devisees against the executor.   The Decretals of Gregory disclose that a little later the Church compelled executors to carry out their testator's will,[41] and Bracton says in terms that legatees and devisees of houses in town or of an usufruct could sue in the ecclesiastical courts.[42]   As we have seen, in the case of houses in town the executor ceased to intervene, the ecclesiastical remedy against him became superfluous and devisees obtained a remedy directly

---

[39] Heusler, Gewere, 479 *et seq.* See Glanv. VII., Ch. 9, where the Church is shown to have the settlement of the question whether the will was reasonably made. Cf. *ib.* Ch. 1., § 3.

[40] Glanv. VII, Ch. 6 and 8.

[41] Decret. Greg. III. Tit. 26, cap. 19. A.D. 1235.

[42] Bract. fol. 407b, 61a, b.

against deforciants in the King's courts. But with regard to legacies, although after a time the Chancery became a competing, and finally, by St. 20 & 21 Vict. Ch. 77, s. 23, the exclusive jurisdiction, as late as James I. "the Lord Chancellor Egerton would say, the Ecclesiastical Courts were more proper for Legacies, and sometimes would send them thither." [43]

These courts were unable to deal with uses in the fulness of their later development. But the chief instances of feoffment upon trust, other than to the uses of a last will or for distribution after death, of which there is any record until sometime after the Chancery had become a separate court under Edward III. were for the various fraudulent purposes detailed in the successive petitions and statutes which have come down to us. [44] It should be mentioned too, that there are some traces of an attempt by *cestuis que use* who were strangers to the feoffment to enforce the trust by way of a condition in their favor, and it seems to have been put that way sometimes in the conveyances. [45]

For a considerable time, then, it would seem that both feoffors and other *cestuis que use* were well

[43] Nurse *v.* Bormes, Choyce Cases in Ch. 48. See further Glen *v.* Webster, 2 Lee, 31. As to common law, see Deeks *v* Strutt, 5 T.R. 690; Atkins *v.* Hill, Cowper, 284, and cases cited.

[44] Petition of Barons, C. 25 (Hen. III. A.D. 1258), Annals of Burton (Rolls ed.), 422; *id.* Stubbs, Select Charters; Irish Stat. of Kilkenny, 3 Ed. II., Ch. 4; Stat. 50 Ed. III., Ch. 6; 1 R. II., Ch. 9; 2 R. II., Stat. 2, Ch. 3; 7 R. II, Ch. 12; 15 R. II., Ch. 5; 4 Hen. IV., Ch. 7. See also Statute of Marlebridge, 52 Hen. III., Ch. 6.

[45] 2 Rot. Parl. 79 (3 R. II., Nos. 24, 25); *ib.* 60, 61 (2 R. II. Nos. 25, 26).

enough protected. The first complaint we hear is under Henry IV. It is of the want of a remedy when property is conveyed by way of *affiance* to perform the will of the grantors and feoffors and the feoffees make wrongful conveyances.[46] As soon as the need was felt, the means of supplying it was at hand. Nothing was easier than for the ecclesiastics who presided in Chancery to carry out there, as secular judges, the principles which their predecessors had striven to enforce in their own tribunals under the rival authority of the Church. As Chancellors they were free from these restrictions which confined them as churchmen to suits concerning matrimony and wills. Under Henry V. we find that *cestuis que use* had begun to resort to equity,[47] whereas under Richard II. the executors and feoffees of Edward III. had brought their bill for instructions before the Judges in Parliament.[48] In the next reign (Henry VI.) bills by *cestuis que use* become common. The foundations of the claim is the *fides*, the trust reposed and the obligation of good faith, and that circumstance remains as a mark at once of the Teutonic source of the right and the ecclesiastical origin of the jurisdiction.

If the foregoing argument is sound, it will be seen that the doctrine of uses is as little the creation of the subpoena, or of decrees requiring personal obedi-

---

[46] 3 Rot. Parl. 511 (4 Hen. IV., No. 112, A.D. 1402).

[47] Dodd *v.* Browning, 1 Cal., Ch. xiii; Rothenhale *v.* Wychingham, 2 Cal. Ch. iii.

[48] 2 Rot. Parl. 60, 61 (2 R. II., Nos. 25, 26).

ence, as it is an improvement invented in a relatively high state of civilization which the common law was too archaic to deal with. It is true, however, that the form of the remedy reacted powerfully upon the conception of the right. When the executor ceased to intervene between testator and devisee the connection between devises and uses was lost sight of And the common law courts having refused to protect even actual pernors of profits, as has been explained, the only place where uses were recognized by that name was the Chancery. Then, by an identification of substantive and remedial rights familiar to students, a use came to be regarded as merely a right to a subpoena. It lost all character of a *jus in rem,* and passed into the category of choses in action.[49] I have shown elsewhere the effect of this view in hampering the transfer of either the benefit or burden of uses and trusts.[50]

II. CONTRACT

I must now say a few words of the only other substantive doctrine of which I have discovered any trace in the first period of English Equity. This is a view of Contract, singularly contradicting the

[49] Co. Lit. 272b; Bacon, Reading on Stat. of Uses, Works (ed. Spedding), VII., p. 398.

[50] The Common Law, ch. 11; see especially pp. 399, 407–409, and, in addition to the books cited on p. 408, notes 1 and 2; Fitz. Abr. *Subpena,* pl. 22; Dalamere *v.* Barnard, Plowden, 346, 352; Pawlett *v.* Attorney-General, Hardres, 465, 469; Co. Lit. 272b; W. Jones, 127.

popular notion that the common law borrowed Consideration from the Chancery. The requirement of consideration in all parol contracts is simply a modified generalization of the requirement of *quid pro quo* to raise a debt by parol. The latter, in certain cases at least, is very ancient, and seems to be continuous with the similar doctrine of the early Norman and other continental sources which have been much discussed in Germany.[51]

I may remark by way of parenthesis that this requirement did not extend to the case of a surety, who obviously did not receive a *quid pro quo* in the sense of the older books and yet could bind himself by parol from the time of the Somma to Edward III,

[51] Somma, II., C. 26, §§ 2, 3, in 7 Ludewig, Reliq. Manuscript. pp. 313, 314; Grand Coustumier, C. 88 and 90; Statutum Walliae, 12 Ed. I; *"Si vero Debitor venerit, necesse habet Actor exprimere petitionem, et rationem sue petitionis, videlict, quod tenetur ei in centum marcis, quas sibi accomodavit, cujus solutionis dies preteriit, vel pro terra vel pro equo, vel pro aliis rebus seu catallis quibuscunque sibi venditis, vel pro arreragiis redditus non provenientis de tenementis, vel de aliis contractibus,"* etc. Y. B. 39 Ed. III., 17, 18, *"issint il est quid pro quo"*; 3 Hen. VI. 36, pl. 33; 7 Hen. VI. 1, pl. 3; 9 Hen. VI. 52, pl. 35; 11 Hen. VI. 35, pl. 30 at fol. 38; 37 Hen. VI. 8, pl. 18. See also *"Justa debendi causa"* in Glanv. X. C. 3; Dial. de Scacc. ii., C. 1 and 9; Fitz. Abr., Dett, pl. 139; Y. B. 43 Ed. III. 11, pl. 1. Form of Count given by 1 Britton (ed. Nichols), 161, 162, pl. 12; Y. B. 20 & 21 Ed. I. App. 488, "Marchandise" ground of debt. Sohm, Eheschliessung, p. 24; I Franken, Französ. Pfandr., § 4, p. 43; Schulte, Reichs- u. Rechtsgesch. § 156 (4th ed.), p. 497. Consideration is first mentioned in equity in 31 Hen. VI., Fitz., Abr. *Subpena*, pl. 23; Y. B. 37 Hen. VI. 13, pl. 3, and by the name *quid pro quo*. So in substance as to assumpsit; Y. B. 3 Hen. VI. 36, pl. 33.

The interpretation of Fleta, II, C. 60, § 25 by the present writer in The Common Law, 266, is rightly criticised in Pollock, Contr. (3rd ed.), 266, as appear by comparing the more guarded language of Bracton, 15b.

and even later where the custom of various cities kept up the ancient law.[52] Sohm has collected evidence that suretyship was a formal contract in the time of the folk laws, in aid of his theory that the early law knew only two contracts; the real, springing from sale or barter and requiring a *quid pro quo;* and the formal, developed from the real at an early date by a process which has been variously figured.[53] I do not attempt to weigh the evidence of the continental sources, but in view of the clear descent of surety-ship from the giving of hostages, and the fact that it appears as a formless contract in the early Norman and Anglo-Norman Law, I find it hard to believe that it owed its origin to form any more than to *quid pro quo.* Tacitus says that the Germans would gamble their personal liberty and pay with their persons if they lost.[54] The analogy seems to me suggestive. I know no warrant for supposing that the *festuca* was necessary to a bet.

[52] Somma, I., C. 62, II. C. 24; 7 Ludewig, 264, 309; Grand Coustum. C. 89 (cf. Bract, fol. 149b, § 6); The Common Law, 260, 264. See, besides authorities there cited, F. N. B. 122 K; *ib.* I in marg., 137 C; Y. B. 43 Ed. III, 11, pl. 1; 9 Hen. V. 14, pl. 23. Car. M. Cap. Langob, A.D. 813, ch. 12, *"Si quis pro alterius debito se pecuniam suam promiserit redditurum in ipsa promissione est retinendus,"* cited Löning, Vetragsbruch, 62, n. 1.

In 2 Gesta Hen. II. (Ben. Abbas, Rolls ed.), 136, sureties make oath to surrender themselves if the agreement is broken. Sohm, Eheschliessung, 48, goes so far as to argue that the oath was simply one substitute for the Salic formal contract. But I find no evidence that the oath was necessary in England unless for ecclesiastical jurisdiction. 2 Gesta Hen. II., p. 137.

[53] See, e.g., 1 Franken Französ. Pfandr. § 16, pp. 209–216; § 18, pp. 241 *et seq.; ib.,* 261–266.

[54] Germ. 24.

I go one step further, and venture hesitatingly to suggest that cases which would now be generalized as contract may have arisen independently of each other from different sources, and have persisted side by side for a long time before the need of generalization was felt or they were perceived to tend to establish inconsistent principles. Out of barter and sale grew the real contract, and if the principle of that transaction was to be declared universal, every contract would need a *quid pro quo*. Out of the giving of hostages, familiar in Caesar's time, grew the guaranty of another's obligation, and if this was to furnish the governing analogy, every promise purporting to be seriously made would bind. But the two familiar contracts kept along together very peaceably until logic, that great destroyer of tradition, pushed suretyship into the domain of covenant, and the more frequent and important real contract succeeded in dividing the realm of debt with instruments under seal.[55]

To return to Equity. In the Diversity of Courts (*Chancery*) it is said that "a man shall have remedy in Chancery for covenants made without specialty, if the party have sufficient witness to prove the cove-

[55] Y. B. 18 Ed. III., 13, pl. 7; 44 Ed. III. 21, pl 23; 43 Ed. III, 11 pl. 1. So warranty, which had been merely an incident of a sale (*Lex Salica*, C. 47; Glanv. X., C. 15 and 17), came to be looked at as a covenant, Y. B. 44 Ed. III. 27, pl. 1; and at a later date bailment was translated into contract. As a further illustration, I may add that in modern times Consideration has still been dealt with by way of remuneration (see e.g. 2 Bl. Comm., 444; I Tidd's Practice, C. 1, as to assumpsit), and only very recently has been resolved into a detriment to the promisee, in all cases.

nants, and yet he is without remedy at the common law." This was in 1525, under Henry VIII., and soon afterwards the contrary was decided.[56] But the fact that a decision was necessary confirms the testimony of the passage quoted as to what had been the tradition of the Chancery. I do not propose to consider whether thus broadly stated it corresponded to any doctrine of early law, or whether any other cases could be found, besides that of the surety, in which a man could bind himself by simply saying that he was bound. For although the meaning of the tradition had been lost in the time of Henry VIII., when the text-book spoke of covenants generally, the promise with which Equity had dealt was a promise *per fidem*. Thus, under Edward IV.,[57] a subpoena was sued in the Chancery alleging that the defendant had made the plaintiff the procurator of his benefice and promised him *per fidem* to hold him harmless for the occupation, and then showing a breach. The Chancellor (Stillington) said that "in that he is damaged by the non-performance of the promise he shall have his remedy here." And to go back to the period to which this article is devoted, we find in the reign of Richard II. a bill brought upon a promise to grant the reversion of certain lands to the plaintiff, setting forth that the plaintiff had come to London and spent money relying upon the *affiance* of the defendant, and that as he had no specialty, and nothing in writing of the aforesaid covenant, he

[56] Cary, Rep. in Ch. 5, Choyce Cases in Ch. 49.
[57] Y. B. 8 Ed., IV., 4, pl. 2; Fitz, Abr. *Subpena*, pl. 7.

had no action at the common law.[58]   This is all the direct evidence, but slight as it is, it is sufficient to prove an ancient genealogy, as I shall try to show.

Two centuries after the Conquest there were three well-known ways of making a binding promise: Faith, Oath, and Writing.[59]   The plighting of one's faith or troth here mentioned has been shown by Sohm and others to be a descendant of the Salic *Fides facta*, and I do not repeat their argument.[60] It still survives in that repertory of antiquities, the marriage ceremony, and is often mentioned in the old books.[61]

Whether this plighting of faith (*fides data, fides facta*) was a formal contract or not in the time of the Plantagenets, and whether or not it was ever

[58] Whalen v. Huchyndin, 2 Cal. Ch. ii.

[59] Compare Letter of Gregory IX. to Henry III., Jan. 10, 1233, in 1 Royal Letters, Henry III. (Rolls ed.), p. 551, "*Possessiones . . . fide ac juramentis a te praestitis de non revocandis eisdem, sub litterarum tuarum testimoniis concessisti,*" with Sententia Rudolfi Regis, A.D. 1277, Pertz, Monumenta, Leges II, p. 412: "*Quaesivimus . . . utrum is qui se datione fidei vel juramento corporaliter prestito, vel patentibus suis litteris, ad obstagium vel solutionem alicujus debiti ad certum terminum obligavit, nec in ipso termino adimplevit ad quod taliter se adstrinxit de jure posset . . . per iulicium occupari? Et promulgatum extitit communiter ab omnibus, quod is, qui modo predicto . . . promisso non paruit, valeat, ubicumque inveniatur, auctoritate iudiciaria conveniri.*"

[60] *Lex Salica* (Merkel), Ch. 50; *Lex Ripuaria*, Ch. 58 (60), § 21; Sohm, Eheschliessung, 48, 49, notes; I. Franken Französ. Pfandr. 264, n. 2.

[61] Eadmer (Rolls ed.), 7, 8, 25; Dial. de Scacc., II. C. 19; 2 Gesta Hen. II. (Ben. Abbas), 134–137; 3 Roger Hoved. (Rolls ed.), 145; Glanv. VII., C. 18; X., C. 12; 1 Royal Letters, Henry III. (Rolls ed.), 308; Bract. 179b. Cf. id. 175a, 406b, etc.; Reg. Majest. II., C. 48, § 10; C. 57, § 10; Abbrev. Plac. 31, col. 1 (2 Joh. Norf. rot. 21); 22 Ass. pl. 70, fol. 101.

proceeded upon in the King's courts, it sufficiently appears from Glanvill and Bracton that the royal remedies were only conceded *de gratia* if ever.[62] The royal remedies were afforded at first only by way of privilege and exception, and, as I have already shown, never extended to all the ancient customs which prevailed in the popular tribunals. But if the King failed the Church stood ready. For a long time, and with varying success, it claimed a general jurisdiction in case of *laesio fidei*.[63] Whatever the limit of this vague and dangerous claim it clearly extended to breach of *fides data*. And even after the Church had been finally cut down to marriages and wills, as shown in the last note, it retained jurisdiction over contracts incident to such matters for breach of faith, and, it seems, might proceed by way of spiritual censure and penance even in other cases.[64]

[62] Glanv. X., C. 8; Bract. 100a.

[63] The fluctuations of the struggle may be traced in the following passages: "*Item generaliter omnes de fidei laesione vel juramenti transgressione quaestiones in foro ecclesiastico tractabantur.*" A.D. 1190. 2 Diceto (Rolls ed.), 87; 2 Matt. Paris, Chron. Maj. (Rolls ed.), 368. "*Placita de debitis quae fide interposita debentur vel absque interpositione fidei sint in justitia Regis.*" Const. Clarend. C. 15; Glanv. X., C. 12; Letter of Thomas à Becket to the Pope, A. D. 1167, 1 Rog. Hoved. (Rolls ed.), 254. Agreement between Richard and the Norman clergy in 1190, Diceto and Matt. Par. *ubi supra*. As to suits for breach of faith, outside of debts, in the Courts Christian, circa 1200, Abbrev. Plac. 31, col. 1 (2 Joh.), Norf. rot. 21. "*Prohibetur ecclesiasticus judex tracture omnes causas contra laicos, nisi sint de matrimonio vel testamento.*" A.D. 1247, 4 Matt. Paris (Rolls ed.), 614. Resistance to this, Annals of Burton (Rolls ed.), 417, 423; cf. *ib.* 256. But this prohibition fixed the boundaries of ecclesiastical jurisdiction.

[64] 22 Lib. Ass., pl. 70, fol. 101. Cf. Glanv. VII., C. 18, "*propter*

Thus the old contracts lingered along into the reign of Edward III. until the common law had attained a tolerably definite theory which excluded them on substantive grounds, and the Chancery had become a separate Court. The clerical Chancellors seem for a time to have asserted successfully in a different tribunal the power of which they had been shorn as ecclesiastics, to give a remedy for contracts for which the ordinary King's Courts afforded none. But, I think, I have now proved that in so doing they were not making reforms or introducing new doctrines, but were simply retaining some relics of ancient custom which had been dropped by the common law, but had been kept alive by the Church.

mutuam affidationem quae fieri solet" Bract. fol. 175a, 406b, 407, 412b; Y. B. 38 Hen. VI. 29, pl. 2. But covenant was the only remedy if the contract had been put in writing; Y. B. 45 Ed. III. 24, pl. 30.

THE LAW

SUFFOLK BAR ASSOCIATION DINNER,
FEBRUARY 5, 1885*

Mr. Chairman and Gentlemen of the Bar:

The Court and the Bar are too old acquaintances to speak much to each other of themselves, or of their mutual relations. I hope I may say we are too old friends to need to do it. If you did not believe it already, it would be useless for me to affirm that, in the judges' half of our common work, the will at least is not wanting to do every duty of their noble office; that every interest, every faculty, every energy, almost every waking hour, is filled with their work; that they give their lives to it, more than which they cannot do. But if not of the Bench, shall I speak of the Bar? Shall I ask what a court would be, unaided? The law is made by the Bar, even more than by the Bench; yet do I need to speak of the learning and varied gifts that have given the Bar of this State a reputation throughout the whole domain of the common law? I think I need not, nor of its high and scrupulous honor. The world has its fling at lawyers sometimes, but its very denial is an admission. It feels, what I believe to be the truth, that of all secular professions this has the highest standards.

* From *Speeches* (1913), printed by Little, Brown & Co.

And what a profession it is! No doubt every-thing is interesting when it is understood and seen in its connection with the rest of things. Every calling is great when greatly pursued. But what other gives such scope to realize the spontaneous energy of one's soul? In what other does one plunge so deep in the stream of life — so share its passions, its battles, its despair, its triumphs, both as wit-ness and actor?

But that is not all. What a subject is this in which we are united — this abstraction called the Law, wherein, as in a magic mirror, we see reflected, not only our own lives, but the lives of all men that have been! When I think on this majestic theme, my eyes dazzle. If we are to speak of the law as our mistress, we who are here know that she is a mistress only to be wooed with sustained and lonely passion — only to be won by straining all the facul-ties by which man is likest to a god. Those who, having begun the pursuit, turn away uncharmed, do so either because they have not been vouchsafed the sight of her divine figure, or because they have not the heart for so great a struggle. To the lover of the law, how small a thing seem the novelist's tales of the loves and fates of Daphnis and Chloe! How pale a phantom even the Circe of poetry, transform-ing mankind with intoxicating dreams of fiery ether, and the foam of summer seas, and glowing green-sward, and the white arms of women! For him no less a history will suffice than that of the moral life of his race. For him every text that he de-

ciphers, every doubt that he resolves, adds a new
feature to the unfolding panorama of man's destiny
upon this earth. Nor will his task be done until, by
the farthest stretch of human imagination, he has
seen as with his eyes the birth and growth of society,
and by the farthest stretch of reason he has understood the philosophy of its being. When I think
thus of the law, I see a princess mightier than she
who once wrought at Bayeux, eternally weaving into
her web dim figures of the ever-lengthening past —
figures too dim to be noticed by the idle, too symbolic
to be interpreted except by her pupils, but to the
discerning eye disclosing every painful step and every
world-shaking contest by which mankind has worked
and fought its way from savage isolation to organic
social life.

But we who are here know the Law even better
in another aspect. We see her daily, not as an-
thropologists, not as students and philosophers, but
as actors in a drama of which she is the providence
and overruling power. When I think of the Law
as we know her in the courthouse and the market,
she seems to me a woman sitting by the wayside,
beneath whose overshadowing hood every man shall
see the countenance of his deserts or needs. The
timid and overborne gain heart from her protecting
smile. Fair combatants, manfully standing to their
rights, see her keeping the lists with the stern and
discriminating eye of even justice. The wretch who
has defied her most sacred commands, and has
thought to creep through ways where she was not,

finds that his path ends with her, and beholds beneath her hood the inexorable face of death.

Gentlemen, I shall say no more. This is not the moment for disquisitions. But when for the first time I was called to speak on such an occasion as this, the only thought that could come into my mind, the only feeling that could fill my heart, the only words that could spring to my lips, were a hymn to her in whose name we are met here to-night — to our mistress, the Law.

THE PROFESSION OF THE LAW

CONCLUSION OF A LECTURE DELIVERED TO UNDER-
GRADUATES OF HARVARD UNIVERSITY,
ON FEBRUARY 17, 1886 *

AND now, perhaps, I ought to have done. But I
know that some spirit of fire will feel that his main
question has not been answered. He will ask, What
is all this to my soul? You do not bid me sell
my birthright for a mess of pottage; what have you
said to show that I can reach my own spiritual possibilities through such a door as this? How can the
laborious study of a dry and technical system, the
greedy watch for clients and practice of shopkeepers'
arts, the mannerless conflicts over often sordid interests, make out a life? Gentlemen, I admit at once
that these questions are not futile, that they may
prove unanswerable, that they have often seemed
to me unanswerable. And yet I believe there is an
answer. They are the same questions that meet
you in any form of practical life. If a man has
the soul of Sancho Panza, the world to him will be
Sancho Panza's world; but if he has the soul of an
idealist, he will make — I do not say find — his
world ideal. Of course, the law is not the place
for the artist or the poet. The law is the calling of

* From *Speeches* (1913), printed by Little, Brown & Co.

thinkers. But to those who believe with me that not the least godlike of man's activities is the large survey of causes, that to know is not less than to feel, I say — and I say no longer with any doubt — that a man may live greatly in the law as well as elsewhere; that there as well as elsewhere his thought may find its unity in an infinite perspective; that there as well as elsewhere he may wreak himself upon life, may drink the bitter cup of heroism, may wear his heart out after the unattainable. All that life offers any man from which to start his thinking or his striving is a fact. And if this universe is one universe, if it is so far thinkable that you can pass in reason from one part if it to another, it does not matter very much what that fact is. For every fact leads to every other by the path of the air. Only men do not yet see how, always. And your business as thinkers is to make plainer the way from some thing to the whole of things; to show the rational connection between your fact and the frame of the universe. If your subject is law, the roads are plain to anthropology, the science of man, to political economy, the theory of legislation, ethics, and thus by several paths to your final view of life. It would be equally true of any subject. The only difference is in the ease of seeing the way. To be master of any branch of knowledge, you must master those which lie next to it; and thus to know anything you must know all.

Perhaps I speak too much the language of intellectual ambition. I cannot but think that the scope for intellectual, as for physical adventure, is narrowing. I look for a future in which the ideal will be content and dignified acceptance of life, rather than aspiration and the passion for achievement. I see already that surveys and railroads have set limits to our intellectual wildernesses — that the lion and the bison are disappearing from them, as from Africa and the no longer boundless West. But that undelightful day which I anticipate has not yet come. The human race has not changed, I imagine, so much between my generation and yours but that you still have the barbaric thirst for conquest, and there is still something left to conquer. There are fields still open for occupation in the law, and there are roads from them that will lead you where you will.

But do not think I am pointing you to flowery paths and beds of roses — to a place where brilliant results attend your work, which shall be at once easy and new. No result is easy which is worth having. Your education begins when what is called your education is over — when you no longer are stringing together the pregnant thoughts, the "jewels five-words-long," which great men have given their lives to cut from the raw material, but have begun yourselves to work upon the raw material for results which you do not see, cannot predict, and which may be long in coming — when you take the fact which life offers you for your appointed task. No man has earned the right to intellectual ambition until he has learned to lay his course by a star which he has never seen — to dig by the divining rod for springs which he may never reach. In saying this, I point to that which will make your study heroic. For I say to you in all sadness of conviction, that to think great thoughts you must be heroes as well as idealists. Only when you have worked alone — when you have felt around you a black gulf of solitude more isolating than that which surrounds the dying man, and in hope and in despair have trusted to your own unshaken will — then only will you have achieved. Thus only can you gain the secret isolated joy of the thinker, who knows that, a hundred years after he is dead and forgotten, men who never heard of him will be moving to the measure of his thought — the subtile rapture of a postponed power, which the world knows not because it has no external trappings, but which to his prophetic vision is more real than that which commands an army. And if this joy should not be yours, still it is only thus that you can know that you have done what it lay in you to do — can say that you have lived, and be ready for the end.

ON RECEIVING THE DEGREE OF DOCTOR OF LAWS

YALE UNIVERSITY COMMENCEMENT,
JUNE 30, 1886 *

MR. PRESIDENT AND GENTLEMEN:

I KNOW of no mark of honor which this country has to offer that I should value so highly as this which you have conferred upon me. I accept it proudly as an accolade, like the little blow upon the shoulder from the sword of a master of war which in ancient days adjudged that a soldier had won his spurs and pledged his life to decline no combat in the future.

The power of honor to bind men's lives is not less now than it was in the Middle Ages. Now as then it is the breath of our nostrils; it is that for which we live, for which, if need be, we are willing to die. It is that which makes the man whose gift is the power to gain riches sacrifice health and even life to the pursuit. It is that which makes the scholar feel that he cannot afford to be rich.

One would sometimes think, from the speech of young men, that things had changed recently, and that indifference was now the virtue to be cultivated. I never heard any one profess indifference to a boat race. Why should you row a boat race? Why endure long months of pain in preparation for a fierce half-hour that will leave you all but dead? Does any one ask the question? Is there any one who would not go through all its costs, and more, for the moment when anguish breaks into triumph — or even for the glory of having nobly lost? Is life less than a boat race? If a man will give all the blood in his body to win the one, will he not spend all the might of his soul to prevail in the other?

I know, Mr. President, that there is a motive above even honor which may govern men's lives. I know that there are some rare spirits who find the inspiration of every moment, the aim of every act, in holiness. I am enough of a Puritan, I think, to conceive the exalted joy of those who look upon themselves only as instruments in the hands of a higher power to work out its designs. But I think that most men do and must reach the same result under the illusion of self-seeking. If the love of honor is a form of that illusion, it is no ignoble one. If it does not lift a man on wings to the sky, at least it carries him above the earth and teaches him those high and secret pathways across the branches of the forest the travellers on which are only less than winged.

Not the least service of this great University and its sister from which I come is, that by their separate teaching and by their mutual rivalry they have fostered that lofty feeling among their graduates. You have done all that a university can do to fan the spark in me. I will try to maintain the honor you have bestowed.

THE USE OF LAW SCHOOLS *

ORATION BEFORE THE HARVARD LAW SCHOOL ASSOCI-
ATION, AT CAMBRIDGE, NOVEMBER 5, 1886, ON
THE 250TH ANNIVERSARY OF HARVARD
UNIVERSITY

IT is not wonderful that the graduates of the Law
School of Harvard College should wish to keep alive
their connection with it. About three quarters of
a century ago it began with a Chief Justice of the
Supreme Court of Massachusetts for its Royall Professor. A little later, one of the most illustrious
judges who ever sat on the United States Supreme
Bench — Mr. Justice Story — accepted a professor-
ship in it created for him by Nathan Dane. And
from that time to this it has had the services of great
and famous lawyers; it has been the source of a
large part of the most important legal literature
which the country has produced; it has furnished a
world-renowned model in its modes of instruction;
and it has had among its students future chief justices and justices, and leaders of state bars and of
the national bar too numerous for me to thrill you
with the mention of their names.

It has not taught great lawyers only. Many who
have won fame in other fields began their studies

* From *Speeches* (1913), printed by Little, Brown & Co.

here. Sumner and Phillips were among the Bachelors of 1834. The orator whom we shall hear in a day or two appears in the list of 1840 alongside of William Story, of the Chief Justice of this State, and of one of the Associate Justices, who is himself not less known as a soldier and as an orator than he is as a judge. Perhaps, without revealing family secrets, I may whisper that next Monday's poet also tasted our masculine diet before seeking more easily digested, if not more nutritious, food elsewhere. Enough. Of course we are proud of the Harvard Law School. Of course we love every limb of Harvard College. Of course we rejoice to manifest our brotherhood by the symbol of this Association.

I will say no more for the reasons of our coming together. But by your leave I will say a few words about the use and meaning of law schools, especially of our law school, and about its methods of instruction, as they appear to one who has had some occasion to consider them.

A law school does not undertake to teach success. That combination of tact and will which gives a man immediate prominence among his fellows comes from nature, not from instruction; and if it can be helped at all by advice, such advice is not offered here. It might be expected that I should say, by way of natural antithesis, that what a law school does undertake to teach is law. But I am not ready to say even that, without a qualification. It seems to me that nearly all the education which men can get from others is moral, not intellectual. The main part of intellectual education is not the acquisition of facts, but learning how to make facts live. Culture, in the sense of fruitless knowledge, I for one abhor. The mark of a master is, that facts which before lay scattered in an inorganic mass, when he shoots through them the magnetic current of his thought, leap into an organic order, and live and bear fruit. But you cannot make a master by teaching. He makes himself by aid of his natural gifts.

Education, other than self-education, lies mainly in the shaping of men's interests and aims. If you convince a man that another way of looking at things is more profound, another form of pleasure more subtile than that to which he has been accustomed — if you make him really see it — the very nature of man is such that he will desire the profounder thought and the subtiler joy. So I say the business of a law school is not sufficiently described when you merely say that it is to teach law, or to make lawyers. It is to teach law in the grand manner, and to make great lawyers.

Our country needs such teaching very much. I think we should all agree that the passion for equality has passed far beyond the political or even the social sphere. We are not only unwilling to admit that any class or society is better than that in which we move, but our customary attitude towards every one in authority of any kind is that he is only the lucky recipient of honor or salary above the average, which any average man might as well receive as he. When the effervescence of democratic negation extends its workings beyond the abolition of external distinctions of rank to spiritual things — when the passion for equality is not content with founding social intercourse upon universal human sympathy, and a community of interests in which all may share, but attacks the lines of Nature which establish orders and degrees among the souls of men — they are not only wrong, but ignobly wrong. Modesty and reverence are no less virtues of freemen than the democratic feeling which will submit neither to arrogance nor to servility.

To inculcate those virtues, to correct the ignoble excess of a noble feeling to which I have referred, I know of no teachers so powerful and persuasive as the little army of specialists. They carry no banners, they beat no drums; but where they are, men learn that bustle and push are not the equals of quiet genius and serene mastery. They compel others who need their help, or who are enlightened by their teaching, to obedience and respect. They set the examples themselves; for they furnish in the intellectual world a perfect type of the union of democracy with discipline. They bow to no one who seeks to impose his authority by foreign aid; they hold that science like courage is never beyond the necessity of proof, but must always be ready to prove itself against all challengers. But to one who has shown himself a master, they pay the proud reverence of men who know what valiant combat means, and who reserve the right to combat against their leader even, if he should seem to waver in the service of Truth, their only queen.

In the army of which I speak, the lawyers are not the least important corps. For all lawyers are specialists. Not in the narrow sense in which we sometimes use the word in the profession — of persons who confine themselves to a particular branch of practice, such as conveyancing or patents — but specialists who have taken all law to be their province; specialists because they have undertaken to master a special branch of human knowledge — a branch, I may add, which is more immediately connected with all the highest interests of man than any other which deals with practical affairs.

Lawyers, too, were among the first specialists to be needed and to appear in America. And I believe it would be hard to exaggerate the goodness of their influence in favor of sane and orderly thinking. But lawyers feel the spirit of the times like other people. They, like others, are forever trying to discover cheap and agreeable substitutes for real things. I fear that the bar has done its full share to exalt that most hateful of American words and ideals, "smartness," as against dignity of moral feeling and profundity of knowledge. It is from within the bar, not from outside, that I have heard the new gospel that learning is out of date, and that the man for the times is no longer the thinker and the scholar, but the smart man, unencumbered with other artillery than the latest edition of the Digest and the latest revision of the Statutes.

The aim of a law school should be, the aim of the Harvard Law School has been, not to make men smart, but to make them wise in their calling — to start them on a road which will lead them to the abode of the masters. A law school should be at once the workshop and the nursery of specialists in the sense which I have explained. It should obtain for teachers men in each generation who are producing the best work of that generation. Teaching should not stop, but rather should foster, production. The "enthusiasm of the lecture-room," the contagious interest of companionship, should make the students partners in their teachers' work. The ferment of genius in its creative moment is quickly imparted. If a man is great, he makes others believe in greatness; he makes them incapable of mean ideals and easy self-satisfaction. His pupils will accept no substitute for realities; but at the same time they learn that the only coin with which realities can be bought is life.

Our School has been such a workshop and such a nursery as I describe. What men it has turned out I have hinted already, and do not need to say; what works it has produced is known to all the world. From ardent coöperation of student and teacher have sprung Greenleaf on Evidence, and Stearns on Real Actions, and Story's epoch-making Commentaries, and Parsons on Contracts, and Washburn on Real Property; and, marking a later epoch, Langdell on Contracts and on Equity Pleading, and Ames on Bills and Notes, and Gray on Perpetuities, and I hope we soon may add Thayer on Evidence. You will notice that these books are very different in character from one another, but you will notice also how many of them have this in common — that they have marked and largely made an epoch.

There are plenty of men nowadays of not a hundredth part of Story's power who could write as good statements of the law as his, or better. And when some mediocre fluent book has been printed, how often have we heard it proclaimed, "Lo, here is a greater than Story!" But if you consider the state of legal literature when Story began to write, and from what wells of learning the discursive streams of his speech were fed, I think you will be inclined to agree with me that he has done more than any other English-speaking man in this century to make the law luminous and easy to understand.

But Story's simple philosophizing has ceased to satisfy men's minds. I think it might be said with safety, that no man of his or of the succeeding generation could have stated the law in a form that deserved to abide, because neither his nor the succeeding generation possessed or could have possessed the historical knowledge, had made or could have made the analyses of principles, which are necessary before the cardinal doctrines of the law can be known and understood in their precise contours and in their innermost meanings.

The new work is now being done. Under the influence of Germany, science is gradually drawing legal history into its sphere. The facts are being scrutinized by eyes microscopic in intensity and panoramic in scope. At the same time, under the influence of our revived interest in philosophical speculation, a thousand heads are analyzing and generalizing the rules of law and the grounds on which they stand. The law has got to be stated over again; and I venture to say that in fifty years we shall have it in a form of which no man could have dreamed fifty years ago. And now I venture to add my hope and my belief, that, when the day comes which I predict, the Professors of the Harvard Law School will be found to have had a hand in the change not less important than that which Story has had in determining the form of the textbooks of the last half-century.

Corresponding to the change which I say is taking place, there has been another change in the mode of teaching. How far the correspondence is conscious, I do not stop to inquire. For whatever reason, the Professors of this School have said to themselves more definitely than ever before, We will not be contented to send forth students with nothing but a rag-bag full of general principles — a throng of glittering generalities, like a swarm of little bodiless cherubs fluttering at the top of one of Correggio's pictures. They have said that to make a general principle worth anything you must give it a body; you must show in what way and how far it would be applied actually in an actual system; you must show how it has gradually emerged as the felt reconciliation of concrete instances no one of which established it in terms. Finally, you must show its historic relations to other principles, often of very different date and origin, and thus set it in the perspective without which its proportions will never be truly judged.

In pursuance of these views there have been substituted for text-books more and more, so far as practicable, those books of cases which were received at first by many with a somewhat contemptuous smile and pitying contrast of good old days, but which now, after fifteen years, bid fair to revolutionize the teaching both of this country and of England.

I pause for a moment to say what I hope it is scarcely necessary for me to say — that in thus giving in my adhesion to the present methods of instructions I am not wanting in grateful and appreciative recollection (alas! it can be only recollection now) of the earlier teachers under whom I studied. In my day the Dean of this School was Professor Parker, the ex-Chief Justice of New Hampshire, who I think was one of the greatest of American judges, and who showed in the chair the same qualities that had made him famous on the bench. His associates were Parsons, almost if not quite a man of genius, and gifted with a power of impressive statement which I do not know that I have ever seen equalled; and Washburn, who taught us all to realize the meaning of the phrase which I already have quoted from Vangerow, the "enthusiasm of the lecture-room." He did more for me than the learning of Coke and the logic of Fearne could have done without his kindly ardor.

To return, and to say a word more about the

theory on which these books of cases are used. It
long has seemed to me a striking circumstance, that
the ablest of the agitators for codification, Sir James
Stephen, and the originator of the present mode of
teaching, Mr. Langdell, start from the same premises
to reach seemingly opposite conclusions. The number of legal principles is small, says in effect Sir
James Stephen, therefore codify them; the number
of legal principles is small, says Mr. Langdell, therefore they may be taught through the cases which
have developed and established them. Well, I think
there is much force in Sir James Stephen's argument,
if you can find competent men and get them to undertake the task; and at any rate I am not now going
to express an opinion that he is wrong. But I am
certain from my own experience that Mr. Langdell
is right; I am certain that when your object is not
to make a bouquet of the law for the public, nor
to prune and graft it by legislation, but to plant its
roots where they will grow, in minds devoted hence-
forth to that one end, there is no way to be compared to Mr. Langdell's way. Why, look at it
simply in the light of human nature. Does not a
man remember a concrete instance more vividly
than a general principle? And is not a principle
more exactly and intimately grasped as the unex-
pressed major premise of the half-dozen examples
which mark its extent and its limits than it can be
in any abstract form of words? Expressed or un-
expressed, is it not better known when you have
studied its embryology and the lines of its growth

than when you merely see it lying dead before you on the printed page?

I have referred to my own experience. During the short time that I had the honor of teaching in the School, it fell to me, among other things, to instruct the first-year men in Torts. With some misgivings I plunged a class of beginners straight into Mr. Ames's collection of cases, and we began to discuss them together in Mr. Langdell's method. The result was better than I even hoped it would be. After a week or two, when the first confusing novelty was over, I found that my class examined the questions proposed with an accuracy of view which they never could have learned from text-books, and which often exceeded that to be found in the text-books. I at least, if no one else, gained a good deal from our daily encounters.

My experience as a judge has confirmed the belief I formed as a professor. Of course a young man cannot try or argue a case as well as one who has had years of experience. Most of you also would probably agree with me that no teaching which a man receives from others at all approaches in importance what he does for himself, and that one who simply has been a docile pupil has got but a very little way. But I do think that in the thoroughness of their training, and in the systematic character of their knowledge, the young men of the present day start better equipped when they begin their practical experience than it was possible for their predecessors to have been. And although no school can boast a monopoly of promising young men, Cambridge, of course, has its full proportion of them at our bar; and I do think that the methods of teaching here bear fruits in their work.

I sometimes hear a wish expressed by the impatient, that the teaching here should be more practical. I remember that a very wise and able man said to a friend of mine when he was beginning his professional life, "Don't know too much law," and I think we all can imagine cases where the warning would be useful. But a far more useful thing is what was said to me as a student by one no less wise and able — afterwards my partner and always my friend — when I was talking as young men do about seeing practice, and all the other things which seemed practical to my inexperience, "The business of a lawyer is to know law." The professors of this Law School mean to make their students know law. They think the most practical teaching is that which takes their students to the bottom of what they seek to know. They therefore mean to make them master the common law and equity as working systems, and think that when that is accomplished they will have no trouble with the improvements of the last half-century. I believe they are entirely right, not only in the end they aim at, but in the way they take to reach that end.

Yes, this School has been, is, and I hope will be, a centre where great lawyers perfect their achievements, and from which young men, even more inspired by their example than instructed by their teaching, go forth in their turn, not to imitate what their masters have done, but to live their own lives more freely for the ferment imparted to them here. The men trained in this School may not always be the most knowing in the ways of getting on. The noblest of them must often feel that they are committed to lives of proud dependence — the dependence of men who command no factitious aids to success, but rely upon unadvertised knowledge and silent devotion; dependence upon finding an appreciation which they cannot seek, but dependence proud in the conviction that the knowledge to which their lives are consecrated is of things which it concerns the world to know. It is the dependence of abstract thought, of science, of beauty, of poetry and art, of every flower of civilization, upon finding a soil generous enough to support it. If it does not, it must die. But the world needs the flower more than the flower needs life.

I said that a law school ought to teach law in the grand manner; that it had something more to do than simply to teach law. I think we may claim for our School that it has not been wanting in greatness. I once heard a Russian say that in the middle class of Russia there were many specialists; in the upper class there were civilized men. Perhaps in America, for reasons which I have mentioned, we need specialists even more than we do civilized men. Civilized men who are nothing else are a little apt to think that they cannot breathe the American atmosphere. But if a man is a specialist, it is most desirable that he should also be civilized; that he should have laid in the outline of the other sciences, as well as the light and shade of his own; that he should be reasonable, and see things in their proportion. Nay, more, that he should be passionate, as well as reasonable — that he should be able not only to explain, but to feel; that the ardors of intellectual pursuit should be relieved by the charms of art, should be succeeded by the joy of life become an end in itself.

At Harvard College is realized in some degree the palpitating manifoldness of a truly civilized life. Its aspirations are concealed because they are chastened and instructed; but I believe in my soul that they are not the less noble that they are silent. The golden light of the University is not confined to the undergraduate department; it is shed over all the schools. He who has once seen it becomes other than he was, forevermore. I have said that the best part of our education is moral. It is the crowning glory of this Law School that it has kindled in many a heart an inextinguishable fire.

NOTE. — The orator referred to above was James Russell Lowell; the poet was Oliver Wendell Holmes.

AGENCY*

I

I PROPOSE in these lectures to study the theory of agency at common law, to the end that it may be understood upon evidence, and not merely by conjecture, and that the value of its principles may be weighed intelligently. I first shall endeavor to show why agency is a proper title in the law. I then shall give some general reasons for believing that the series of anomalies or departures from general rule which are seen wherever agency makes its appearance must be explained by some cause not manifest to common sense alone; that this cause is, in fact, the survival from ancient times of doctrines which in their earlier form embodied certain rights and liabilities of heads of families based on substantive grounds which have disappeared long since, and that in modern days these doctrines have been generalized into a fiction, which, although nothing in the world but a form of words, has reacted upon the law and has tended to carry its anomalies still farther. That fiction is, of course, that, within the scope of the agency, principal and agent are one. I next shall examine the early law of England upon every branch of the subject — tort, contract, possession, ratification — and show the working of survival or fiction in each. If

* *Harvard Law Review*, Vol. IV. (1891).

I do not succeed in reducing the law of all these branches to a common term, I shall try to show that at least they all equally depend upon fiction for their present existence. I shall prove incidentally that agency in its narrower sense presents only a special application of the law of master and servant, and that the peculiar doctrines of both are traceable to a common source. Finally I shall give my reasons for thinking that the whole outline of the law is the resultant of a conflict at every point between logic and good sense — the one striving to work fiction out to consistent results, the other restraining and at last overcoming that effort when the results become too manifestly unjust.

A part of my task has been performed and my general view indicated in my book on the Common Law. It remains to discuss the matter systematically and in detail, giving due weight to the many difficulties or objections which are met with in the process.

My subject extends to the whole relation of master and servant — it is not confined to any one branch; so that when I choose the title "Agency," I do not use it in the strict sense just referred to, but as embracing everything of which I intend to treat.

The first question proposed is why agency is a proper title in the law. That is to say, Does agency bring into operation any new and distinct rules of law? Do the facts which constitute agency have attached to them legal effects which are peculiar to it,

or is the agency only a dramatic situation to which
principles of larger scope are applied? And if
agency has rules of its own incapable of being further generalized, what are they?

If the law went no farther than to declare a man
liable for the consequences of acts specifically commanded by him with knowledge of circumstances
under which those consequences were the natural
results of those acts, it would need no explanation
and introduce no new principle. There may have
been some difficulty in arriving at this conclusion
when the intervening agent was a free person and
himself responsible. Speaking without special investigation, I do not remember any case in early
law in which one could charge himself thus in contract or even in tort. Taking the allied case of joint
trespassers, although it long has been settled that
each wrong-doer is liable for the entire damages, the
objection that "the battery of one cannot be the
battery of the other" prevailed as late as James I.[1]
It is very possible that liability even for the commanded acts of a free person first appeared as an
extension of the liability of an owner for similar acts
by his slave.

But however this may be, it is plain good sense
to hold people answerable for wrongs which they
have intentionally brought to pass, and to recognize
that it is just as possible to bring wrongs to pass
through free human agents as through slaves, animals, or natural forces. This is the true scope and

[1] Sampson v. Cranfield, I Bustr. 157 (T. 9 Jac.).

meaning of *"Qui facit per alium facit per se,"* and the English law has recognized that maxim as far back as it is worth while to follow it.[2] So it is only applying the general theory of tort to hold a man liable if he commands an act of which the natural consequence, under the circumstances known to him, is harm to his neighbor, although he has forbidden the harm. If a trespass results, it is as much the trespass of the principal as if it were the natural, though unwished for, effect of a train of physical causes.[3] In such cases there is nothing peculiar to master and servant; similar principles have been applied where independent contractors were employed.[4]

No additional explanation is needed for the case of a contract specifically commanded. A difficulty has been raised concerning cases where the agent has a discretion as to the terms of the contract, and it has been called "absurd to maintain that a contract which in its exact shape emanates exclusively from a particular person is not the contract of such person [*i.e.*, the agent], but is the contract of another."[5] But I venture to think that the absurdity is the other

[2] In Tort: Y. B. 32 Ed. I., 318, 320 (Harwood); 22 Ass. pl. 43, fol. 94; 11 Hen. IV. 90, pl. 47; 9 Hen. VI. 53, pl. 37; 21 Hen. VI., 39; 4 Ed. IV. 36; Dr. and Stud., II., C. 42; Seaman and Browning's Case, 4 Leon. 123, pl. 249 (M. 31 Eliz.). Conveyance: Fitz. Abr. *Annuitie*, pl. 51 (H. 33, Ed. I.), where the maxim is quoted. Account: 4 Inst. 109.

[3] Gregory *v.* Piper, 9 B. & C. 591. Cf. The Common Law, 53, 54, and Lect. 3 and 4.

[4] Bower *v.* Peate, 1, Q. B. D. 321.

[5] Thöl, Handelsrecht, § 70, cited in Wharton Agency, § 6.

way, and that there is no need of any more complex machinery in such a case than where the agent is a mere messenger to express terms settled by his principal in every detail. Suppose that the principal agrees to buy a horse at a price fixed by another. The principal makes the contract, not the referee who settles the price. If the agreement is communicated by messenger, it makes no difference. If the messenger is himself the referee, the case is still the same. But that is the case of an agent with discretionary powers, no matter how large they may be. So far as he expresses his principal's assent to be bound to terms to be fixed by the agent, he is a mere messenger; in fixing the terms he is a stranger to the contract, which stands on the same footing as if it had been made before his personal function began. The agent is simply a voice affording the marks provided by the principal's own expression of what he undertakes. Suppose a wager determined in amount as well as event by the spinning of a teetotum, and to be off if numbers are turned up outside certain limits; is it the contract of the teetotum?

If agency is a proper title of our *corpus juris*, its peculiarities must be sought in doctrines that go farther than any yet mentioned. Such doctrines are to be found in each of the great departments of the law. In tort, masters are held answerable for conduct on the part of their servants, which they not only have not authorized, but have forbidden. In contract, an undisclosed principal may bind or may be bound to another, who did not know of his very existence at the time he made the contract. By a few words of ratification a man may make a trespass or a contract his own in which he had no part in fact. The possession of a tangible object may be attributed to him although he never saw it, and may be denied to another who has it under his actual custody or control. The existence of these rules is what makes agency a proper title in the law.

I do not mean to assume in advance that these rules have a common origin because they are clustered round the same subject. It would be possible to suggest separate reasons for each, and going farther still, to argue that each was no more than an application, even though a misapplication, of general principles.

Thus, in torts it is sometimes said that the liability of the master is "in effect for employing a careless servant," repeating the reason offered by the pseudo-philosophy of the Roman jurists for an exceptional rule introduced by the praetor on grounds of public policy.[6] This reason is shown to be unsound by the single fact that no amount of care in selection will exonerate the master;[7] but still it might be argued that, whether right or wrong, this or some other notion of policy had led to the first of the rules which I selected as a peculiar, and that at most the liability of a master for his servant's torts is only a mistaken conclusion from the general theory of tort.

[6] Parke, B., in Sharrod v. London & N. W. Ry. Co., 4 Exch. 580, 585 (1849); 1 Austin, Jurisprudence, Lect. 26, 3d Ed., p. 513. Cf. The Common Law, 15, 16.

[7] Dansey v. Richardson, 3 El. & Bl., 144, 161.

Then with regard to undisclosed principals in contract, it might be said that it was no hardship to hold a man bound who had commanded his servant to bind him. And as to the other and more difficult half of the doctrine, the right of an undisclosed principal to sue, it might be observed that it was first asserted in cases of debt,[8] where the principal's goods were the consideration of the liability, and that the notion thus started was afterwards extended to other cases of simple contract. Whether the objection to the analogy and to the whole rule were duly considered or not, it might be urged, there is no connection other than a purely dramatic one between the law of agency in torts and in contracts, or between the fact of agency and the rule, and here, as there, nothing more is to be found than a possibly wrong conclusion from the general postulates of the department of law concerned.

Ratification, again, as admitted by us, the argument would continue, merely shows that the Roman maxim *"ratihabitio mandato comparatur"* has become imbedded in our law, as it has been from the time of Bracton.

Finally, the theory of possession through servants would be accounted for by the servant's admission of his master's present right to deal with the thing at will, and the absence of any claim or intent to assert a claim on his part, coupled with the presence of such a claim on the part of the master.

---

[8] Scrimshire *v.* Alderton, 2 Strange, 1182 (H. 16 G. II). Cf. Gurratt *v.* Cullum (T. 9 Anne, B.R.), stated in Scott *v.* Surman, Willes, 400, at p. 405 (H. 16 G. II.) and in Buller, N. P. 42.

But the foregoing reasoning is wholly inadequate to justify the various doctrines mentioned, as I have shown in part and as I shall prove in detail hereafter. And assuming the inadequacy to be proved, it cannot but strike one as strange that there should run through all branches of the law a tendency to err in the same direction. If, as soon as the relation of master and servant comes in, we find the limits of liability for, or gain by, others' acts enlarged beyond the scope of the reasons offered or of any general theory, we not only have good ground for treating that relation separately, but we fairly may suspect that it is a cause as well as a concomitant of the observed effects.

Looking at the whole matter analytically it is easy to see that if the law did identify agents with principals, so far as that identification was carried the principal would have the burden and the benefit of his agent's torts, contracts, or possession. So, framing a historical hypothesis, if the starting-point of the modern law is the *patria potestas*, a little study will show that the fiction of identity is the natural growth from such a germ.

There is an antecedent probability that the *patria potestas* has exerted an influence at least upon existing rules. I have endeavored to prove elsewhere that the unlimited liability of an owner for the torts of his slave grew out of what had been merely a privilege of buying him off from a surrender to the vengeance of the offended party, in both the early Roman and the early German law. I have shown, also, how the unlimited liability thus established was extended by the praetor in certain cases to the misconduct of free servants.[9] Of course it is unlikely that the doctrines of our two parent systems should have been without effect upon their offspring, the common law.

The Roman law, it is true, developed no such universal doctrines of agency as have been worked out in England. Only innkeepers and shipowners (*nautae, caupones, stabularii*) were made answerable for the misconduct of their free servants by the praetor's edict. It was not generally possible to acquire rights or to incur obligations through the acts of free persons.[10] But, so far as rights of property, possession,[11] or contract [12] could be acquired through others not slaves, the law undoubtedly started from slavery and the *patria potestas*.

It will be easy to see how this tended toward a fictitious identification of agent with principal, although within the limits to which it confined agency the Roman law had little need and made little use of the fiction. Ulpian says that the act of the family cannot be called the act of the *paterfamilias* unless it is done by his wish.[13] But as all the family rights and obligations were simply attributes of the *persona* of the family head, the summary expression for the members of the family as means of loss or gain

---

9 The Common Law, 9, 15–20.
10 Inst. 2, 9, § 5; D. 44, 7, 11; D. 45, 1, 126, § 2.
11 Inst. 2, 9, esp. §§ 4, 5. Cf. D. 41, 1, 53.
12 Inst. 3, 17; D. 41, 1, 53; D. 45, 1, 38, § 17.
13 D. 43, 16, 1., §§11–13.

would be that they sustained that *persona, pro hac vice*. For that purpose they were one with the *paterfamilias*. Justinian's Institutes tell us that the right of a slave to receive a binding promise is derived *ex persona domini*.[14] And with regard to free agents, the commentators said that in such instances two persons were feigned to be one.[15]

Such a formula, of course, is only derivative. The fiction is merely a convenient way of expressing rules which were arrived at on other grounds. The Roman praetor did not make innkeepers answerable for their servants because "the act of the servant was the act of the master," any more than because they had been negligent in choosing them. He did so on substantive grounds of policy — because of the special confidence necessarily reposed in innkeepers. So when it held that a slave's possession was his owner's possession, the practical fact of the master's power was at the bottom of the decision.[16]

But when such a formula is adopted, it soon acquires an independent standing of its own. Instead of remaining only a short way of saying that when from policy the law makes a master responsible for his servant, or because of his power gives him the benefit of his slave's possession or contract, it treats him *to that extent* as the tort-feasor, possessor, or contractee, the formula becomes a reason in itself for

---

[14] Inst. 3, 17, pr. 18, in the older editions.

[15] D. 45, 1, 38, § 17, Elzevir ed., Gothofred. note 74, Cf. D. 44, 2, 4, note 17.

[16] The Common Law, 228.

making the master answerable and for giving him rights. If "the act of the servant is the act of the master," or master and servant are "considered as one person," then the master must pay for the act if it is wrongful, and has the advantage of it if it is right. And the mere habit of using these phrases, where the master is bound or benefited by his servant's act, makes it likely that other cases will be brought within the penumbra of the same thought on no more substantial ground than the way of thinking which the words have brought about.

I shall examine successively the English authorities with regard to agency in tort, contract, ratification, and possession. But some of those authorities are of equal importance to every branch of the proposed examination, and will prove in advance that the foregoing remarks are not merely hypothetical. I therefore begin with citations sufficient to establish that family headship was recognized as a factor in legal rights and duties; that this notion of headship was extended by analogy so as to cover the relation of a master to freemen filling a servile place for the time being, and that the relations thus embraced were generalized under the misleading fiction of identity.

The *familia*, Bracton says, embraces "those who are regarded in the light of serfs, such as, etc. So, too, as well freemen as serfs, and those over whom one has the power of command." [17]

[17] *"Et etiam familiae appellatio eos complectitur qui loco servorum habentur, sicut sunt mercenarii et conductitii. Item tam liberi quam servi, et quibus poterit imperari."* Bract., fol. 171b.

In West's *Symboleography,*[18] a work which was published towards the beginning of the reign of James I., and which, though mainly a form book, gives several glimpses of far-reaching insight, we read as follows:

"The person is he which either agreeth or offendeth, and beside him none other.

"And both may be bound either mediately, or immediately.

"Immediately, if he which is bound doe agree.

"Mediately, when if he, which by nature differeth from him, but not by law, whereby as by some bond he is fained to be all one person, doth contract, or offend, of which sort in some cases be those which be in our power, as a wife, a bondman, servant, a factor, an Attourney, or Procurator, exceeding their authority."

Here we see that the *patria potestas* is the substantive ground, that it is extended to cover free agents, who are not even domestic servants, and that it finds its formal expression in the fiction of identity.

So, at the beginning of the next reign, it was said that an action for fire, due to the negligence of a wife, or servant, lay *"vers patrem familias."* [19]   The extension of the liability, as shown by West, is sometimes expressed in later books by saying that it is not confined to cases where the party stands in the

[18] Lib. I., § 3, *ad fin.* "Of the Fact of Man."
[19] Shelley and Barr's Case, I Roll. Abr. 2, pl. 7 (M.I Car.I.).

relation of *paterfamilias* to the wrong-doer;[20] but
this only means that the rule extends to other servants besides domestic servants, and admits the
analogy or starting-point.[21]

Every one is familiar with the fiction as applied
to married women. The early law dealt with married women on the footing of servants. It called
both wives and servants chattels.[22] The wife was
said to be in the nature of a servant,[23] and husband
and wife were only one person in law.[24] So far was
this identification carried, so far was the *persona* of
the wife swallowed up in and made part of the husband's, that whereas, in general, assigns could not
vouch upon a warranty unless they were expressly
mentioned in it,[25] a husband always could vouch
upon a warranty made to his wife before marriage.
By marriage, as was said in Simon Simeon's case
"it vested in the person of the husband." That is
to say, although what actually happened was that
the right to enforce a contract was transferred to a
stranger, in theory of law there was no transfer, because the stranger had become the same person as
the contractee.[26]

20 Bac. Abr., Master and Servant, K; Smith's Master and Servant,
3d ed, 260.
21 Laugher *v.* Pointer, 5 B. & C., 547, 554 (1826). Cf. Bush *v.*
Steinman, I Bos. & P. 404 (1709).
22 Y. B. 19 Hen. VI. 31, pl. 59; 2 Roll. Abr. 546 (D).
23 I Roll. Abr. 2, pl. 7.
24 Dial. de Scaccario II., Ch. 18.; Bract., fol. 429b; Y. B. 22 Hen.
VI. 38, pl. 6; Litt. §§ 168, 191; 3 Salk. 46; Com. Dig. *Baron & Feme*
(D); 1 Bl. Comm. 442.
25 The Common Law, 375, n. 2, 401, n. 1.
26 Simon Simeon's Case, Y. B. 30 Ed. III 14; s.c. *ib.* 6; 29 Ed.

Of course the identification between husband and wife, although by no means absolute, was far more complete than that between master and menial servant, just as in the latter case it went farther than in that of an agent employed for some particular transaction. Even in the case of villeins, while the lord might take advantage of their possession or their title, he could not take advantage of contracts or warranties made to them.[27] But the idea and its historical starting-point were the same throughout. When considering the later cases, the reader will remember that it is incontrovertably established that a wife was on the footing of a servant, that the consequences of the relation were familiarly expressed in terms of the fiction of identity, and, therefore, that the applicability of this fiction to the domestic relations generally must have been well known to the courts long before the date of the principal decisions, which it will be my task to interpret.

I now take up the liability of a master for the torts of his servant at common law. This has been supposed in England to have been manufactured out of the whole cloth, and introduced by the decision

III. 48. I have seen no reason to change the views expressed in The Common Law, Lecture XI., to meet the suggestions of Prof. Ames in 3 Harv. Law Rev. 388, n. 6. Undoubtedly the letter of credit was known in the reign of Henry III. 1 Royal Letters, Hen. III. 315. But the modern theory of contract applied to letters of credit, in my opinion, was not the theory on which assigns got the benefit of a warranty. Norcross v. James, 140 Mass. 188.

[27] Y. B. 22 Ass. pl. 27, fol. 93; Co. Lit. 117a.

in Michael *v.* Alestree [28] in the reign of Charles II. In view of the historical antecedents it would be very extraordinary if such a notion were correct. I venture to think that it is mistaken, and that the principle has gradually grown to its present form from beginnings of the earliest date. I also doubt whether Michael *v.* Alestree is an example for the principle in question. It rather seems to me a case in which the damage complained of was the natural consequence of the very acts commanded by the master, and which, therefore, as I have said above, needs no special or peculiar doctrine to account for it. It was an action on the case against master and servant; "for that the Defendants in *Lincoln's-Inn Fields,* a place where People are always going to and fro about their Business, brought a Coach with two ungovernable Horses, *& eux improvide incaute & absque debita consideratione ineptitudinis loci* there drove them to make them tractable and fit them for a Coach; and the Horses, because of their Ferocity, being not to be managed, ran upon the Plaintiff, and . . . wounded him: The master was absent," but both defendants were found guilty. "It was moved in Arrest of Judgment, That no *Sciens* is here laid of the Horses being unruly, nor any Negligence alledged, but *e contra,* that the Horses were ungovernable: Yet judgment was given for the Plaintiff, for it is alledged that it was *improvide & absque debita consideratione ineptitudinis loci;* and it shall be intended the Master Sent the servant to train the

---

[28] 2 Levinz, 172; S.C. 3 Keble, 650, 1 Ventris, 295 (T. 28 Car. II).

Horses there." [29]   In other words, although there was no negligence averred in the mode of driving the horses at the instant of the accident, but, *e contra,* that the horses were ungovernable, which was the scope of the defendant's objection, there was negligence in driving ungovernable horses for the purpose of breaking them in a public place, and that was averred, and was averred to have been done negligently.   Furthermore, it was averred to have been done negligently by the defendant, which was a sufficient allegation on its face, and would be supported by proof that the defendant, knowing the character of the horses, ordered his servant to break them in a public resort.   Indeed, the very character of the command (to break horses) imports sufficient knowledge; and when a command is given to do the specified act complained of, it always may be laid as the act of the party giving the order.[30]

When I come to investigate the true history of this part of the law, notwithstanding the likelihood which I have pointed out that it was a continuation and development of what I have traced in one or both of the parent systems, I must admit that I am met with a difficulty.   Even in Bracton, who writes under the full influence of the Roman law, I have failed to find any passage which distinctly asserts the civil liability of masters for their servants' torts apart from command or ratification.   There is one text, to be sure, which seems corrupt as it stands and which

[29] 2 Lev. 172.
[30] Sup., p. 51, 52.

could be amended by conjecture so as to assert it. But as the best manuscripts in Lincoln's Inn substantially confirm the printed reading, conjecture would be out of place.[31]

On the other hand, I do find an institution which may or may not have been connected with the Anglo-Saxon laws touching the responsibility of masters, but which, at any rate, equally connects liability of a different sort with family headship.

At about the time of the Conquest, what was known as the *Frithborh,* or frankpledge, either was introduced or grew greatly in importance. Among other things, the master was made the pledge of his servants, to hand them over to justice or to pay the fine himself. *"Omnes qui servientes habent, eorum sint francplegii,"* was the requirement of William's laws. Bracton quotes the similar provisions of Edward the Confessor, and also says that in some counties a man is held to answer for the members of his family.[32] The quasi-criminal liability of master for man is found as late as Edward II. alongside of the other rules of frankpledge, with which this discussion is not concerned. Fitzherbert's Abridgment[33] reads as follows: "Note that if the servant (*serviens*) of any lord while in his service (*in servicio suo existens*) commits a felony and is convicted, although after the felony (the master) has not

[31] Bract., fol. 115a.
[32] *"Tenebitur ille, in quibusdam partibus, de cujus fuerint familia et manupastu."* Bract., fol. 124b; i.e., for the persons under his *patria potestas.* LL. Gul. I., C. 52; LL. Edw. Conf., C. 21 (al. 20).
[33] *Corone,* pl. 428 (8 Ed. II. It canc.).

received him, he is to be amerced, and the reason is because he received him 'in bourgh.' " Bracton, in like manner, says that the master is bound *"Emendare"* for certain torts of his servant,[34] meaning, as I take it, to pay a fine, not damages.

But true examples of the peculiar law of master and servant are to be found before Edward II. The maxim *respondeat superior* has been applied to the torts of inferior officers from the time of Edward I. to the present day. Thus that chapter of the Statute of Westminster the Second,[35] which regulates distresses by sheriffs or bailiffs, makes the officer disregarding its provisions answerable, and then continues, *"si non habeat ballivus unde reddat reddat superior suus."* So a later chapter of the same statute, after subjecting keepers of jails to an action of debt for escapes in certain cases, provides that if the keeper is not able to pay, his superior, who committed the custody of the jail to him shall be answerable by the same writ.[36] So, again, the eighteenth chapter of the Articuli super Chartas [37] gives a writ of waste to wards, for waste done in their lands in the king's hands by escheators or sub-escheators, "against the escheator for his act (if he have whereof to answer), and if he have not, his master shall answer (*'si respoigne son sovereign'*) by like pain concerning the

---

[34] Bract., fol. 158b, 171a, b, 172b. Cf. Ducange, *"Emenda."*

[35] St. 13 Ed. I., St. I, Ch. 2, § 3.

[36] Ch. II. *ad finem.* *"Et si custos gaole non habeat per quod justicietur vel unde solvat respondeat superior suus qui custodiam hujusmodi gaole sibi commisit per idem breve."*

[37] St. 28 Ed. I., Ch. 18.

damages, as is ordained by the statute for them that do waste in wardships." A case of the time of Edward II. interpreting the above statute concerning jailers is given in Fitzherbert's Abridgment,[38] and later similar cases are referred to in Coke's Fourth Institute.[39]

It may be objected that the foregoing cases are all statutory. But the same principle seems to have been applied apart from any statute except that which gave counties the power to elect coroners, to make the county of Kent answerable to the king for a coroner's default, as well as in other instances which will be mentioned later.[40] Moreover, early statutes are as good evidence of prevailing legal conceptions as decisions are.

But again it may be objected that there were special grounds of public policy for requiring those who disposed of public offices of profit to appoint persons "for whom they will answer at their peril," in the words of another similar statute as to clerks in the King's Courts.[41] It might be said with truth

---

[38] *Dette,* pl. 172 (M. 11 Ed. II.).

[39] 4 Inst. 114; "45 E. 3, 9, 10, *Prior datife et removeable suffer eschape, respondeat superior.* 14 E. 4, *Pur insufficiency del bailie dun libertie respondeat dominus libertatis.* Vid. 44 E. 3, 13; 50 E. 3, 5; 14 H. 4, 22; 11 H. 6, 52; 30 H. 6, 32."

[40] See the writ of H. 14 Ed. III, ex parte, Remem. Regis, rot. 9, in Scacc. in 4 Inst. 114, and less fully in 2 Inst. 175. "*Et quia ipse coronator electus erat per comitatum juxta formam statuti, etc., ita quod in defectu ejusdem coronatoris totus comitatus ut elector et superior, etc. (tenetur), habeant regi respondere, praecip. (praeceptum fuit) nunc vic. quod de terris et tenementis (hominum) hujusmodi totius comitatus in balliva sua fieri fac.,*" etc. See the other references in 4 Inst. 114, and further Y. B. 49 Ed. III. 25, 26, pl. 3.

[41] St. 2 Hen. VI., Ch. 10.

that the responsibility was greater than in the case of private servants, and it might be asked whether *respondeat superior* in its strict sense is not an independent principle which is rather to be deemed one of the causes of the modern law, than a branch from a common stem. It certainly has furnished us with one of the inadequate reasons which have been put forward for the law as it is — that somebody must be held who is able to pay the damages.

The weight of the evidence seems to me to overcome these objections. I think it most probable that the liability for under-officers was a special application of conceptions drawn from the family and the power of the family head over his servants. Those conceptions were in existence, as I have shown. From a very early date, under-officers are called servants of their superior, as indeed it seems to be implied that they are, by the word *"sovereign"* or even *"superior,"* in the statutes which have been cited. "Sovereign" is used as synonymous with master in Dyer.[42] In the Y. B., II Edward IV. 1, pl. 1, it is said, "If I make a deputy, I am always officer, and he performs the office in my right and as my servant"; and from that day to this, not only has the same language been repeated,[43] but, as I shall show, one of the chosen fields for the express

[42] Alford *v.* Eglisfield, Dyer, 230b, pl. 56. The passage will be cited later in dealing with factors. See also Y. B. 27 Hen. VIII. 24, pl. 3.

[43] Parkes *v.* Mosse, Cro. Eliz. 181 (E. 32 Eliz.); Wheteley *v.* Stone, 2 Roll. Abr. 556, pl. 14; S. C. Hobart, 180; 1 Bl. Comm., 345, 346.

use of the fiction of identity is the relation of superior and under-officer.

Under Edward III. it was held that if an abbot has a wardship, and a co-canon commits waste, the abbot shall be charged by it, "for that is adjudged the deed of the abbot." [44] This expression appears to me not only to apply the rule *respondeat superior* beyond the case of public officers, but to adopt the fiction of identity as a mode of explaining the rule.

An earlier record of the same reign, although it turned on the laws of Oleron, shows that the King's Court would in some cases hold masters more strictly accountable for their servants' torts than is even now the case. A ship-master was held liable in trespass *de bonis asportatis* for goods wrongfully taken by the mariners, and it was said that he was answerable for all trespasses on board his ship. [45]

A nearly contemporaneous statute is worth mentioning, although it perhaps is to be construed as referring to the fines which have been mentioned above, or to other forfeitures, and not to civil damages. It reads, "That no merchant nor other, of what condition that he be, shall lose or forfeit his goods nor merchandizes for the trespass and forfeiture of his servant, unless he do it by the commandment or procurement of his master, or that he hath offended in the office in which his master hath set him, or in other manner, that the master be holden

---

[44] Y. B. 49 Ed. III, 25, 26, pl. 3.

[45] Brevia Regis in Turr. London, T. 24 Ed. III., No. 45, Bristol, printed in Molloy, Book 2, Ch. 3, § 16.

to answer for the deed of his servant by the law-merchant, as elsewhere is used."[46] The statute limits a previously existing liability, but leaves it open that the master still shall be holden to answer for the deed of his servant in certain cases, including those of the servant's offending in the office in which the master hath set him. It is dealing with merchants, to be sure, but is another evidence that the whole modern law is of ancient extraction.

It must be remembered, however, that the cases in which the modern doctrines could have been applied in the time of the Year Books were exceedingly few. The torts dealt with by the early law were almost invariably wilful. They were either prompted by actual malevolence, or at least were committed with full foresight of the ensuing damage.[47] And as the judges from an early day were familiar with the distinction between acts done by a man on his own behalf and those done in the capacity of servant,[48] it is obvious that they could not have held masters generally answerable for such torts unless they were prepared to go much beyond the point at which their successors have stopped.[49]

[46] St. 27 Ed. III., St. 2, cap. 19.

[47] The Common Law, 3, 4, 101–103. I do not mean as a matter of articulate theory, but as a natural result of the condition of things. As to very early principles of liability see now Dr. Brunner's most learned and able discussion in Sitzungsberichte der kön. Preuss. Akademie der Wissensch., XXXV., July 10, 1890. *Uber absichtlose Missethat im Altdeutschen Strafrechte.* Some of the cases mentioned by him, such as Beowulf, 2435, had come to my notice.

[48] See, e.g., Gascoigne in Y. B. 7 Hen. IV. 34, 35, pl. 1.

[49] Cf. Dr. and Stud. Dial. 2, Ch. 42 (A.D. 1530).

Apart from frauds[50] and intentional trespasses against the master's will[51] I know of only one other case in the Year Books which is important to this part of my subject. That, however, is very important. It is the case concerning fire,[52] which was the precedent relied on by Lord Holt in deciding Turberville *v.* Stampe,[53] which in its turn has been the starting-point of the later decisions on master and servant.[54] I therefore shall state it at length.

Beaulieu sued Finglam, alleging that the defendant so negligently guarded his fire that for want of due guard of the same the plaintiff's houses and goods were burned. Markham (J.), "A man is held to answer for the act of his servant or of his guest (*hosteller*) in such case; for if my servant or my guest puts a candle on a beam (*en un pariet*), and the candle falls in the straw, and burns all my house, and the house of my neighbor also, in this case I shall answer to my neighbor for the damage which he has, *quod concedebatur per curiam.* Horneby [of counsel], Then he should have had a writ, *Quare domum suam ardebat vel exarsit.* Hull [of counsel], That will be against all reason to put blame or default in a man where there is (*il ad*) none in

[50] Y. B. 9 Hen. VI. 53, pl. 37.

[51] Y. B. 13 Hen. VII. 15, pl. 10. Cf. Keilway, 3b, pl. 7 (M. 12 Hen. VII.).

[52] Y. B. 2 Hen. IV. 18, pl. 6.

[53] Carthew, 425, shows that the Year Book was cited. And the language of Lord Holt, reported in 1 Ld. Raym. 264, shows that he had it before his mind.

[54] Brucker *v.* Fromont, 6 T. R. 659; M'Manus *v.* Crickett, 1 East, 106; Patten *v.* Rea, 2 C. B. N. S. 606.

him; for negligence of his servants cannot be called his feasance. Thirning [C. J.], If a man kills (*tue ou occist*) a man by misfortune he will forfeit his goods, and he must have his charter of pardon *de grace. Ad quod Curia concordat.* Markham, I shall answer to my neighbor for him who enters my house by my leave or my knowledge, or is entertained (*hoste*) by me or by my servant, if he does, or any one of them does such a thing, as with a candle (*come de chandel*), or other thing, by which feasance the house of my neighbor is burned; but if a man from outside my house, against my will, puts the fire in the straw of my house, or elsewhere, by which my house is burned and also the houses of my neighbors are burned, for that I shall not be held to answer to them, etc., for this cannot be said to be through ill-doing (*male*) on my part, but against my will." Horneby then said that the defendant would be ruined if this action were maintained against him. Thirning (C. J.), "What is that to us? It is better that he should be undone wholly, than that the law should be changed for him.[55] Then they were at issue that the plaintiff's house was not burned by the defendant's fire."

The foregoing case affords some ground for the argument which was vainly pressed in Turberville *v.* Stampe, that the liability was confined to the house.[56] Such a limit is not unsupported by analogy. By the old law a servant's custody of his master's things was

[55] Y. B. 2 Hen. IV. 18, pl. 6.
[56] See also I Bl. Comm. 431; Noy's Maxims, Ch. 44.

said to be the master's possession within his house, but the servant's on a journey outside of it.[57] So an innkeeper was liable for all goods within the inn whether he had the custody of them or not.[58] So in the case which has been mentioned above, a master was said to be responsible for the acts of his servants on board ship. It will be noticed also that the responsibility of a householder seems to be extended to his guests. From that day to this there have been occasional glimpses of a tendency to regard guests as part of the *familia* for the purposes of the law.[59] And in view of the fact that by earlier law if a guest was allowed to stop in the house three days, he was called *hoghenehine* or *agenhine*, that is, *own hine* or servant of the host, it may be thought that we have here an echo of the *frithborh*.[60] But with whatever limits and for whatever occult causes, the responsibility of the head of the house for his servants was clearly recognized, and, it would seem, the identification of the two, notwithstanding a statement by counsel, as clear as ever has been made since, of the objections to the doctrine.

The later cases in the Year Books are of wilful wrongs, as I have said, and I now pass to the subsequent reports. Under Elizabeth a defendant justified taking sheep for toll under a usage to have toll of strangers' sheep driven through the vill by

---

[57] Y. B. 21 Hen. VII. 14, pl. 21; The Common Law, 226.

[58] Y. B. 42 Ass. pl. 17, fol. 260; 42 Ed. III. 11, pl. 13.

[59] Y. B. 13 Ed. IV. 10, pl. 5; Southcote v. Stanley, 1 H. N. 247, 250.

[60] Bract., fol. 124b; LL. Gul. I., Ch. 48; LL. Edw. Conf., Ch. 23.

strangers, and if he were denied by such stranger driving them, to distrain them. The defendant alleged that the plaintiff, the owner of the sheep, was a stranger, but did not allege that the driver was. But the court sustained the plea, saying, "The driving of the servant is the driving of the master; and if he be a foreigner, that sufficeth." [61]

I leave on one side certain cases which often have been cited for the proposition that a master is chargeable for his servant's torts, because they may be explained otherwise and make no mention of it.[62] The next evidence of the law to which I refer is the passage from West's *Symboleography* which was given in full at the outset, and which gives the modern doctrine of agency as well as the fiction of identity in their full development. There are two nearly contemporaneous cases in which unsuccessful attempts were made to hold masters liable for wilful wrongs of their servants, in one for a piracy,[63] in the other for a fraud.[64] They are interesting chiefly as showing that the doctrine under discussion

[61] Smith *v.* Shepherd, Cro. Eliz., 710; M. 41 & 42 Eliz. B. R.

[62] The most important is Lord North's case, Dyer, 161a (T. 4 & 5 Phil. & M.); but there the master was a bailee bound to return at his peril (cf. The Common Law, 175–179. In Dyer, 238b, pl. 38 (E. 7 Eliz.), a customer of a port was said to be liable to the penalties for a false return, although he made it through the concealment of his deputy. One or both of these cases are cited in Waltham *v.* Mulgar, Moore, 776; Southern *v.* How, Popham, 143; Boson *v.* Sandford, 1 Shower, 101; Lane *v.* Cotton, 12 Mod. 472, 489, etc.

[63] Waltham *v.* Mulgar, Moore, 776 (P. 3 Jac. 1.).

[64] Southern *v.* How, Cro. Jac. 468; s. c. Popham, 143; 2 Roll. Rep. 5, 26; Bridgman, 125, where the special verdict is set forth.

was in the air, but that its limits were not definitely fixed. The former sought to carry the rule *respondeat superior* to the full extent of the early statutes and cases which have been referred to, and cited the Roman law for its application to public affairs. The latter cites Doctor and Student. West also, it will have been noticed, indicates Roman influence.

Omitting one or two cases on the liability of the servant, which will be mentioned shortly, I come once more to a line of authorities touching public officers. I have said that although there was a difference in the degree of responsibility, under-officers always have been said to be servants.

Under Charles II. this difference was recognized, but it was laid down that "the high sheriff and under-sheriff is one officer," and on that ground the sheriff was held chargeable.[65] Lord Holt expressed the same thought: "What is done by the deputy is done by the principal, and it is the act of the principal," or, as it is put in the margin of the report, "Act of deputy may forfeit office of principal, because it is *quasi* his act." [66] Later still, Blackstone repeats from the bench the language of Charles's day. "There is a difference between master and servant, but a sheriff and all his officers are considered in cases like this as one person." So his associate judge, Gould, "I consider [the under-sheriff's clerk] as standing in the place of, and representing the very

---

[65] Cremer *v.* Humberston, 2 Keble, 352 (H. 19 & 20 Car. II.).

[66] Lane *v.* Cotton, 1 Salk, 17, 18; s.c. 1 Ld. Raym. 646; Com. 100 (P. 12 W. III.).

persons of . . . the sheriffs themselves." [67]   Again, the same idea is stated by Lord Mansfield: "For all civil purposes the act of the sheriff's bailiff is the act of the sheriff." [68]   The distinction taken above by Blackstone did not prevent his saying in his *Commentaries* that under-officers are servants of the sheriff; [69] and in Woodgate *v.* Knatchbull,[70] Ashurst, J., after citing the words of Lord Mansfield, adds, "This holds, indeed, in most instances with regard to servants in general"; and Blackstone says the same thing in a passage to be quoted hereafter.

Having thus followed down the fiction of identity with regard to one class of servants, I must now return once more to Lord Holt's time. In Boson *v.* Sanford,[71] Eyres, J., says that the master of a ship is no more than a servant, "the power which he hath is by the civil law, Hob. 111, and it is plain the act or default of the servant shall charge the owner." Again, in Turberville *v.* Stampe,[72] Lord Holt, after beginning according to the Roman law that "if my servant throws dirt into the highway I am indictable," continues, "So in this case, if the defendant's servant kindled the fire in the way of husbandry and proper for his employment, though he had no express com-

---

[67] Saunderson *v.* Baker, 3 Wilson, 309 s.c. 2 Wm. Bl. 832; (T. 12 G. III. 1772).

[68] Ackworth *v.* Kempe, Douglas, 40, 42 (M. 19 Geo. III. 1778).

[69] I Bl. Comm. 345, 346.

[70] 2 T. R. 148, 154 (1787).

[71] I Shower, 101. 107 (M. 2 Wm. III.).

[72] I Ld. Raym. 264 (M. 9 Wm. III.); s. c. 3 *id.* 250, Carthew, 425, Com. 32, 1 Salk. 13, Skinner, 681, 12 Mod. 151, Comb. 459, Holt, 9.

mand of his master, yet the master shall be liable
to an action for damages done to another by the fire;
for it shall be intended, that the servant had authority from his master, it being for his master's benefit."
This is the first of a series of cases decided by Lord
Holt [73] which are the usual starting-point of modern
decisions, and it will be found to be the chief authority relied on by cases which have become leading in
their turn.[74] It therefore is interesting to note that
it only applied the principles of Beaulieu v. Finglam,
in the Year Book 2 Henry IV., to a fire outside the
house, that the illustration taken from the Roman
law shows that Lord Holt was thinking of the responsibility of a *paterfamilias,* and that in another
case within three years [75] he made use of the fiction
of identity.

I may add, by way of confirmation, that Blackstone, in his *Commentaries,* after comparing the
liability of the master who "hath the superintendence
and charge of all his household" if any of his family
cast anything out of his house into the street, with
that of the Roman *paterfamilias,*[76] further observes
that the "master may frequently be answerable for
his servant's misbehavior, but never can shelter himself from punishment by laying the blame on his

[73] Jones v. Hart, 2 Salk. 441; *s.c.* 1 Ld. Raym. 738, 739 (M. 10
Wm. III); Middleton v. Fowler, 1 Salk 282 (M. 10 Wm.
III); Hern v. Nichols, 1 Salk. 289.
[74] Brucker v. Fromont, 6 T.R. 659; M'Manus v. Crickett, 1 East,
106; Patten v. Rea, 2 C.B. N.S. 606 (1857).
[75] Lane v. Cotton, 1 Salk. 17, 18.
[76] See also Noy's *Maxims,* Ch. 44.

agent. The reason of this is still uniform and the same; that the wrong done by the servant is looked upon in law as the wrong of the master himself." [77]

There is another line of cases which affords striking and independent evidence that the law of master and servant is a survival from slavery or other institution of like effect for the present purpose, and that the identification of the two parties was carried out in some cases to its logical result. If a servant, although a freeman, was treated for the purposes of the relation as if he were a slave who only sustained the *persona* of his master, it followed that when the master was liable, the servant was not. There seems to have been a willingness at one time to accept the conclusion. It was said under James and Charles I. that the sheriff only was liable if an under-sheriff made a false return, "for the law doth not take notice of him." [78] So it was held in the latter reign that case does not lie against husband and wife for negligently keeping their fire in their house, "because this action lies on the . . . custom . . . against *patrem familias* and not against a servant or a *feme covert* who is in the nature of a servant." [79] So Rolle says that "if the servant of an innkeeper sells wine which is corrupt, knowing this, action of deceit lies not against the servant, for he did this only as

[77] Bl. Comm. 431, 432.

[78] Cremer & Tookley's Case, Godbolt, 385, 389 (Jac. I.); Laicock's Case, Latch, 187 (H. 2 Car. I.).

[79] Shelley & Burr, 1 Roll. Abr. 2, pl. 7 (M. 1 Car. I.). Cf. I Bl. Comm. 431; Com. Dig., *Action on the case for negligence*, A. C.

servant." [80]   So as to an attorney maliciously acting
in a case where he knew there was no cause of action.
"For that what he does is only as servant to another,
and in the way of his calling and profession." [81]

Later this was cut down by Lord Holt to this rule
that a servant is not liable for a neglect (i.e. a non-
feasance), "for they must consider him only as a
servant"; "but for a misfeasance an action will lie
against a servant or deputy, but not *quatenus* a
deputy or servant, but as a wrong-doer." [82]   That is
to say, although it is contrary to theory to allow a
servant to be sued for conduct in his capacity as such,
he cannot rid himself of his responsibility as a freeman, and may be sued as a free wrong-doer.   This,
of course, is the law to-day. [83]   Yet as late as Blackstone's Commentaries it was said that "if a smith's
servant lames a horse while he is shoeing him, an
action lies against the master, and not against the
servant. [84]

I think I now have traced sufficiently the history
of agency in torts.   The evidence satisfies me that
the common law has started from the *patria potestas*

[80] Roll. Abr. 95 (T), citing no authority, and adding, "*Contra,*
9 Hen. VI., 53b." The contradiction is doubtful.

[81] Anon., I Mod. 209, 210 (H. 27 & 28, Car II.).   Cf. Barker *v.*
Braham, 2 W. Bl. 866, 869.

[82] Lane *v.* Cotton, 12 Mod. 472, 488, T. 13 W. III. Cf. Mors *v.*
Slew, 3 Keble, 135 (23 & 24 Car. II., 1671, 1672); also Mires *v.*
Solebay, 2 Mod. 242, 244 (T. 29 Car. II.), for an exception by
Scroggs, C. J.

[83] Sands *v.* Childs, 3 Lev. 351, 352; Perkins *v.* Smith, 3 Wilson, 328
(1752).

[84] 1 Bl. Comm. 431; Bac. Abr., Master and Servant, K. It is enough
simply to refer to the law as to the liability of married women.

and the *firthborh*, — whether following or simply helped by the Roman law, it does not matter, — and that it has worked itself out to its limits through the formula of identity. It is true that liability for another as master or principal is not confined to family relations; but I have shown partly, and shall complete the proof later, that the whole doctrine has been worked out in terms of master and servant and on the analogies which those terms suggested.

AGENCY.*

II

THE history of agency as applied to contract is
next to be dealt with.[1] In this branch of the law there
is less of anomaly and a smaller field in which to
look for traces of fiction than the last. A man is not
bound by his servant's contracts unless they are
made on his behalf and by his authority, and that
he should be bound then is plain common-sense. It
is true that in determining how far authority extends,
the question is of ostensible authority and not of
secret order. But this merely illustrates the general
rule which governs a man's responsibility for his
acts throughout the law. If, under the circumstances
known to him, the obvious consequence of the principal's own conduct in employing the agent is that
the public understand him to have given the agent
certain powers, he gives the agent these powers. And
he gives them just as truly when he forbids their
exercise as when he commands it. It seems always
to have been recognized that an agent's ostensible
powers were his real powers![2] and on the other hand
it always has been the law that an agent could not

* *Harvard Law Review.* Vol. V. No. 1.
[1] *4 Harv. Law Rev.* 345.
[2] Y. B. 27 Ass., pl. 5, fol. 133; Anon., 1 Shower, 95; Nickson *v.*
Brohan, 10 Mod. 109, etc.

bind his principal beyond the powers actually given in the sense above explained.

There is, however, one anomaly introduced by agency even into the sphere of contract, — the rule that an undisclosed principal may sue or be sued on a contract made by an agent on his behalf; and this must be examined, although the evidence is painfully meagre. The rule would seem to follow very easily from the identification of agent and principal, as I shall show more fully in a moment. It is therefore well to observe at the outset that the power of contracting through others, natural as it seems, started from the family relations, and that it has been expressed in the familiar language of identification.

Generally speaking, by the Roman law contractual rights could not be acquired through free persons who were strangers to the family. But a slave derived a standing to accept a promise to his master *ex persona domini.*[3] Bracton says that contracts can be accepted for a principal by his agent; but he starts from the domestic relations in language very like that of the Roman jurisconsults. An obligation may be acquired through slaves or free agents in our power, if they take the contract in the name of their master.[4]

It was said under Henry V. that a lease made by

---

[3] Inst. 3. 17, pr. See Gaius, 3, §§ 164-166.

[4] "Videndum etiam est per quas personas acquirator obligatio, et sciendum quod per procuratores, et per liberos, quos sub potestate nostra habemus, et per nosmetipsos, et filios nostros et per liberos homines servientes nostros." Bract., fol. 100 *b*. So, "Etiam dormienti per servum acquiritur, ut per procuratorem, si nomine domini stipuletur." Bract., fol. 28 *b.*

the seneschal of a prior should be averred as the lease of the prior,[5] and under James I. it was held that an assumpsit to a servant for his master was properly laid as an assumpsit to the master.[6] West's *Symboleography* belongs to the beginnings of the same reign. It will be remembered that the language which has been quoted from that work applies to contracts as well as to torts. A discussion in the Year Book, 8 Edward IV., fol. 11, is thus abridged in Popham: "My servant makes a contract, or buys goods to my use; I am liable, and it is my act."[7] Baron Parke explains the requirement that a deed executed by an agent should be executed in the name of his principal, in language repeated from Lord Coke: "The attorney is . . . put in place of the principal and represents his person."[8] Finally, Chitty, still speaking of contracts, says, like West, that "In point of law the master and servant, or principal and agent, are considered as one and the same person."[9]

I have found no early cases turning upon the law of undisclosed principal. It will be remembered that the only action on simple contract before Henry VI., and the chief one for a good while after, was debt,

[5] Y. B, 8 H. V. 4, pl. 17.

[6] Seignior & Wolmer's Case, Godbolt, 360 (T. 21 Jac.). Cf. Jordan's Case, Y. B. 27 H. VIII. 24, pl. 3.

[7] Drope v. Theyar, Popham, 178, 179 (P. 2 Car. I.).

[8] Hunter v. Parker, 7 M. & W. 322, 343 (1840); Combes's Case, 9 Rep, 75 a, 76 b, 77 (T. 11 Jac.). The fiction of identity between principle and agent was fully stated by Hobbes, who said many keen things about the law. Leviathan, Part I. Ch. 16. "Of Persons, Authors, and things Personated." Also De Homine, I. C. 15. De Homine Fictitio.

[9] 1 Bl. Comm. 429, note.

and that this was founded on a *quid pro quo* received by the debtor. Naturally, therefore, the chief question of which we hear in the earlier books is whether the goods came to the use of the alleged debtor.[10] It is at a much later date, though still in the action of debt, that we find the most extraordinary half of the rule under consideration first expressly recognized. In Scrimshire *v.* Alderton[11] (H. 16 G. II.) a suit was brought by an undisclosed principal against a purchaser from a *del credere* factor. Chief Justice Lee "was of opinion that this new method [*i.e.*, of the factor taking the risk of the debt for a larger commission] had not deprived the farmer of his remedy against the buyer." And he was only prevented from carrying out his opinion by the obstinacy of the jury at Guildhall. The language quoted implies that the rule was then well known, and this, coupled with the indications to be found elsewhere, will perhaps warrant the belief that it was known to Lord Holt.

Scott *v.* Surman,[12] decided at the same term that Scrimshire *v.* Alderton was tried, refers to a case of T. 9 Anne, Gurratt *v.* Cullum,[13] in which goods were sold by factors to J. S. without disclosing their principal. The factors afterwards went into bankruptcy. Their assignee collected the debt, and the principal then sued him for the money. "And this matter being

[10] Fitz. Abr. *Dett,* pl. 3 (T. 2 R. II.). Cf. Alford *v.* Eglisfield, Dyer, 230 *b* (T. 6 Eliz.), and notes.

[11] 2 Strange, 1182.

[12] Willes, 400, at p. 405 (H. 16 G. II.).

[13] Also reported in Buller, N. P. 42. Cf. Whitecomb *v.* Jacob, 1 Salk. 160 (T. 9 Anne).

referred by Holt for the opinion of the King's Bench, judgment was given on argument for the plaintiff. Afterwards at Guildhall, before Lord Chief Justice Parker, this case was cited and allowed to be law, because though it was agreed that payment by J. S. to [the factors] with whom the contract was made would be a discharge to J. S. against the principal, yet the debt was not in law due to them, but to the person whose goods they were . . . and being paid to the defendant who had no right to have it, it must be considered in law as paid for the use of him to whom it was due." This explanation seems to show that Chief Justice Parker understood the law in the same way as Chief Justice Lee, and, if it be the true one, would show that Lord Holt did also. I think the inference is somewhat strengthened by other cases from the Salkeld MSS. cited in Buller's *Nisi Prius*.[14] Indeed I very readily should believe that at a much earlier date, if one man's goods had come to another man's hand by purchase, the purchaser might have been charged, although he was unknown and had dealt through a servant,[15] and that perhaps he might have been, in the converse case of the goods belonging to an undisclosed master.[16]

[14] Gonzales *v.* Sladen; Thorp *v.* How (H. 13 W. III.); Buller, N.P. 130.

[15] See Goodbaylie's Case, Dyer, 230 *b*, pl. 56, n.; Truswell *v.* Middleton, 2 Roll. R. 269, 270. Note, however, the insistence on the servant being known as such in Fitz. Abr. *Dett*, pl. 3; 27 Ass., pl. 5, fol. 133.

[16] Consider the doubt as to ratifying a distress made "generally not showing his intent nor the cause wherefore he distrained" in Godbolt, 109, pl. 129 (M. 28 & 29 Eliz.). Suppose the case had been contract instead of tort, and with actual authority, would the same doubt have been felt?

The foregoing cases tend to show, what is quite probable, that the doctrine under discussion began with debt. I do not wish to undervalue the argument that may be drawn from this fact, that the law of undisclosed principal has no profounder origin than the thought that the defendant, having acquired the plaintiff's goods by way of purchase, fairly might be held to pay for them in an action of contract, and that the rule then laid down has been extended since to other contracts.[17]

But suppose what I have suggested be true, it does not dispose of the difficulties. If a man buy's B.'s goods of A., thinking A. to be the owner, and B. then sues him for the price, the defendant fairly may object that the only contract which he has either consented or purported to make is a contract with A., and that a stranger, to both the intent and the form of a voluntary obligation cannot sue upon it. If the contract was made with the owner's consent, let the contractee bring his action. If it was made without actual or ostensible authority, the owner's right's can be asserted in an action of tort. The general rule in case of a tortious sale is that the owner cannot waive the tort and sue in assumpsit.[18] Why should the fact that the seller was secretly acting in the owner's behalf enlarge the owner's rights as against a third person? The extraordinary character of the doctrine is still clearer when it is held that under a

[17] Sims v. Bond, 5 B. & Ad. 389, 393 (1833). Cf. Bateman v. Phillips, 15 East, 272 (1812).

[18] Berkshire Glass Co. v. Wolcott, 2 Allen (Mass.) 227.

contract purporting to be made with the plaintiff and another jointly, the plaintiff may show that the two ostensible joint parties were agents for himself alone, and thus set up a several right in the teeth of the words used and of the ostensible transaction, which gave him only a joint one.[19]

Now, if we apply the formula of identification and say that the agent represents the person of the owner, or that the principal adopts the agent's name for the purposes of that contract, we have at once a formal justification of the result. I have shown that the power of contracting through agents started from the family, and that principal and agent were identified in contract as well as in tort. I think, therefore, that the suggested explanation has every probability in its favor. So far as Lord Holt is concerned, I may add that in Gurratt v. Cullum the agent was a factor, that a factor in those days always was spoken of as a servant, and that Lord Holt was familiar with the identification of servant and master. If he was the father of the present doctrine, it is fair to infer that the technical difficulty was consciously or unconsciously removed from his mind by the technical fiction. And the older we imagine the doctrine to be, the stronger does a similar inference become. For just in proportion as we approach the archaic stage of the law, the greater do we find the technical obstacles in the way of any one attempting to enforce a contract except the actual party to it, and the greater

[19] Spurr v. Cass, L. R. 5 Q. B. 656. See further, Sloan v. Merrill, 135 Mass. 17, 19.

therefore must have been the need of a fiction to overcome them.[20]

The question which I have been considering arises
in another form with regard to the admission of oral
evidence in favor of or to charge a principal, when a
contract has been made in writing, which purports
on its face to be made with or by the alleged agent
in person. Certainly the argument is strong that
such evidence varies the writing, and if the Statute
of Frauds applies, that the statute is not satisfied unless the name of the principal appears. Yet the contrary has been decided. The step was taken almost
sub silentio.[21] But when at last a reason was offered,
it turned on, or at least was suggested by, the notion
of the identity of the parties. It was in substance
that the principal "is taken to have adopted the name
of the [agent] as his own, for the purpose of such contracts," as it was stated by Smith in his Leading
Cases, paraphrasing the language of Lord Denman in
Trueman *v.* Loder.[22]

I gave some evidence at the beginning of this discussion, that notions drawn from the *familia* were

---

[20] Cf. The Common Law, Ch. x. and xi. "Unsere heutigen Ans-
chauungen . . . können sich nur schwer in ursprüngliche Rechts-
zustände hineinfinden, in welchen . . . bei Contrahirung oder Zahlung
einer Schuld die handelnden Subjecte nicht als personae fungibiles
galten." Brunner, Zulässigkeit der Anwaltschaft im französ, etc. Rechte.
(Zeitschr. für vergleich. Rechtswissenschaft.) Norcross *v.* James, 140
Mass. 188, 189.

[21] Bateman *v.* Phillips, 15 East, 272 (1812); Garrett *v.* Handley, 4
B. & C. 664 (1825); Higgins *v.* Senior, 8 M. & W. 834, 844 (1841).

[22] 11 Ad. & El. 595; s. c. 3 P. & D. 267, 271 (1840); 2 Sm. L. C.,
8th ed., 408, note to Thompson *v.* Davenport; Byington *v.* Simpson, 134
Mass. 169, 170.

applied to free servants, and that they were extended
beyond the domestic relations. All that I have quoted
since tends in the same direction. For when such
notions are applied to freemen in a merely contractual
state of service it is not to be expected that their influence should be confined to limits which became
meaningless when servants ceased to be slaves. The
passage quoted from Bracton proved that already
in his day the analogies of domestic service were
applied to relations of more limited subjection. I
have now only to complete the proof that agency in
the narrower sense, the law familiar to the higher
and more important representatives employed in
modern business, is simply a branch of the law of
master and servant.

First of the attorney. The primitive lawsuit was
conducted by the parties in person. Counsel, if they
may be called so, were very early admitted to conduct the formal pleadings in the presence of the party
who was thus enabled to avoid the loss of his suit,
which would have followed a slip on his part in uttering the formal words, by disavowing the pleading of
his advocate. But the Frankish law very slowly
admitted the possibility of giving over the conduct
of a suit to another, or of its proceeding in the absence
of the principals concerned. Brunner has traced the
history of the innovation by which the appointment
of an attorney (i.e., *loco positus*) came generally to
be permitted, with his usual ability. It was brought
to England with the rest of the Norman law, was
known already to Glanvill, and gradually grew to

its present proportions. The question which I have to consider, however, is not the story of its introduction, but the substantive conception under which it fell when it was introduced.

If you were thinking of the matter *a priori* it would seem that no reference to history was necessary, at least to explain the client's being bound in the cause by his attorney's acts. The case presents itself like that of an agent authorized to make a contract in such terms as he may think advisable. But as I have hinted, whatever common-sense would now say, even in the latter case it is probable that the power of contracting through others was arrived at in actual fact by extending the analogy of slaves to freemen. And it is at least equally clear that the law had need of some analogy or fiction in order to admit a representation in lawsuits. I have given an illustration from Iceland in my book on the Common Law. There the conduct of a suit was transferred from Thorgier to Mord "as if he were the next of kin." [23] In the Roman law it is well known that the same difficulty was experienced. The English law agreed with the Northern sources in treating attorneys as sustaining the *persona* of their principal. The result may have been worked out in a different way, but that fundamental thought they had in common. I do not inquire into the recondite causes, but simply observe the fact.

Bracton says that the attorney represents the

[23] The Common Law, 359. See Brunner, in 1 Holtzendorff, Encyc. II. 3, A. 1, § 2, 3d ed., p. 166. 1 Stubbs, Const. Hist. 82.

persona of his principal in nearly everything.[24] He was "put in the place of" his principal, *loco positus* (according to the literal meaning of the word *attorney*), as every other case in the *Abbreviatio Placitorum* shows. The *essoign de malo lecti* had reference to the illness of the attorney as a matter of necessity.[25] But, in general, the attorney was dealt with on the footing of a servant, and he is called so as soon as his position is formulated. Such is the language of the passage in West's *Symboleography* which I have quoted above, and the anonymous case which held an attorney is not liable for maliciously acting in a cause which he knew to be unfounded.[26] When, therefore, it is said that the "act of the attorney is the act of his client," it is simply the familiar fiction concerning servants applied in a new field. On this ground it was held that the client was answerable in trespass, for assault and false imprisonment, where his attorney had caused the party to be arrested on a void writ, wholly irrespective, it would seem, of any actual command or knowledge on the part of the client;[27] and in trespass *quare clausum*, for an officer's breaking a man's house and taking his goods by command of an attorney's agent without the actual knowledge either of the client or the attorney. The court said that the client was "answerable for the

24 "Attornatus fere in omnibus personam domini representat." Bract., fol. 342 *a*. See LL. Hen. I. 42, § 2.
25 Bract., fol. 342 *a*. Cf. Glanv. XI., C. 3.
26 Anon., 1 Mod. 209, 210 (H. 27 & 28 Car. II.).
27 Parsons *v.* Loyd, 3 Wils. 341, 345; s. c. 2 W. Bl. 845 (M. 13 G. III. 1772); Barker *v.* Braham, 2 W. Bl. 866, 868, 869; s. c. 3 Wils. 368.

act of his attorney, and that [the attorney] and his agent [were] to be considered as one person." [28]

The only other agent of the higher class that I think it necessary to mention is the factor. I have shown elsewhere that he is always called a servant in the old books.[29] West's language includes factors as well as attorneys. Servant, factor, and attorney are mentioned in one breath and on a common footing in the Year Book, 8 Edward IV., folio 11 *b*. So Dyer,[30] "if a purveyor, factor, or servant make a contract for his sovereign or master." So in trover for money against the plaintiff's "servant and factor." [31] It is curious that in one of the first attempts to make a man liable for the fraud of another, the fraudulent party was a factor. The case was argued in terms of master and servant.[32] The first authority for holding a master answerable for his servant's fraud is another case of a factor.[33] Nothing is said of master and servant in the short note in Salkeld. But in view of the argument in Southern *v.* How, just referred to, which must have been before Lord Holt's mind, and the invariable language of the earlier books, including Lord Holt's own when arguing Morse *v.* Slue ("Factor, who is servant at the master's

---

[28] Bates *v.* Pilling, 6 B. & C. 38 (1826).

[29] The Common Law, 228, n. 3, 181. See further generally, 230, and n. 4, 5.

[30] Alford *v.* Eglisfield, Dyer, 230 *b*, pl. 56.

[31] Holiday *v.* Hicks, Cro. Eliz. 638, 661, 746. See further, Malyne's Lex. Merc., Pt. I. Ch. 16; Molloy, Book 3, Ch. 8, § 1; Williams *v.* Millington, 1 H. Bl. 81, 82.

[32] Southern *v.* How, Cro. Jac. 468; s. c. Popham, 143.

[33] Hern *v.* Nichols, 1 Salk. 289.

dispose"),[34] it is safe to assume that he considered the case to one of master and servant, and it always is cited as such.[35]

To conclude this part of the discussion, I repeat from my book on the Common Law [36] that as late as Blackstone agents appear under the general head of servants; that the precedents for the law of agency are cases of master and servant, when the converse is not the case; and that Blackstone's language on this point is express: "There is yet a fourth species of servants, if they may be so called, being rather in a superior, a ministerial, capacity; such as *stewards, factors,* and *bailiffs;* whom, however, the law considers as servants *pro tempore,* with regard to such of their acts as affect their master's or employer's property." [37]

Possession is the third branch of the law in which the peculiar doctrines of agency are to be discovered, and to that I now pass.

The Roman law held that the possession of a slave was the possession of his master, on the practical ground of the master's power.[38] At first it confined possession through others pretty closely to things in custody of persons under the *patria potestas* of the possessor (including prisoners *bona fide* held as slaves). Later the right was extended by a constitution of Severus.[39] The common law in like manner

[34] Mors *v.* Slew, 3 Keble, 72.
[35] Smith, Master and Servant, 3d ed., 266.
[36] P. 228 *et seq.* [37] 1 Bl. Comm. 427.
[38] The Common Law, 228; Gaius, 3, §§ 164–166.
[39] Inst. 2, 9, §§ 4, 5; C. 7. 32. 1.

allowed lords to appropriate lands and chattels purchased by their villeins, and after they had manifested their will to do so, the occupation of the villeins was taken to be the right of their lords.[40] As at Rome, the analogies of the *familia* were extended to free agents. Bracton allows possession through free agents, but the possession must be held in the name of the principal;[41] and from that day to this it always has been the law that the custody of the servant is the possession of the master.[42]

The disappearance of the servant under the *persona* of his master, of which a trace was discovered in the law of torts, in this instance has remained complete. Servants have no possession of property in their custody as such.[43] The distinction in this regard between servants and all bailees whatsoever [44] is fundamental, although it often has been lost sight of. Hence a servant can commit larceny [45] and cannot maintain trover.[46] A bailee cannot commit larceny [47]

[40] Littleton, § 177. Cf. Bract. fol. 191 *a*; Y. B. 22 Ass., pl. 37, fol. 93; Litt., § 172; Co. Lit. 117 *a*.

[41] Bract., fol. 28 *b*, 42 *b*, 43, etc.; Fleta, IV., C. 3, § 1, C. 10, § 7, C. 11, § 1.

[42] Wheteley *v.* Stone, 2 Roll. Abr. 556, pl. 14; s. c. Hobart, 180; Drope *v.* Theyar, Popham, 178, 179.

[43] The Common Law, 227.

[44] The Common Law, 174, 211, 221, 243; Hallgarten *v.* Oldham, 135 Mass. 1, 9.

[45] Y. B. 13 Ed. IV. 9, 10, pl. 5; 21 H. VII. 14, pl. 21.

[46] The Common Law, 227, n. 2. The distinction mentioned above, under torts, between servants in the house and on a journey, led to the servant's being allowed an appeal of robbery, without prejudice to the general principle. Heydon & Smith's Case, 13 Co. Rep. 67, 69; Drope *v.* Theyar, Popham, 178, 179; Coombs *v.* Hundred of Bradley, 2 Salk. 613, pl. 2; ib., pl. 1. [47] 2 Bish. Crim. Law, § 833, 7th ed.

and can maintain trover.[48]   In an indictment for
larceny against a third person the property cannot
be laid in a servant,[49] it may be laid in a bailee.[50]
A servant cannot assert a lien;[51] a bailee, of course,
may, even to the exclusion of the owner's right to the
possessory actions.[52]

Here, then, is another case in which effects have
survived their causes. But for survival and the fiction of identity it would be hard to explain why in this
case alone the actual custody of one man should be
deemed by the law to be the possession of another
and not of himself.

A word should be added to avoid a misapprehension
of which there are signs in the books, and to which
I have adverted elsewhere,[53] A man may be a servant for some other purpose, and yet not a servant in
his possession. Thus, an auctioneer or a factor is a
servant for purposes of sale, but not for purposes
of custody. His possession is not that of his principal, but, on the contrary, is adverse to it, and held
in his own name, as is shown by his lien. On the
other hand, if the fiction of identity is adhered to,
there is nothing to hinder a man from constituting
another his agent for the sole purpose of maintain-
ing his possession, with the same effect as if the agent
were a domestic servant, and in that case the principal would have possession and the agent would not.

[48] The Common Law, 174, 243.   [49] 2 East, P. C. 652, 653.
[50] Kelyng, 39.
[51] Bristow v. Whitmore, 4 De G. & J. 325, 334.
[52] Lord v. Price, L. R. 9 Ex. 54; Owen v. Knight, 4 Bing. N. C. 54 57
[53] The Common Law, 233.

Agency is comparatively unimportant in its bearing on possession, for reasons connected with procedure. With regard to chattels, because a present right of possession is held enough to maintain the possessory actions, and therefore a bailor, upon a bailment terminable at his will, has the same remedies as a master, although he is not one. With regard to real estate, because the royal remedies, the assizes, were confined to those who had a feudal seisin, and the party who had the seisin could recover as well when his lands were subject to a term of years as when they were in charge of agents or servants.[54]

Ratification is the only doctrine of which the history remains to be examined. With regard to this I desire to express myself with great caution, as I shall not attempt to analyze exhaustively the Roman sources from which it was derived. I doubt, however, whether the Romans would have gone the length of the modern English law, which seems to have grown to its present extent on English soil.

Ulpian said that a previous command to dispossess another would make the act mine, and, although opinion was divided on the subject, he thought that ratification would have the same effect. He agreed with the latitudinarian doctrine of the Sabinians, who compared ratification to a previous command.[55] The Sabinians' "comparison" of ratification to mandate may have been a mere figure of speech to explain the natural conclusion that if one accepts possession

[54] Bract., fol. 207 a. Cf. ib., 220. Heusler, Gewere, 126.
[55] D. 43, 16, 1, §§ 12, 14. Cf. D. 46, 3, 12, § 4.

of a thing which has been acquired for him by wrongful force, he is answerable for the property in the same way as if he had taken it himself. It therefore is hardly worth while to inquire whether the glossators were right in their comment upon this passage, that the taking must have been in the name of the assumed principal, — a condition which is ambiguously mentioned elsewhere in the Digest.[56]

Bracton copied Ulpian,[57] still, so far as I have observed, not going beyond cases of distress [58] and disseisin.[59] The first reported cases known to me are again assizes of novel disseisin.[60]

But later decisions went much beyond this point, as may be illustrated by one of them.[61] In trespass *de bonis asportatis* the defendant justified as bailiff. After charging the inquest Gascoigne said that "if the defendant took the chattels claiming property in himself for a heriot, although the lord afterward agreed to that taking for services due him, still he [the defendant] cannot be called his bailiff for that time. But had he taken them without command, for services due the lord, and had the lord afterwards agreed to his taking, he shall be adjudged as bailiff, although he was nowhere his bailiff before that tak-

---

[56] D. 43, 26, 13. (Pomponius).   [57] Bract., fol. 171 *b*.

[58] Fol. 158 *b*, 159 *a*.

[59] Fol. 171. But note that by ratification "suam facit injuriam, et ita tenetur ad utrumque, ad restitutionem, s. [et] ad pœnam." Ibid., *b*.

[60] Y. B. 30 Ed. I. 128 (Horwood) (where, however, the modern doctrine is stated and the Roman maxim is quoted by the judge); 38 Ass., pl. 9, fol. 223; s. c. 38 Ed. III. 18; 12 Ed. IV. 9, pl. 23; Plowden, 8 *ad fin*, 27, 31.

[61] Y. B. 7 H. IV. 34, 35, pl. 1.

ing." A ratification, according to this, may render lawful *ab initio* an act which without the necessary authority is a good cause of action, and for which the authority was wanting at the time that it was done. Such is still the law of England.[62] The same principle is applied in a less startling manner to contract, with the effect of giving rights under them to persons who had none at the moment when the contract purported to be complete.[63] In the case of a tort, it follows, of course, from what has been said, that if it is not justified by the ratification, the principal in whose name and for whose benefit it was done is answerable for it.[64]

Now it may be argued very plausibly that the modern decisions have only enlarged the comparison

[62] Godbolt, 109, 110, pl. 129; s. c. 2 Leon, 196, pl. 246 (M. 28 & 29 Eliz.); Hull v. Pickersgill, 1 Brod. & B. 282; Muskett v. Drummond, 10 B. & C. 153, 157; Buron v. Denman, 2 Exch. 167 (1848); Secretary of State in Council of India v. Kamachee Boye Sahaba, 13 Moore, P. C. 22 (1859), 86; Cheetham v. Mayor of Manchester, L. R. 10 C. P. 249; Wiggins v. United States, 3 Ct. of Cl. 412. But see Bro. Abr., *Trespass*, pl. 86; Fitz, Abr., *Bayllie*, pl. 4.

[63] Wolff v. Horncastle, 1 Bos. & P. 316 (1798). See further, Spittle v. Lavender, 2 Brod, & B. 452 (1821).

[64] Bract. 159 a, 171 b; Bro., *Trespass*, pl. 113; Bishop v. Montague, Cro. Eliz. 824; Gibson's Case, Lane, 90; Com. Dig., *Trespass*, c. 1; Sanderson v. Baker, 2 Bl. 832; s. c. 3 Wils. 309; Barker v. Braham, 2 Bl. 866, 868; s. c. 3 Wils. 368; Badkin v. Powell, Cowper, 476, 479; Wilson v. Tumman, 6 Man. & Gr. 236, 242; Lewis v. Read, 13 M. & W. 834; Buron v. Denman, 2 Exch. 167, 188; Bird v. Brown, 4 Exch. 786, 799; Eastern Counties Ry. v. Broom, 6 Exch. 314, 326, 327; Roe v. Birkenhead, Lancashire, & Cheshire Junction Ry., 7 Exch. 36, 44; Ancona v. Marks, 7 H. & N. 686, 695; Perley v. Georgetown, 7 Gray, 464; Condit v. Baldwin, 21 N. Y. 219, 225; Exum v. Brister, 35 Miss. 391; G. H. & S. A. Ry. v. Donahoe, 56 Tex. 162; Murray v. Lovejoy, 2 Cliff. 191, 195. (See 3 Wall. 1, 9.)

of the Sabinians into a rule of law, and carried it to
its logical consequences. The *comparatur* of Ulpian
has become the *aequiparatur* of Lord Coke,[65] it might
be said; ratification has been made equivalent to
command, and that is all. But it will be seen that this
is a very great step. It is a long way from holding
a man liable as a wrongful disseizor when he has accepted the wrongfully-obtained possession, to allowing him to make justifiable an act which was without
justification when it was done, and, if that is material,
which was followed by no possession on the part of
the alleged principal.[66] For such a purpose why should
ratification be equivalent to a previous command?
Why should my saying that I adopt or approve of a
trespass in any form of words make me responsible
for a past act? The act was not mine, and I cannot
make it so. Neither can it be undone or in any wise
affected by what I may say.[67]

But if the act was done by one who affected to
personate me, new considerations come in. If a man
assumes the status of my servant *pro hac vice*, it lies
between him and me whether he shall have it or not.
And if that status is fixed upon him by my subsequent
assent, it seems to bear with it the usual consequence

[65] Co. Lit. 207 *a;* 4 Inst. 317. It is *comparatur* in 30 Ed. I. 128;
Bract. 171 *b.*

[66] Buron *v.* Denman, 2 Exch. 167 (1848).

[67] Ratification had a meaning, of course, when the usual remedy for
wrongs was a blood-feud, and the head of the house had a choice
whether he would maintain his man or leave him to the vengeance of
the other party. See the story of Howard the Halt, 1 Saga Library,
p. 50, Ch. 14, end. Compare "although he has not received him" in
Fitz. Abr., *Corone*, pl. 428, cited 4 Harv. Law Rev. 355.

as incident that his acts within the scope of his employment are my acts. Such juggling with words of course does not remove the substantive objections to the doctrine under consideration, but it does formally reconcile it with the general framework of legal ideas.

From this point of view it becomes important to notice that, however it may have been in the Roman law, from the time of the glossators and of the canon law it always has been required that the act should have been done in the name or as agent of the person assuming to ratify it. "Ratum quis habere non potest quod ipsius nomine non est gestum." [68] In the language of Baron Parke in Buron *v.* Denman,[69] "a subsequent ratification of an act done *as agent* is equal to a prior authority." And all the cases from that before Gascoigne downwards have asserted the same limitation.[70] I think we may well doubt whether ratification would ever have been held equivalent to command in the only cases in which that fiction is of the least importance had it not been for the further circumstance that the actor had assumed the position of a servant for the time being. The grounds for the doubt become stronger if it be true that the liability even for commanded acts started from the case of owner and slave.

[68] Sext. Dec. 5. 12. de Reg. Jur. (Reg. 9). It made the difference between excommunication and a mere sin in case of an assault upon one of the clergy. Ibid. 5, 11, 23.

[69] 2 Exch. 167.

[70] *Supra.* See also Fuller & Trimwell's Case, 2 Leon, 215, 216; New England Dredging Co. *v.* Rockport Granite Co., 149 Mass. 381, 382; Bract., fol. 28 *b*, 100 *b*.

In any event, ratification like the rest of the law of agency reposes on a fiction, and whether the same fiction or another, it will be interesting in the conclusion to study limits which have been set to its workings by practical experience.

What more I have to say concerning the history of agency will appear in my treatment of the last proposition which I undertook to maintain. I said that finally I should endeavor to show that the whole outline of the law, as it stands to-day, is the resultant of a conflict between logic and good sense — the one striving to carry fictions out to consistent results, the other restraining and at last overcoming that effort when the results become too manifestly unjust. To that task I now address myself.

I assume that common-sense is opposed to making one man pay for another man's wrong, unless he actually has brought the wrong to pass according to the ordinary canons of legal responsibility, — unless, that is to say, he has induced the immediate wrong-doer to do acts of which the wrong, or, at least, wrong, was the natural consequence under the circumstances known to the defendant. I assume that common-sense is opposed to allowing a stranger to my overt acts and to my intentions, a man of whom I have never heard, to set up a contract against me which I had supposed I was making with my personal friend. I assume that common-sense is opposed to the denial of possession to a servant and the assertion of it for a depositary, when the only difference between the two lies in the name by which the custodian is called. And I assume that the opposition of common-sense is intensified when the foregoing doctrines are complicated by the additional absurdities introduced by ratification. I therefore assume that common sense is opposed to the fundamental theory of agency, although I have no doubt that the possible explanations of its various rules which I suggested at the beginning of this chapter, together with the fact that the most flagrant of them now-a-days often presents itself as a seemingly wholesome check on the indifference and negligence of great corporations, have done much to reconcile men's minds to that theory. What remains to be said I believe will justify my assumption.

I begin with the constitution of the relation of master and servant, and with the distinction that an employer is not liable for the torts of an independent contractor, or, in other words, that an independent contractor is not a servant. And here I hardly know whether to say that common-sense and tradition are in conflict, or that they are for once harmonious. On the one side it may be urged that when you have admitted that an agency may exist outside the family relations, the question arises where you are to stop, and why, if a man who is working for another in one case is called his servant, he should not be called so in all. And it might be said that the only limit is found, not in theory, but in common-sense, which steps in and declares that if the employment is well recognized as very distinct, and all the circumstances are such as to show that it would be mere folly to pretend that the employer could exercise control in any practical sense, then the fiction is at an end. An evidence of the want of any more profound or logical reason might be sought in the different circumstances that have been laid hold of as tests, the objections that might be found to each, and in the fact that doubtful cases are now left to the jury.[71]

On the other hand, it might be said that the master is made answerable for the consequences of the negligent acts "of those whom the law denominates *his* servants, because," in the language of that judg-

---

[71] Among the facts upon which stress has been laid are the following: 1. Choice. Kelly *v.* Mayor of New York, 11 N. Y. 432, 436. See Walcott *v.* Swampscott, 1 Allen, 101, 103. But although it is true that the employer has not generally the choice of the contractor's servants, he has the choice of the contractor, yet he is no more liable for the contractor's negligence than for that of his servant. 2. Control. Sadler *v.* Henlock, 4 El. & Bl. 570, 578 (1855). Yet there was control in the leading case of Quarman *v.* Burnett, 6 M. & W. 499 (1840), where the employee was held not to be the defendant's servant. Cf. Steel *v.* Lester, 3 C. P. D. 121 (1877). 3. A round sum paid. But this was true in Sadler *v.* Henlock, *sup.*, where the employee was held to be a servant. 4. Power to discharge. Burke *v.* Norwich & W. R.R., 34 Conn. 474 (1867). See Lane *v.* Cotton, 12 Mod. 472, 488, 489. But apart from the fact that this can only be important as to persons removed two stages from the alleged master, and not to determine whether a person directly employed by him is a servant or contractor, the power to discharge a contractor's servants may be given to the contractee without making him their master. Reedie *v.* London & Northwestern Ry. Co., 4 Exch. 244, 258. Robinson *v.* Webb, 11 Bush (Ky.), 464–5. Notoriously distinct calling, Milligan *v.* Wedge, 12 Ad. & E. 737 (1840) ; Linton *v.* Smith, 8 Gray (Mass.), 47. This is a practical distinction, based on common-sense, not directly on a logical working out of the theory of agency. Moreover, it is only a partial test. It does not apply to all the cases.

In doubtful cases the matter seems to be left to the jury, that ever-ready sword for the cutting of Gordian knots, as difficult questions of law generally are.

ment which settled the distinction under consideration,[72] "such servants represent the master himself, and their acts stand upon the same footing as his own." That although the limits of this identification are necessarily more or less vague, yet all the proposed tests go to show that the distinction rests on the remoteness of personal connection between the parties, and that as the connection grows slighter, the likeness to the original case of menials grows less. That a contractor acts in his own name and on his own behalf, and that although the precise point at which the line is drawn may be somewhat arbitrary, the same is true of all legal distinctions, and that they are none the worse for it, and that wherever the line is drawn it is a necessary one, and required by the very definition of agency. I suppose this is the prevailing opinion.

I come next to the limit of liability when the relation of master and servant is admitted to exist. The theory of agency as applied to free servants no doubt requires that if the servant commits a wilful trespass or any other wrong, when employed about his own business, the master should not be liable. No free man is servant all the time. But the cases which exonerate the master could never have been decided as the result of that theory alone. They rather represent the revolt of common-sense from the whole doctrine when its application is pushed far enough to become noticeable.

[72] Littledale, J., in Laugher v. Pointer, 5 B. & C. 547, 553 (T. 7 G. IV. 1826).

For example, it has been held that it was beyond
the scope of a servant's employment to go to the further side of a boundary ditch, upon a neighbor's land,
and to cut bushes there for the purpose of clearing
out the ditch, although the right management of
the master's farm required that the ditch should
be cleaned, and although the servant only did what
he thought necessary to that end, and although the
master relied wholly upon his servant's judgment in
the entire management of the premises.[73]

Mr. Justice Keating said, the powers given to the
servant "were no doubt very wide, but I do not see
how they could authorize a wrongful act on another
person's land or render his employers liable for a
wilful act of trespass." It is true that the act could
not be authorized in the sense of being made lawful,
but the same is true of every wrongful act for which
the principal is held. As to the act being wilful, there
was no evidence that it was so in any other sense than
that which every trespass might be said to be, and
as the judge below directed a verdict for the defendant, there were no presumptions adverse to the
plaintiff in the case. Moreover, it has been said elsewhere that even a wilful act in furtherance of the
master's business might charge him.[74]

Mr. Justice Grove attempted to draw the line in
another way. He said, "There are some things which

[73] Bolingbroke v. Swindon Local Board, L. R. 9 C. P. 575 (1874). Cf.
Lewis v. Read, 13 M. & W. 834; Haseler v. Lemoyne, 5 C. B. N. S. 530.

[74] Howe v. Newmarch, 12 Allen, 49 (1866). See also cases as to
fraud, inf., and cf. Craker v. Chicago & N. W. Ry. Co., 36 Wisc. 657,
669 (1875).

may be so naturally expected to occur from the wrongful or negligent conduct of persons engaged in carrying out an authority given, that they may be fairly said to be within the scope of the employment." But the theory of agency would require the same liability for both those things which might and those which might not be so naturally expected, and this is only revolt from the theory. Moreover, it may be doubted whether a case could be found where the servant's conduct was more naturally to be expected for the purpose of accomplishing what he had to do.[75]

The truth is, as pretty clearly appears from the opinions of the judges, that they felt the difficulty of giving a rational explanation of the doctrine sought to be applied, and were not inclined to extend it. The line between right and wrong corresponded with the neighbor's boundary line, and therefore was more easily distinguishable than where it depends on the difference between care and negligence, and it was just so much easier to hold that the scope of the servant's employment was limited to lawful acts.

I now pass to fraud. It first must be understood that, whatever the law may be, it is the same in the case of agents, *stricto sensu,* as of other servants. As has been mentioned, the fraudulent servant was a factor in the first reported decision that the master was liable.[76] Now if the defrauded party not merely has a right to repudiate a contract fraudulently obtained, or in general to charge a defendant to the

[75] Cf. Harlow *v.* Humiston, 6 Cowen, 189 (1826).
[76] Hern *v.* Nichols, 1 Salk. 289.

extent that he has derived a benefit from another's fraud, but may hold him answerable *in solidum* for the damage caused by the fraudulent acts of his servant in the course of the latter's employment, the ground can only be the fiction that the act of the servant is the act of the master.

It is true that in the House of Lords [77] Lord Selborne said that the English cases "proceeded, not on the ground of any imputation of vicarious fraud to the principal, but because (as it was well put by Mr. Justice Willes in Barwick's case[78]) "with respect to the question whether a principal is answerable for the act of his agent in the course of his master's business, no sensible distinction can be drawn between the case of fraud and the case of any other wrong." But this only puts off the evil day. Why is the principal answerable in the case of any other wrong? It is, as has been seen, because, in the language of Mr. Justice Littledale, the "servants represent the master himself, and their acts stand upon the same footing as his own." [79] Indeed Mr. Justice Willes, in the very judgment cited by Lord Selborne, refers to Mr. Justice Littledale's judgment for the general principle. So Lord Denman, in Fuller *v.* Wilson,[80] "We think the principal and his agent

[77] Houldsworth *v.* City of Glasgow Bank, 5 App. Cas. 317, 326, 327 (1880).

[78] L. R. 2 Ex. 259.

[79] Laugher *v.* Pointer, 5 B. & C. 547, 553. See Williams *v.* Jones, 3 H. & C. 602, 609.

[80] 3 Q. B. 58, 67; s. c. reversed on another ground, but admitting this principle, ib. 77 and 1009, 1010 (1842).

are for this purpose identified." I repeat more distinctly the admission that no fiction is necessary to account for the rule that one who is induced to contract by an agent's fraud may rescind as against the innocent principal. For whether the fraud be imputed to the principal or not, he has only a right to such a contract as has been made, and that contract is a voidable one. But when you go beyond that limit and even outside the domain of contract altogether to make a man answer for any damages caused by his agent's fraud, the law becomes almost inconceivable without the aid of the fiction. But a fiction is not a satisfactory reason for changing men's rights or liabilities, and common-sense has more or less revolted at this point again and has denied the liability. The English cases are collected in Houldsworth v. City of Glasgow Bank.[81]

When it was attempted to carry identification one step further still, and to unite the knowledge of the principal with the statement of the agent in order to make the latter's act fraudulent, as in Cornfoot v. Fowke,[82] the absurdity became more manifest and dissent more outspoken. As was most accurately said by Baron Wilde in a later case.[83] "The artificial identification of the agent and principal, by bringing the words of the one side with the knowledge of the other, induced the apparent logical consequence of

---

[81] 5 App. Cas. 317. See The Common Law, p. 231.

[82] 6 M. & W. 358 (1810). It is not necessary to consider whether the case was rightly decided or not, as I am only concerned with this particular ground.

[83] Udell v. Atherton, 7 H. & N. 172, 184 (1861).

fraud. On the other hand, the real innocence of both agent and principal repelled the notion of a constructive fraud in either. A discordance of views, varying with the point from which the subject was looked at, was to be expected." The language of Lord Denman, just quoted, from Fuller *v.* Wilson, was used with reference to this subject.

The restrictions which common-sense has imposed on the doctrine of undisclosed principal are well-known. An undisclosed principal may sue on his agent's contract, but his recovery is subject to the state of accounts between the agent and third person.[84] He may be sued, but it is held that the recovery will be subject to the state of accounts between principal and agent, if the principal has paid fairly before the agency was discovered; but it is, perhaps, doubtful whether this rule or the qualification of it is as wise as the former one.[85]

Then as to ratification. It has nothing to do with estoppel,[86] but the desire to reduce the law to general principles has led some courts to cut it down to that point.[87] Again, the right to ratify has been limited by considerations of justice to the other party. It has been said that the ratification must take place

[84] Rabone *v.* Williams, 7 T. R. 360 (1785); George *v.* Clagett, 7 T. R. 359 (1797); Carr *v.* Hinchcliff, 4 B. & C. 547 (1825); Borries *v.* Imperial Ottoman Bank, L. R. 9 C. P. 38 (1873); Semenza *v.* Brinsley, 18 C. B. N. s. 467, 477 (1865); *Ex parte* Dixon, 4 Ch. D 133.

[85] Armstrong *v.* Stokes, L. R. 7 Q. B. 598, 610; Irvine *v.* Watson, 5 Q. B. D. 414.

[86] See Metcalf *v.* Williams, 144 Mass. 452, 454, and cases cited.

[87] Doughaday *v.* Crowell, 3 Stockt. (N.J.) 201; Bird *v.* Brown, 4 Exch. 788, 799.

at a time and under circumstances when the would-be
principal could have done the act;[88] and it has
been so held in some cases when it was manifestly
just that the other party should know whether the
act was to be considered the principal's or not, as in
the case of an unauthorized notice to quit, which the
landlord attempts to ratify after the time of the
notice has begun to run.[89] But it is held that bringing an action may be subsequently ratified.[90]

I now take up pleading. It is settled that an
assumpsit [91] to or by a servant for his master may
be laid as an assumpsit to or by the master. But
these are cases where the master has commanded the
act, and, therefore, as I have shown in the beginning
of this discussion, may be laid on one side. The same
thing is true of a trespass commanded by the
master.[92] But when we come to conduct which the
master has not commanded, but for which he is responsible, the difficulty becomes greater. It is, nevertheless, settled that in actions on the case the negligence of the servant is properly laid as the negligence
of the master,[93] and if the analogy of the substantive
law is to be followed, and the fiction of identity is
to be carried out to its logical results, the same would
be true of all pleading. It is so held with regard to
fraud. "The same rule of law which imputes to the

[88] Bird v. Brown, 4 Exch. 788.
[89] Doe v. Goldwin, 2 Q. B. 143.
[90] Ancona v. Marks, 7 H. & N. 686.
[91] Seignior and Wolmer's Case, Godboldt, 360.
[92] Gregory v. Piper, 9 B. & C. 591.
[93] Brucker v. Fromont, 6 T. R. 659 (1796).

principal the fraud of the agent and makes him answerable for the consequences justifies the allegation that the principal himself committed the wrong." [94]   Some American cases have applied the same view to trespass,[95] and have held that this action could be maintained against a master whose servant had committed a trespass for which he was liable although he had not commanded it. But these decisions, although perfectly reasonable, seem to have been due rather to inadvertence than to logic, in the first instance, and the current of authority is the other way. Baron Parke says, "The maxim '*Qui facit per alium, facit per se*' renders the master liable for all the negligent acts of the servant in the course of his employment, but that liability does not make the *direct* act of the servant the *direct* act of the master. Trespass will not lie against him; case will, in effect, for employing a careless servant." [96]   Considered as reasoning, it would be hard to unite more errors in as many words. *"Qui facit per alium, facit per se"* as an axiom admitted by common-sense goes no farther than to make a man liable for commanded trespasses, and for them trespass lies. It it be extended beyond that point it simply embodies the fiction, and the precise point of the fiction is that the direct act of one is treated as if it were the direct act

---

[94] Comstock, Ch. J., in Bennett *v.* Judson, 21 N. Y. 238 (1860) ; acc. Barwick *v.* English Joint Stock Bank, L R. 2 Ex. 259 (1867).

[95] Andrew *v.* Howard, 36 Vt. 248 (1863) ; May *v.* Bliss, 22 Vt. 477 (1850).

[96] Sharrod *v.* London & N. W. Ry Co., 4 Exch. 580, 585 (1849). Cf. Morley *v.* Gaisford, 2 H. Bl. 442 (1795).

of another. To avoid this conclusion a false reason is given for the liability in general.[97]   It is, as has been shown, the fallacy of the Roman jurists, and is disposed of by the decisions that no amount of care in the choice of one's servant will help the master in a suit against him.[98]   But although the reasoning is bad, the language expresses the natural unwillingness of sensible men to sanction an allegation that the defendant directly brought force to bear on the plaintiff, as the proper and formal allegation, when as a matter of fact it was another person who did it by his independent act, and the defendant is only answerable because of a previous contract between himself and the actual wrong-doer.[99]   Another circumstance may have helped. Usually the master is not liable for his servant's wilful trespasses, and, therefore, the actions against him stand on the servant's negligence as the alternative ground on which anybody is responsible. There was for a time a confused idea that when the cause of action was the defendant's negligence, the proper form of action was always case.[100]   Of course if this was true it applied equally to the imputed negligence of a servant. And thus there was the further possibility of confounding the question of the proper form of action with the

---

[97] The same reason is given in M'Manus v. Crickett, 1 East, 106, 108 (1800). Compare 1 Harg. Law Tracts, 347; Walcott v. Swampscott, 1 Allen, 101, 103; Lane v. Cotton, 12 Mod. 472, 488, 489.

[98] Dansey v. Richardson, 3 El. & Bl. 144, 161.

[99] M'Manus v. Crickett, 1 East, 106, 110 (1800); Brucker v. Fromont, 6 T. R. 659 (1796).

[100] Ogle v. Barnes, 8 T. R. 188 (1799). Cf. Leame v. Bray, 3 East, 593 (1803).

perfectly distinct one whether the defendant was liable at all.

I come finally to the question of damages. In those States where exemplary damages are allowed, the attempt naturally has been made to recover such damages from masters when their servant's conduct has been such as to bring the doctrine into play. Some courts have had the courage to be consistent.[101] "What is the principle," it is asked, "upon which this rule of damages is founded? It is that the act of the agent is the act of the principal himself. . . . The law has established, to this extent, their legal unity and identity. . . . This legal unity of the principal and agent, in respect to the wrongful or tortious, as well as the rightful acts, of the agent, done in the course of his employment, is an incident which the law has wisely attached to the relation, from its earliest history." "If then the act of the agent be the act of the principal in law, and this legal identity is the foundation of the responsibility of the principal, there can be no escape from his indemnity to the full extent of civil responsiblity." An instruction that the jury might give punitive damages was upheld, and the plaintiff had judgment for $12,000. Whatever may be said of the practical consequences or the English of the opinion from which these extracts are made, it has the merit of going to the root of the matter with great keenness. On the other

---

[101] New Orleans, Jackson, & Great Northern R. R. Co. v. Bailey, 40 Miss. 395, 452, 453, 456 (1866); acc. Atlantic & G. W. Ry. Co. v. Dunn, 19 Ohio St. 162.

hand, other courts, more impressed by the monstrosity of the result than by the *elegantia juris*, have peremptorily declared that it was absurd to punish a man who had not been to blame, and have laid down the opposite rule without hesitation.[102]

I think I now have made good the propositions which I undertook at the beginning of this essay to establish. I fully admit that the evidence here collected has been gathered from nooks and corners, and that although in the mass it appears to me imposing, it does not lie conspicuous upon the face of the law. And this is equivalent to admitting, as I do, that the views here maintained are not favorites with the courts. How can they be? A judge would blush to say nakedly to a defendant: "I can state no rational ground on which you should be held liable, but there is a fiction of law which I must respect and by which I am bound to say that you did the act complained of, although we both know perfectly well that it was done by somebody else whom the plaintiff could have sued if he had chosen, who was selected with the utmost care by you, who was in fact an eminently proper person for the employment in which he was engaged, and whom it was not only your right to employ, but much to the public advantage that you should employ." That would not be a satisfactory form in which to render a decision against a master, and it is not pleasant even to admit to one's self that

[102] Hagar *v.* Providence & Worcester R.R., 3 R. I. 88 (1854); Cleghorn *v.* New York Central & Hudson River R.R., 56 N. Y. 44 (1874). Cf. Craker *v.* Chicago & N. W. R.R., 36 Wis. 657 (1875).

such are the true grounds upon which one is deciding. Naturally, therefore, judges have striven to find more intelligible reasons, and have done so in the utmost good faith; for whenever a rule of law is in fact a survival of ancient traditions, its ancient meaning is gradually forgotten, and it has to be reconciled to present notions of policy and justice, or to disappear.

If the law of the agency can be resolved into mere applications of general and accepted principles, then my argument fails; but I think it cannot be, and I may suggest, as another ground for my opinion beside those which I have stated heretofore, that the variety of reasons which have been offered for the most important application of the fiction of identity, the liability of the master for his servant's torts, goes far to show that none of those reasons are good. Baron Parke, as we have seen, says that case is brought in effect for employing a negligent servant. Others have suggested that it was because it was desirable that there should be some responsible man who could pay the damages.[103] Mr. Justice Grove thinks that the master takes the risk of such offences as it must needs be should come.

I admit my scepticism as to the value of any such general considerations, while on the other hand I should be perfectly ready to believe, upon evidence, that the law could be justified as it stands when applied to special cases upon special grounds.[104]

[103] See Williams v. Jones, 3 H. & C. 256, 263; 1 Harg. Law Tracts, 347.
[104] Cf. what is said as to common carriers in The Common Law, 204, 205.

There should have been added to the illustrations of a man's responsibility within his house, given in the former article, that of a vassal for attempts on the chastity of his lord's daughter or sister "tant com elle est Damoiselle en son Hostel," in Ass. Jerusalem, c. 205, 217, ed. 1690. The origin of the liability of innkeepers never has been studied, so far as I know Beaumanoir, c. 36, seems to confine the liability to things intrusted to the innkeeper, and to limit it somewhat even in that case, and to suggest grounds of policy. The English law was more severe, and put it on the ground that the guest for the time had come to be under the innkeeper's protection and safety. 42 Ass., pl. 17, fol. 260. A *capias* was refused on the ground that the defendant was not in fault, but an *elegit* was granted. 42 Ed. III. 11, pl. 13. Notwithstanding the foregoing reason given for it, the liability was confined, at an early date, to those exercising a common calling (*common hostler*). 11 Hen. IV. 45, pl. 18. See The Common Law, 183-189, 203. See further, 22 Hen. VI. 21, pl. 38; pl. 8. And note a limitation of liability in cases of taking by the king's enemies, similar to that of bailees. Plowden, 9, and note in margin; The Common Law, 177, 182, 199, 201. The references to the custom of England, or to the *lex terræ*, are of no significance. The Common Law, 188. See further, the titles of Glanvill and Bracton. Other citations could be given if necessary.

PRIVILEGE, MALICE, AND INTENT *

THE law of torts as now administered has worked itself into substantial agreement with a general theory. I should sum up the first part of the theory in a few words, as follows: Actions of tort are brought for temporal damage. The law recognizes temporal damage as an evil which its object is to prevent or to redress, so far as is consistent with paramount considerations to be mentioned. When it is shown that the defendant's act has had temporal damage to the plaintiff for its consequence, the next question is whether that consequence was one which the defendant might have foreseen. If common experience has shown that some such consequence was likely to follow the act under the circumstances known to the actor, he is taken to have acted with notice, and is held liable, unless he escapes upon the special grounds to which I have referred, and which I shall mention in a moment. The standard applied is external, and the words malice, intent, and negligence, as used in this connection, refer to an external standard. If the manifest probability of harm is very great, and the harm follows, we say that it is done maliciously or intentionally; if not so great, but still considerable, we say that the harm is

* *Harvard Law Review*, Vol. VIII, 1. (1894.)

done negligently; if there is no apparent danger, we call it mischance.

Furthermore, so far as liability for an act depends upon its probable consequences without more, the liability usually is not affected by the degree of the probability if it is sufficient to give the defendant reasonable warning. In other words, for this purpose commonly it does not matter whether the act is called malicious or negligent. To make a *primâ facie* case of trespass or libel, if the likelihood of bringing force to bear on the plaintff's person or of bringing him into contempt goes to the height expressed by the word negligence, as above explained, it need not go higher. There are exceptions, at least in the criminal law. The degree of danger under the known circumstances may make the difference between murder and manslaughter.[1] But the rule is as I have stated. The foregoing general principles I assume not to need further argument.[2]

But the simple test of the degree of manifest danger does not exhaust the theory of torts. In some cases, a man is not liable for a very manifest danger unless he actually intends to do the harm complained of. In some cases, he even may intend to do the harm and yet not have to answer for it: and, as I think, in some cases of this latter sort, at least, actual malice may make him liable when without it he would not have been. In this connection I mean

[1] 2 Bigelow, Fraud, 117, n. 3; Commonwealth *v.* Pierce, 138 Mass., 165. Compare Hanson *v.* Globe Newspaper Co., 159 Mass., 293.
[2] See The Common Law, Ch. 2, 3, 4.

by malice a malevolent motive for action, without
reference to any hope of a remoter benefit to oneself
to be accomplished by the intended harm to another.[3]
The question whether malice in this sense has any
effect upon the extent of a defendant's rights and
liabilities, has arisen in many forms. It is familiar
in regard to the use of land in some way manifestly
harmful to a neighbor. It has been suggested, and
brought to greater prominence, by boycotts, and
other combinations for more or less similar purposes,
although in such cases the harm inflicted is only a
means, and the end sought to be attained generally
is some benefit to the defendant. But before discussing that, I must consider the grounds on which
a man escapes liability in the cases referred to, even
if his act is not malicious.

It will be noticed that I assume that we have got
past the question which is answered by the test of
the external standard. There is no dispute that the
manifest tendency of the defendant's act is to inflict
temporal damage upon the plaintiff. Generally, that
result is expected, and often at least it is intended.
And the first question that presents itself is why the
defendant is not liable without going further. The
answer is suggested by the commonplace, that the
intentional infliction of temporal damage, or the
doing of an act manifestly likely to inflict such
damage and inflicting it, is actionable if done without
just cause.[4] When the defendant escapes, the court

[3] See Rideout v. Knox, 148 Mass., 368, 373.

[4] Walker v. Cronin, 107 Mass., 555, 562; Mogul Steamship Co. v.
McGregor, 23 Q.B.D. 598, 613, 618.

is of opinion that he has acted with just cause. There are various justifications. In these instances, the justification is that the defendant is privileged knowingly to inflict the damage complained of.

But whether, and how far, a privilege shall be allowed is a question of policy. Questions of policy are legislative questions, and judges are shy of reasoning from such grounds. Therefore, decisions for or against the privilege, which really can stand only upon such grounds, often are presented as hollow deductions from empty general propositions like *sic utere tuo ut alienum non laedas*, which teaches nothing but a benevolent yearning, or else are put as if they themselves embodied a postulate of the law and admitted of no further deduction, as when it is said that, although there is temporal damage, there is no wrong; whereas, the very thing to be found out is whether there is a wrong or not, and if not, why not.

When the question of policy is faced it will be seen to be one which cannot be answered by generalities, but must be determined by the particular character of the case, even if everybody agrees what the answer should be. I do not try to mention or to generalize all the facts which have to be taken into account; but plainly the worth of the result, or the gain from allowing the act to be done, has to be compared with the loss which it inflicts. Therefore, the conclusion will vary, and will depend on different reasons according to the nature of the affair.

For instance, a man has a right to set up a shop

in a small village which can support but one of the kind, although he expects and intends to ruin a deserving widow who is established there already. He has a right to build a house upon his land in such a position as to spoil the view from a far more valuable house hard by. He has a right to give honest answers to inquiries about a servant, although he intends thereby to prevent his getting a place. But the reasons for these several privileges are different. The first rests on the economic postulate that free competition is worth more to society than it costs. The next, upon the fact that a line must be drawn between the conflicting interests of adjoining owners, which necessarily will restrict the freedom of each; [5] upon the unavoidable philistinism which prefers use to beauty when considering the most profitable way of administering the land in the jurisdiction taken as one whole; upon the fact that the defendant does not go outside his own boundary; and upon other reasons to be mentioned in a moment. The third, upon the proposition that the benefit of free access to information, in some cases and within some limits, outweighs the harm to an occasional unfortunate. I do not know whether the principle has been applied in favor of a servant giving a character to a master.

Not only the existence but the extent or degree of the privilege will vary with the case. Some privileges are spoken of as if they were absolute, to borrow the language familiar in cases of slander. For

[5] See Middlesex Company v. McCue, 149 Mass. 103, 104; Boston Ferrule Company v. Hills, 159 Mass. 147, 149, 150.

instance, in any common case, apart from statutory exceptions, the right to make changes upon or in a man's land is not affected by the motive with which the changes are made.   Were it otherwise, and were the doctrine carried out to its logical conclusion, an expensive warehouse might be pulled down on the finding of a jury that it was maintained maliciously, and thus a large amount of labor might be . wasted and lost.   Even if the law stopped short of such an extreme, still, as the motives with which the building was maintained might change, the question would be left always in the air.   There may be other and better reasons than these and those mentioned before, or the reasons may be insufficient.[6]   I am not trying to justify particular doctrines, but to analyze the general method by which the law reaches its decision.

So it has been thought that refusing to keep a man in one's service, if he hired a house of the plaintiff, or dealt with him, was absolutely privileged.[7]   Here the balance is struck between the benefit of unfettered freedom to abstain from making the contract, on the one side, and the harm which may be done by the particular use of that freedom, on the other.

It is important to notice that the privilege is not a general one, maliciously to prevent making con-

[6] See 1 Ames & Smith, Cases on Torts, 750, n.

[7] Heywood v. Tillson, 75 Me. 225; Payne v. Western & Atlantic R. R., 13 Lea, 507. See Capital and Counties Bank v. Henry, 7 App. Cas. 741.

tracts with the plaintiff, but is attached to the particular means employed. It is a privilege to abstain from making a certain kind of contract oneself, whether maliciously, in order to prevent others from contracting with the plaintiff, or for a more harmless motive. Still more important it is, and more to the point of this paper, that, in spite of many general expressions to the contrary, the conclusion does not stand on the abstract proposition that malice cannot make a man liable for an act otherwise lawful. It is said that if this were not so a man would be sued for his motives. But the proposition is no more self-evident than that knowledge of the circumstances under which an act is done cannot affect liability, since otherwise a man would be sued for his knowledge, a proposition which is obviously untrue. In a proper sense, the state of a man's consciousness always is material to his liability, and when we are considering the extent of a man's privilege knowingly to inflict pecuniary loss upon his neighbor, it would not be surprising to find that in some cases motives made all the difference in the world. I pass to the inquiry, whether privilege, sometimes at least, is not dependent upon the motives with which the act complained of is done.

Take a case where, as in the last one, the harm complained of is a malicious interference with business, but where the means employed (the act of the defendant) are different. I assume that the harm is recognized by the law as a temporal damage, that not being the object of this discussion. I assume

also that the defendant's act is not unlawful or a
cause of action unless it is made so by reason of
the particular consequence mentioned, and the defendant's attitude toward that consequence. I assume, finally, that the acts or abstinences of third
persons induced by the defendant are lawful. If a
case could be put where the defendant's act was
justified by no grounds of policy more special or other
than the general one of letting men do what they
want to do, it would present the point which I wish
to raise. Such a case I find hard to imagine, but if
one should occur, I think courts would say that the
benefit of spontaneity was outweighed by the damage
which it caused.[8]   The gratification of ill-will, being
a pleasure, may be called a gain, but the pain on
the other side is a loss more important. Otherwise,
why allow a recovery for a battery? There is no
general policy in favor of allowing a man to do harm
to his neighbor for the sole pleasure of doing harm.

But there is no need to stay in such thin air.
Let us suppose another case of interference with business by an act which has some special grounds of
policy in its favor. Take the case of advice not to
employ a certain doctor, given by one in a position of
authority. To some extent it is desirable that people
should be free to give one another advice. On the

---

[8] Possibly, one is suggested by Keeble v. Hickeringill, 11 East, 574 n.,
and Tarleton v. M'Gawley, Peake, 205 — we may suppose people to
be kept away from the plaintiff by the malicious firing of guns, otherwise lawful. These cases will be found in 1 Ames & Smith, Cases of
Torts, which contains an excellent selection of decisions bearing on the
subject of this article.

other hand, commonly it is not desirable that a man should lose his business. The two advantages run against one another, and a line has to be drawn. So absolute a right of way may not be given to advice as to abstaining from some contracts which have been mentioned. In such a case, probably it would be said that if the advice was believed to be good, and was given for the sake of benefiting the hearers, the defendant would not be answerable. But if it was not believed to be for their benefit, and was given for the sake of hurting the doctor, the doctor would prevail.[9] If the advice was believed to be good, but was volunteered for the sake of doing harm only, courts might differ, but some no doubt would think that the privilege was not made out.[10] What the effect of bad faith without malice would be is outside my subject.

It will be seen that the external standard applied for the purpose of seeing whether the defendant had notice of the probable consequences of his act, has little or nothing to do with the question of privilege. The defendant is assumed to have had notice of the

[9] See Morasse v. Brochu, 151 Mass. 567; Tasker v. Stanley, 153 Mass. 148; Delz v. Winfree, 80 Texas, 400, 405. The cases often are obscure as to the precise nature of the act done, which seems to me a most important fact. In Lumley v. Gye, 2 El. & Bl. 216, the allegation was that the defendant "enticed and procured" the third person to break the contract. In Bowen v. Hall, 6 Q.B.D. 333, the defendant Hall persuaded another to break his contract (pp. 338, 339). In Old Dominion Steamship Co. v. McKenna, 30 Fed. Rep. 48, the defendant "procured plaintiff's workmen" to leave their work, and so on.

[10] See Stevens v. Sampson, 5 Ex. D. 53.

probable consequences of his act, otherwise the question of privilege does not arise. Generally, the harm complained of is not only foreseen but intended. If there is no privilege, the difference between notice of consequences and malice is immaterial. If the privilege is absolute, or extends to malicious acts, of course it extends to those which are not so. If the privilege is qualified, the policy in favor of the defendant's freedom generally will be found to be qualified only to the extent of forbidding him to use for the sake of doing harm what is allowed him for the sake of good. Suppose, for instance, advice is given which manifestly tends to injure the plaintiff, but without thinking of him in fact, and that the advice would be privileged unless given in bad faith or maliciously, if expressly directed against the plaintiff. The advice could not be given maliciously as against the plaintiff unless he either was thought of, or was embraced in a class which was thought of.

Perhaps one of the reasons why judges do not like to discuss questions of policy, or to put a decision in terms upon their views as law-makers, is that the moment you leave the path of merely logical deduction you lose the illusion of certainty which makes legal reasoning seem like mathematics. But the certainty is only an illusion, nevertheless. Views of policy are taught by experience of the interests of life. Those interests are fields of battle. Whatever decisions are made must be against the wishes and opinion of one party, and the distinctions on which they go will be distinctions of degree. Even the economic postulate of the benefit of free competition which I have mentioned above, is denied by an important school.

Let me illustrate further. In England, it is lawful for merchants to combine to offer unprofitably low rates and a rebate to shippers for the purpose of preventing the plaintiff from becoming a competitor, as he has a right to do, and also to impose a forfeiture of the rebate, and to threaten agents with dismissal in case of dealing with him.[11] But it seems to be unlawful for the officer of a trade union to order the members not to work for a man if he supplies goods to the plaintiff, for the purpose of forcing the plaintiff to abstain from doing what he has a right to do.[12]

In the latter case the defendant's act, strictly, was giving an order, not refusing to contract; but perhaps the case would have been decided the same way if the same course had been adopted by unanimous vote of the union.[13] So the right to abstain from contracting is not absolutely privileged as against interference with business. The combination and the intent to injure the plaintiff, without more, do not seem to be the ground. Both those elements were present to an equal degree in the Mogul Steamship Company's case. It is true the jury found malice.

11 Mogul Steamship Company, Limited, v. McGregor, 1892, App. Cas. 25; 23 Q.B.D. 598. See also Bowen v. Matheson, 14 Allen, 499 (1867); Bohn Manufacturing Company v. Hollis, 55 N.W.R. 1119 (Minnesota, 1893).

12 Temperton v. Russell, 1893, 1 Q. B. 715.

13 See Carew v. Rutherford, 106 Mass. 1, and the cases below, as to combination. See, also, the further comments toward the end of this article.

But looking at the evidence, the instructions of the judge, and the judgments, evidently they did not mean that the ultimate motive of the defendants was not to benefit themselves. The defendants meant to benefit themselves by making the plaintiff submit, just as, in the other case, the defendants meant to benefit themselves by driving the plaintiff away. It might be said that the defendants were free not to contract, but that they had no right to advise or persuade the contractors who would have dealt with the plaintiff not to do so, and that, by communicating the union's willingness to deal with the contractors, if they would not deal with the plaintiff, the defendants were using such persuasion. But if this refinement is not a roundabout denial of the freedom not to contract, since a man hardly is free in his abstaining unless he can state the terms or conditions upon which he intends to abstain, at all events the same mode of reasoning could be used in the cases where the defendant escapes. The ground of decision really comes down to a proposition of policy of rather a delicate nature concerning the merit of the particular benefit to themselves intended by the defendants, and suggests a doubt whether judges with different economic sympathies might not decide such a case differently when brought face to face with the issue.

Another illustration may be drawn from other cases upon boycotts. Acts which would be privileged if done by one person for a certain purpose may be held unlawful if done for the same purpose in combination.[14] It is easy to see what trouble may be found in distinguishing between the combination of great powers in a single capitalist, not to speak of a corporation, and the other form of combination.[15] It is a question of degree at what point the combination becomes large enough to be wrong, unless the knot is cut by saying that any combination however puny is so. Behind all is the question whether the courts are not flying in the face of the organization of the world which is taking place so fast, and of its inevitable consequences. I make these suggestions, not as criticisms of the decisions, but to call attention to the very serious legislative considerations which have to be weighed. The danger is that such considerations should have their weight in an inarticulate form as unconscious prejudice or half conscious inclination. To measure them justly needs not only the highest powers of a judge and a training which the practice of the law does not insure, but also a freedom from prepossessions which is very hard to attain. It seems to me desirable that the work should be done with express recognition of its nature. The time has gone by when law is only an unconscious embodiment of the common will. It has become a conscious reaction

[14] See State *v.* Donaldson, 32 N.J. 191; State *v.* Glidden, 55 Conn. 46; Camp *v.* Commonwealth, 84 Va. 927; Lucke *v.* Clothing Cutters' & Trimmers' Assembly No. 7, 507, K. of L., 26 Atl. R. 505; Jackson *v.* Stanfield, 36 N.E.R. 345 (Indiana, 1894); Mogul Steamship Company *v.* McGregor, 23 Q.B.D. 598, 616 (1892); App. Cas. 25, 45. The cases are not quite unanimous. Bohn Manufacturing Co. *v.* Hollis, 55 N.W.R. 1119 (Minnesota, 1893).

[15] 23 Q.B.D. 617.

upon itself of organized society knowingly seeking to determine its own destinies.

To sum up this part of the discussion, when a responsible defendant seeks to escape from liability for an act which he had noticed was likely to cause temporal damage to another, and which has caused such damage in fact, he must show a justification. The most important justification is a claim of privilege. In order to pass upon that claim, it is not enough to consider the nature of the damage, and the effect of the act, and to compare them. Often the precise nature of the act and its circumstances must be examined. It is not enough, for instance, to say that the defendant induced the public, or a part of them, not to deal with the plaintiff. We must know how he induced them. If by refusing to let them occupy a building, or to employ them, the answer may be peremptory in his favor, without regard to other circumstances. If by acts wrongful for other reasons, the answer falls outside my subject. If by advice, or combined action not otherwise unlawful, motive may be a fact of the first importance. It is entirely conceivable that motive, in some jurisdictions, should be held to affect all, or nearly all, claims of privilege. The cases which I have cited, by way of illustration, come from different States, and might not be regarded as being so consistent with each other as I have assumed them to be. But in all such cases the ground of decision is policy; and the advantages to the community, on the one side and the other, are the only matters really entitled to be weighed. I only wish to add that thus far, when the act of a third person is nearer to the harm than the act of the defendant, I have assumed the former to be lawful. I have said nothing as yet of privilege in connection with wrongful acts of others. Also I have left on one side exceptional cases where the act induced by the defendant would have been a tort or a crime had the third person had his knowledge, for instance, the innocent giving of a poisoned apple. If the harm were of a more serious nature than loss of business, that naturally would narrow the privilege, but it is not likely to be so in the cases which I have had in mind.

I now pass to an entirely different class of cases. In these, intent to produce the harm complained of has an importance of its own, as distinguished from notice of danger on the one side, and from actual malice on the other. To begin at a little distance, one of the difficulties which must occur to every one in thinking of the external standard of liability is: if notice so determined is the general ground, why is not a man who sells fire-arms answerable for assaults committed with pistols bought of him, since he must be taken to know the probability that, sooner or later, some one will buy a pistol of him for some unlawful end? I do not think that the whole answer to such questions is to be found in the doctrine of privilege. Neither do I think that any instruction is to be got from the often-repeated discussions as to cause. It is said that the man whose wrong-doing is nearest to the injury is the only cause of it. But, as is pointed out in Hayes v. Hyde Park,[16] a man whose act is nearest to the injury is as much a cause when his act is rightful, as when it is wrongful. Yet an intervening act may not exonerate the defendant.

The principle seems to be pretty well established, in this country at least, that every one has a right to rely upon his fellow-men acting lawfully, and, therefore, is not answerable for himself acting upon the assumption that they will do so, however improbable it may be. There may have been some nibbling at the edges of this rule in strong cases, for instance, where only the slight negligence of a third person intervenes, or where his negligence plays only a subordinate part, but the rule hardly will be disputed. It applies in favor of wrong-doers as well as others. The classical illustration is, that one who slanders another is not liable for the wrongful repetition of the slander without his authority; but the principle is general.[17] If the repetition were privileged, and so rightful, and also were manifestly likely to happen, the law might be otherwise.[18]

But the case is different when a defendant has not stopped at the point of saying, I take it for granted that my neighbors will keep to the law, and I shall not let myself be checked in doing what I like, by the danger which there would be, if they acted un-

[16] 153 Mass. 514.

[17] Ward v. Weeks, 7 Bing. 211, 215; Cuff v. Newark & New York R.R., 6 Vroom, 17, 32; Clifford v. Atlantic Mills, 146 Mass. 47; Tasker v. Stanley, 153 Mass. 148, 150.

[18] Elmer v. Fessenden, 151 Mass. 359, 362, and cases cited. See Hayes v. Hyde Park, 153 Mass. 514.

lawfully; when, instead, he not only has expected
unlawful conduct, but has acted with the intent to
bring about consequences which could not happen
without the help of such unlawful acts on the part of
others. The difference is illustrated by the difference between the general right of a landowner, as
against trespassers, to put his land in what condition
he likes, and his liability, even to trespassers (without notice), for man-traps or dog-spears. In the
latter case, he has contemplated expressly what he
would have had a right to assume would not happen,
and the harm done stands just as if he had been on
the spot and had done it in person. His intent may
be said to make him the last wrong-doer.[19]

So when the wrongful act expected is that of a
third person, and not of the plaintiff, the defendant
may be liable for the consequences of it. There is
no doubt, of course, that a man may be liable for the
unlawful act of another, civilly as well as criminally,
and this now is pretty well agreed when the act is
a breach of contract as well as when it is a tort.[20]
He is liable, if having authority he commands it; he
may be liable if he induces it by persuasion. I do
not see that it matters how he knowingly gives the
other a motive for unlawful action, whether by fear,
fraud, or persuasion, if the motive works. But, in
order to take away the protection of his right to rely

---

[19] Bird v. Holbrook, 4 Bing. 628, 641, 642. See Jordin v. Crump, 8
M. & W. 78; Chenery v. Fitchburg R.R., 160 Mass. 211, 213, 214.

[20] Lumley v. Gye, 2 El. & Bl. 216; 1 Ames & Smith, Cases on
Torts, 600, 612, note by Professor Ames.

upon lawful conduct, you must show that he intended to bring about consequences to which that unlawful act was necessary. Ordinarily, this is the same as saying that he must have intended the unlawful act. To sum the matter up in a rule, where it is sought to make a man answerable for damage, and the act of a third person is nearer in time than the defendant's to the harm, if the third person's act was lawful, it stands like the workings of nature, and the question is whether it reasonably was to be anticipated or looked out for; but if the third person's act was unlawful, the defendant must be shown to have intended consequences which could not happen without the act.[21]

Although actual intention is necessary in this class of cases, malice commonly is not so, except so far as the question of liability for an intervening wrongdoer is complicated with a question of privilege. The damage is assumed to be inflicted unlawfully, since the act of the third person which is nearest to it is assumed to be unlawful. If the defendant has no notice that the third person's act will or may be unlawful, he is free on general principles. But, notwithstanding the reserves of Bowen v. Hall,[22] if he

[21] I venture to refer to a series of cases in which my views will be found illustrated. Hayes v. Hyde Park, 153 Mass. 514; Burt v. Advertiser Newspaper Co., 154 Mass. 238, 347; Tasker v. Stanley, 153 Mass. 148. [Note that, in this case, it did not appear that the conduct advised (the departure of the plaintiff's wife) would have been unlawful in any sense, on the facts assumed as the basis of the advice. It did not appear what those facts were. The question of privilege, therefore, was the main one.] Elmer v. Fessenden, 151 Mass. 359, 362; Clifford v. Atlantic Cotton Mills., 146 Mass. 47.

[22] 6 Q.B.D. 333, 338.

knows the act will be unlawful, it seems plain that persuasion to do it will make him liable as well when not malicious as when malicious. I cannot believe that *bona fide* advice to do an unlawful act to the manifest harm of the plaintiff ought to be any more privileged than such advice, given maliciously, to do a lawful act. Of course, I am speaking of effectual advice. It seems to me hard for the law to recognize a privilege to induce unlawful conduct. But, whether there is such a privilege or not, what I am driving at is, that apart from privilege there is no defence; that is to say, that malice is not material, on any other ground than that of privilege, to liability for the wrongful act of another man.

At this point, then, we have come again upon the question of privilege. When the purpose of the defendant's act is to produce the result complained of by means of illegal acts of third persons, his privilege will be narrower than when he intends to induce only legal acts. As I have said, I do not suppose that the privilege extended to honest persuasion to do harm to the plaintiff by lawful conduct, would extend to similar persuasion to do it by unlawful conduct. Take acts of which the privilege is greater. Could a man refuse to contract with A unless he broke his contract with B? There are cases by respectable courts which look as if he could not.[23] What I have called heretofore the privilege not to contract really

[23] Temperton *v.* Russell (1893), 1 Q.B.D. 715, mentioned above for a different point. In this case, there was the additional element of combination. See the other cases cited above, p. 129, n. 14.

is only the negative side of a privilege to make contracts. I stated it in the negative way in order to make the claim of an absolute privilege more plausible. But the right not to contract in a certain event, and to say that you will not, means nothing unless it is implied that you offer a contract, that is, an act on your part, in the other event. If no such offer is understood, then you simply refuse to contract, whatever happens, which undoubtedly you may do. But there is no absolute privilege to make agreements which are not unlawful on their face, that is to say, which do not necessarily and always tend to produce a result that the law wishes to prevent. An agreement may be unlawful, because under the particular circumstances it tends to produce such a result, although in general harmless.

The question has arisen, how close the connection must be between an agreement — for instance, a sale — and the result sought to be prevented, in order to make the sale unlawful. I presume that the same degree of connection which would have that effect would make the seller liable if the result in question was a tort. In Graves v. Johnson,[24] where intoxicating liquor was found to have been sold in Massachusetts, "with a view to" an illegal resale by the purchaser in Maine, a majority of the court interpreted the words quoted as meaning that the seller intended that the buyer should resell unlawfully, and was understood by the latter to be acting in aid of that purpose, and held the sale unlawful. But it

[24] 156 Mass. 211.

may be conjectured that the decision would have been different if the seller merely had known of the buyer's intent without encouraging or caring about it.

In questions of privilege, the nature of the defendant's act, the nature of the consequences, and the closeness of the bond between them, may vary indefinitely. We may imagine the conduct to be of the most highly privileged kind, like the use of land, and to consist of imposing conditions upon the letting of rooms or the removal of a building cutting off a view. We may imagine the conditions to be stated with intent, but without any persuasion or advice, that they should be satisfied, and we may imagine them to be illegal acts anywhere from murder down to breach of a contract to take the *Herald* for a month. Interesting cases of such a kind might be framed for a moot court, although I hardly expect to meet one in practice. But, as I have said, my object is not to decide cases, but to make a little clearer the method to be followed in deciding them.

LEARNING AND SCIENCE *

SPEECH AT A DINNER OF THE HARVARD LAW SCHOOL
ASSOCIATION IN HONOR OF PROFESSOR
C. C. LANGDELL, JUNE 25, 1895

MR. PRESIDENT AND GENTLEMEN OF THE ASSOCIA-
TION:

As most of those here have graduated from the
Law School within the last twenty-five years, I know
that I am in the presence of very learned men. For
my own part, lately my thoughts have been turned to

> "old, unhappy, far-off things,
> And battles long ago";

and when once the ghosts of the dead fifers of thirty
years since begin to play in my head, the laws are
silent. And yet as I look around me, I think to
myself, like Correggio, "I too am, or at least have
been, a pedagogue." And as such I will venture a
reflection.

Learning, my learned brethren, is a very good
thing. I should be the last to undervalue it, having
done my share of quotation from the Year Books.
But it is liable to lead us astray. The law, so far
as it depends on learning, is indeed, as it has been
called, the government of the living by the dead.

* From *Speeches* (1913), Little, Brown, & Co.

To a very considerable extent no doubt it is inevitable that the living should be so governed. The
past gives us our vocabulary and fixes the limits of
our imagination; we cannot get away from it. There
is, too, a peculiar logical pleasure in making manifest
the continuity between what we are doing and what
has been done before. But the present has a right
to govern itself so far as it can; and it ought always
to be remembered that historic continuity with the
past is not a duty, it is only a necessity.

I hope that the time is coming when this thought
will bear fruit. An ideal system of law should draw
its postulates and its legislative justification from
science. As it is now, we rely upon tradition, or
vague sentiment, or the fact that we never thought
of any other way of doing things, as our only warrant
for rules which we enforce with as much confidence
as if they embodied revealed wisdom. Who here can
give reasons of any different kind for believing that
half the criminal law does not do more harm than
good? Our forms of contract, instead of being made
once for all, like a yacht, on lines of least resistance,
are accidental relics of early notions, concerning
which the learned dispute. How much has reason
had to do in deciding how far, if at all, it is expedient
for the State to meddle with the domestic relations?
And so I might go on through the whole law.

The Italians have begun to work upon the notion
that the foundations of the law ought to be scientific,
and, if our civilization does not collapse, I feel pretty
sure that the regiment or division that follows us

will carry that flag. Our own word seems the last always; yet the change of emphasis from an argument in Plowden to one in the time of Lord Ellenborough, or even from that to one in our own day, is as marked as the difference between Cowley's poetry and Shelley's. Other changes as great will happen. And so the eternal procession moves on, we in the front for the moment; and, stretching away against the unattainable sky, the black spearheads of the army that has been passing in unbroken line already for near a thousand years.

EXECUTORS *

AT the present day executors and administrators hold the assets of the estate in a fiduciary capacity. Their rights and liabilities in respect of the fund in their hands, are very like those of trustees. But this way of regarding them is somewhat modern. I wish to call attention to several changes in the law which have taken place at different times and without reference to each other, for the purpose of suggesting that they are witnesses of an older condition of things in which the executor received his testator's assets in his own right. As usually is the case with regard to a collection of doctrines of which one seeks to show that they point to a more general but forgotten principle, there can be found a plausible separate explanation for each or for most of them, which some, no doubt, will regard as the last word to be said upon the matter.

I have shown elsewhere that originally the only person liable to be sued for the debts of the deceased, if they were disputed and had not passed to judgment in the debtor's lifetime, was the heir.[1] In Glanvill's

---

* *Harvard Law Review*, Vol. IX, 42. (1895.)

[1] Early English Equity, 1 Law Quart. Rev. 165. The Common Law, 348. Bracton 407b, 61, 98a, 101a, 113b. The article referred to in the Law Quarterly Review shows the origin and early functions of the executor. It is not necessary to go into them here.

time, if the effects of the ancestor were not sufficient for the payment of his debts the heir was bound to make up the deficiency out of his own property.[2] In the case of debts to the king, this liability continued as late as Edward III.,[3] royalty like religion being a conservator of archaisms. The unlimited liability was not peculiar to England.[4] While it continued we may conjecture with some confidence that a judgment against the heir was not confined to the property which came to him from his ancestor, and that such property belonged to him outright. At a later date, M. Viollet tells us, the French customary law borrowed the benefit of inventory from the Roman law of Justinian. The same process had taken place in England before Bracton wrote. But in the earliest sources it looks as if the limitation of liability was worked out by a limitation of the amount of the judgment, not by confining the judgment to a particular fund.[5]

---

[2] "Si vero non sufficiunt res defuncti ad debita persolvenda, tunc quidem haeres ejus defectum ipsum de suo tenetur adimplere: ita dico si habuerit aetatem haeres ipse." Glanvill, Lib. 7, C. 8. Regiam Majestatem, Book 2, C. 39, § 3.

[3] 2 Rot. Parl. 240, pl. 35. St. 3 Ed. I., C. 19.

[4] Ass. Jerus., Bourgeois, C. cxciii. 2 Beugnot, 130. Paul Viollet, Hist. du Droit Franç., 2d ed. 829.

[5] Viollet, op. cit. The Common Law, 347, 348. "Haeres autem defuncti tenebitur ad debita preadecessoris sui acquietanda eatenus quatenus ad ipsum pervenerit, sci. de haereditate defuncti, et non ultra," etc. Bracton, 61 a. "Notandum tamen est, quod nullus de antecessoris debito tenetur respondere ultra valorem huius, quod de eius hereditate dignoscitur possidere." Somma, Lib. 2, C. 22, § 5, in 7 Ludewig, Reliq. Manuscript, 308, 309. Grand Coustum. C. 88. Compare also St. Westm. II. (13 Ed. I.), C. 19, as to the liability of the

As was shown in the article above referred to, the executor took the place of the heir as universal successor within the limits which still are familiar, shortly after Bracton wrote.   His right to sue and the right of others to sue him in debt seemed to have been worked out at common law.[6]   It hardly needs argument to prove that the new rights and burdens were arrived at by treating the executor as standing in the place of the heir.   The analogy relied on is apparent on the face of the authorities, and in books of a later but still early date we find the express statement, *executores universales loco haeredis sunt*,[7] or as it is put in *Doctor and Student*, "the heir, which in the laws of England is called an Executor."

Now when executors thus had displaced heirs partially in the courts, the question is what was their position with regard to the property in their hands. Presumably it was like that of heirs at about the beginning of the fourteenth century, but I have had to leave that somewhat conjectural.   The first mode of getting at an answer is to find out, if we can, what was the form of judgment against them.   For if the

ordinary: "*Obligetur decetero Ordinarius ad respondendum de debitis, quatenus bona defuncti sufficiunt eodem modo quo executores hujus modo erespondere tenerentur si testamentum fecisset.*" See the cases stated below. I know of no early precedents or forms of judgments against heirs. I wish that Mr. Maitland would give the world the benefit of his knowledge and command of the sources on the matter. Later the judgments against heirs was limited to assets descended. Townesend, Second Book of Judgments, 67, pl. 26.

[6] Y. B. 20 & 21 Ed. I., 374; 30 Ed. I., 238; 11 Ed. III., 142. Id. 186. (Rolls ed.)

[7] Lyndwood, Provinciale. Lib. 3, Tit. 13, C. 5. (*Statutum bonae memoriae*), note, at word *Intestatis*. Dr. and Stud. Dial. I, Ch. 19.

judgment ran against them personally, and was not
limited to the goods of the deceased in their hands,
it is a more than probable corollary that they held
those assets in their own right. The best evidence
known to me is a case of the year 1292 (21 Ed. I.)
in the Rolls of Parliament.[8] Margery Moygne recovered two judgments against Roger Bertelmeu as
executor of William the goldsmith. In the first case
he admitted the debt and set up matter in discharge.
This was found against him except as to £60, as to
which the finding was in his favor, and the judgment
went against him personally for the residue. In the
second case the claim was for 200 marks, of which
the plaintiff's husband had endowed her *ad ostium
ecclesiae.* The defendant pleaded that the testator
did not leave assets sufficient to satisfy his creditors.
The plaintiff replied that her claim was preferred,
which the defendant denied. The custom of boroughs was reported by four burgesses to be as
the plaintiff alleged, and the plaintiff had a judgment against the defendant generally. The defendant complained of these judgments in Parliament,
and assigned as error that there came to his hands
only £27 at most, and that the two judgments
amounted to £40 and more. The matter was com-
promised at this stage, but enough appears for my
purposes. If the defendant was right in his con-
tention, it would follow in our time that the judgment should be *de bonis testatoris,* yet it does not

---

[8] 1 Rot. Parl. 107, 108. It may be remarked, by the way, that an
excellent example of trustee process will be found in this case.

seem to have occurred to him to make that suggestion. He assumed, as the court below assumed, that the judgment was to go against him personally. The limitation for which he contended was in the amount of the judgment, not in the fund against which it should be directed.

There is some other evidence that at this time, and later, the judgment ran against the executor personally, and that the only limitation of liability expressed by it was in the amount. In the first case known to me in which executors were defeated on a plea of *plene administravit* it was decided that the plaintiff should recover of the defendants "without having regard to whether they had to the value of the demand." [9] Afterwards it was settled that in such cases the judgment for the debt should be of the goods of the deceased, and that the judgment for the damages should be general.[10] But whether the first case was right in its day or not, the material point is the way in which the question is stated. The alternatives are not a judgment *de bonis testatoris* and a general judgment against the defendants, but a judgment against the defendants limited to the amount in their hands, and an unlimited judgment against them.

But if it be assumed that a trace of absolute ownership still was shown in the form of the judg-

---

[9] Y. B. 17 Ed. III. 66, pl. 83.

[10] Y. B. 11 Hen. IV. 5, pl. 11. Skrene in 7 Hen. IV. 12, 13, pl. 8. Martin in 9 Hen. VI. 44, pl. 26. Danby in 11 Hen. VI. 7, 8, pl. 12. Dyer, 32 *a*, pl. 2. 1 Roll. Abr. 931, D. pl. 3. 1 Wms. Saund. 336, n. 10.

ment, when we come to the execution we find a distinction between the goods of the testator and those of the executor already established. In 12 Edward III. a judgment had been recovered against a parson, who had died. His executors were summoned, and did not appear. Thereupon the plaintiff had *fieri facias* to levy on the chattels of the deceased in the executors' hands (*de lever ses chateux qil avoient entre mayns des biens la mort*), and on the sheriff returning that he had taken 20s and that there were no more, execution was granted of the goods of the deceased which the executors had in their hands on the day of their summons, or to the value out of the executors' own goods if the former had been eloigned.[11]

I now pass to two other rules of law for each of which there is a plausible and accepted explanation, but which I connect with each other and with my theme. In former days, I was surprised to read in *Williams on Executors*, that the property in the ready money left by the testator "must of necessity be altered; for when it is intermixed with the executor's own money, it is incapable of being distinguished from it, although he shall be accountable for its value." [12] What right, one asked oneself, has an executor to deal in that way with trust funds? In

---

11 Y. B. 13 Ed. III. 398–401 (A.D. 1338). Acc. 2 Rot. Parl. 397, No. 110 (Ed. III.). See also the intimation of Wychingham, J., in 40 Ed. III. 15, pl. 1. Fleta, Lib. 2, C. 57, § 6.

12 1 Wms. Exors. (7th ed.), 646. In the ninth edition this is qualified slightly by the editor in a note. (9th ed.) 566, 567 and n. (p).

this Commonwealth at least the executor would be guilty of a breach of duty if he mingled money of his testator with his own. Another passage in Williams shows that we must not press his meaning too far. It is stated that money of the testator which can be distinguished does not pass to a bankrupt executor's assignee.[13] The principal passage merely was repeated from the earlier text-books of Wentworth and Toller. In Wentworth the notion appears to be stated as a consequence of the difficulty of distinguishing pieces of money of the same denomination from each other — a most impotent reason.[14] There is no doubt that similar arguments were used in other cases of a later date than Wentworth.[15] But I prefer to regard the rule as a survival, especially when I connect it with that next to be mentioned.

As late as Lord Ellenborough's time it was the unquestioned doctrine of the common law that the executor was answerable absolutely for goods which had come into his possession, and that he was not excused if he lost them without fault, for instance, by robbery.[16] Now it is possible to regard this as

---

[13] 1 Wms. Exors. 9th ed. 559. Howard v. Jemmett, 2 Burr. 1368, 1369, note; Farr v. Newman, 4 T.R. 621, 648.

[14] Wentworth, Executors (14th ed. Philadelphia, 1832), 198.

[15] Whitecomb v. Jacob, 1 Salk. 160; Ford v. Hopkins, 1 Salk, 283, 284; Ryall v. Rolle, 1 Atk. 165, 172; Scott v. Surman, Willes, 400, 403, 404. Rightly condemned *quoad hoc* in *Re* Hallett's Estate, 13 Ch. D. 696, 714, 715. See also Miller v. Race, 1 Burr. 452, 457 S.C. 1 Sm. L. C.

[16] Crosse v. Smith, 7 East, 246, 258.

merely one offshoot of the early liability of bailees which still lingered alive, although the main root had rotted and had been cut a century before by Chief Justice Pemberton, and by the mock learning of Lord Holt.[17]   It is explained in that way by Wentworth,[18] who wrote before the early law of bailment had been changed, but with some suggestions of difference and mitigation.   If this explanation were adopted we only should throw the discussion a little further back, upon the vexed question whether possession was title in primitive law.   But it is undeniable that down to the beginning of this century the greatest common-law judges held to the notion that the executor's liability stood on stronger grounds than that of an ordinary bailee, and this notion is easiest explained as an echo of a time when he was owner of the goods, and therefore absolutely accountable for their value.   In the Chancery, the forum of trusts, it is not surprising to find a milder rule laid down at an earlier date, and no doubt the doctrine of equity now has supplanted that of the common law.[19]

There is no dispute, of course, that in some sense executors and administrators have the property in the goods of the deceased.[20]   I take it as evidence

[17] King v. Viscount Hertford, 2 Shower, 172; Coggs v. Bernard, 2 Ld. Raym. 909.   The Common Law, Lect. 5, esp. p. 195.   Morley v. Morley, 2 Cas. in Ch. 2.

[18] Executors (14th ed.), 234.

[19] Lord Hardwicke in Jones v. Lewis, 2 Ves. Sen. 240, 241 (1751); Job v. Job, 6 Ch. D. 562; Stevens v. Gage, 55 N.H. 175.   See Morley v. Morley, 2 Cas. in Ch. 2 (1678).

[20] Com. Dig. *Administration* (B. 10).   Cf. Wms. Exors. (9th ed.) 558.

how hard the early way of thinking died that as late
as 1792, the King's Bench were divided on the question whether a sheriff could apply the goods of a
testator in the hands of his executor in execution of
a judgment against the executor in his own right, if
the sheriff was notified after seizure that the goods
were effects of the testator. As might have been
expected the judgment was that the sheriff had not
the right, but Mr. Justice Buller delivered a powerful dissent.[21] A little earlier the same court decided
that a sale of the testator's goods in execution of
such a judgment passed the title, and Lord Mansfield laid it down as clear that an executor might
alien such goods to one who knew them to be assets
for the payment of debts, and that he might alien
them for a debt of his own. He added, "If the
debts had been paid the goods are the property of
the executor."[22]

Another singular thing is the form of an executor's right of retainer. "If an executor has as much
goods in his hands as his own debt amounts to, the
property of those goods is altered and rests in himself; that is, he has them as his own proper goods
in satisfaction of his debt, and not as executor."[23]
This proposition is qualified by Wentworth, so far
as to require an election where the goods are more
than the debt.[24] But the right is clear, and if not

[21] Farr v. Newman, 4 T.R. 621.

[22] Whale v. Booth, 4 Doug. 36, 46. See 1 Wms. Exors. (9th ed.)
561, note.

[23] Woodward v. Lord Darcy, Plowden, 184, 185.

[24] Executors (14th ed.), 77, 198, 199.

exercised by the executor in his lifetime passes to his executor.[25] So when an executor or administrator pays a debt of the deceased with his own money he may appropriate chattels to the value of the debt.[26] A right to take money would not have seemed strange, but this right to take chattels at a valuation *in pais* without judgment is singular. It may be a survival of archaic modes of satisfaction when money was scarce and valuations in the country common.[27] But it may be a relic of more extensive title.

The last fact to be considered is the late date at which equity fully carried out the notion that executors hold the assets in trust. In 1750, in a case where one Richard Watkins had died, leaving his property to his nephew and niece, Lord Hardwicke, speaking of a subsequently deceased nephew, William Watkins, said that he "had no right to any specific part of the personal estate of Richard whatever; only a right to have that personal estate accounted for, and debts and legacies paid out of it, and so much as should be his share on the whole account paid to him; which is only a debt, or in the nature of a chose in action due to the estate of Wil-

---

[25] Hopton *v.* Dryden, Prec. Ch. 179. Wentw. Exors. (14th ed.) 77, note, citing 11 Vin. Abr. 261, 263; Croft *v.* Pyke, 3 P. Wms. 179, 183; Burdet *v.* Pix, 2 Brownl. 50.

[26] Dyer, 2*a*; Elliott *v.* Kemp. 7 M. & W. 306, 313.

[27] See, e.g., the application of the trusteed wool to the judgment in 1 Rot. Parl. 108. Assignment of dower *de la pluis beale*, Litt. § 49. Delivery of debtor's chattels by sheriff, St. Westm. II. Ch. 18. Kearns *v.* Cunniff, 138 Mass. 434, 436.

liam."²⁸ In M'Leod *v.* Drummond²⁹ Lord Eldon says that Lord Hardwicke "frequently considered it as doubtful, whether even in the excepted cases any one except a creditor, or a specific legatee, could follow the assets in equity. On the same page, Hill *v.* Simpson, 7 Ves. 152 (1802), is said to have been the first case which gave that right to a general pecuniary legatee.³⁰ Hill *v.* Simpson lays it down that executors in equity are mere trustees for the performance of the will,³¹ but it adds that in many respects and for many purposes third persons are entitled to consider them absolute owners. Toward the end of the last century their fiduciary position began to be insisted on more than had been the case, and the common-law decisions which have been cited helped this tendency of the Chancery.³²

The final step was taken in M'Leod *v.* Drummond,³³ when Lord Eldon established the rights of residuary legatees. "It is said in Farr *v.* Newman that the residuary legatee is to take the money, when made up: but I say, he has in a sense a lien upon the fund, as it is; and may come here for the specific fund." ³⁴

---

²⁸ Thorne *v.* Watkins, 2 Ves. Sen. 35, 36.

²⁹ 17 Ves. 152, 169 (1810).

³⁰ See also M'Leod *v.* Drummond, 14 Ves. 353, 354.

³¹ P. 166. Note the recurrence with a difference to their original position in the early Frankish law. I Law Quart. Rev. 164.

³² See also Scott *v.* Tyler, 2 Dickens, 712, 725, 726.

³³ 17 Ves. 152, 169.

³⁴ See Marvel *v.* Babbitt, 143 Mass. 226; Pierce *v.* Gould, 143 Mass. 234, 235; Mechanics' Savings Bank *v.* Waite, 150 Mass. 234, 235.

I made the decree appealed from in Foster *v.* Bailey, 157 Mass. 160,

162. The particular form which it took, allowing the defendant, the administrator of an administrator, to retain one share of stock and a savings-bank book as security for what might be found due to his intestate on the settlement of his account, and directing him to hand over the rest of the assets, was consented to, in case the defendant had a right to retain anything. I made the decree on the assumption that the change in the position of executor and administrator which I am considering left their rights undisturbed. Of course if the liability were only to account for a balance, the executor of an executor would not be bound to hand over anything more, and could not be compelled to pay anything until the balance was settled. His duty, when established, would not be to deliver specific property, but to pay a sum of money. I do not know what evidence can be found on this point. It is fair to mention that the plea offered in 30 Ed. I. 240, by executor of executors, was that, "We held none of the goods of the deceased on the day when this bill was delivered." But that may be no more than a general form. "Bonz" probably only meant property.

THE BAR AS A PROFESSION *

THE main thoughts of the fine paper on "The Bar as a Profession," by the Lord Chief Justice of England, in the *Companion* of February 13, 1896, are as true for America as for England; but possibly a few local variations on his theme may have their use. It is not likely here that anybody will be prejudiced against business or will take formal views of the dignity of callings such as a hundred years ago put the ministry first, law and medicine next, and below them all other pursuits. The real beliefs of the world to-day are commercial, and money and the means of making it are in no danger of being undervalued.

I should say that one of the good things about the law is that it does not pursue money directly. When you sell goods the price which you get and your own interests are what you think about in the affair. When you try a case you think about the ways to win it and the interests of your client. In the long run this affects one's whole habit of mind, as anyone will notice if he talks much with men.

In the twenty-five years that I have known English lawyers it has seemed to me that a scholastic type of man has more chance of success in England than

* Reprinted from the *Youth's Companion* for 1896.

here, where the men at the top are usually hard fighters.   At all events, scholarliness as a social accomplishment is more important there than here, and this would lead me to lay somewhat less weight upon a university training than is done by the Lord Chief Justice.

I will not go so far as a jesting friend of mine once did and say that the main use of a university education is to learn the humbug of it.   I think it very useful and very important to a man as a man.   But in this country I do not think it quite so important to a lawyer as a lawyer.

A certain amount of education a man must have who constantly is using books.   It will save him trouble if he understands an occasional scrap of Latin when he comes across it.   But a man may sweep juries before him, command the attention of judges, counsel sagely in great affairs, or be a leader in any senate of the country with nothing of the scholarly about him.

I say this not to make light of the good of going to college, but by way of encouragement to those who doubt whether their inability to go there does not take away hope of success in the law.   I have had letters from young men beset with the doubt, and always have told them that it is no ground for despair.

If a man misses a university education it may be made up to him in part by the way we study law in this country; for that also is different from the English way.   I think all the lawyers I know here-

abouts would agree that the place for a young man
to study law is a law school, not a lawyer's office.

We have a great many law schools in the United
States in which a great many able and more or less
distinguished men are teachers. I will mention that
at Cambridge, not by way of invidious comparison,
but as that which I know best. If a young man can
afford to study there for two, or even three years, he
will not regret a month of it when he comes to
practice.

After the law school spend six months in a good
office, to see how things are done, and also perhaps
to get a little of the usual law student's conceit
rubbed off, and then begin. Practice, in Massachusetts at least, is very easily understood.

What needs time is not to learn the routine of
clerk's offices or what a writ looks like, but to master
profoundly and in detail the great body of the law.
This is done far better in a law school in the midst
of a catching enthusiasm than it can be in the listless
solitude of an office, and the companionship and intellectual excitement which are found in the school take
the place to many of the experience which they
missed at an earlier stage.

In a law school the lines of study are marked out,
of course, and the student will not be likely to find
much time for the Roman law. If he studies that,
it will be in his months of waiting for clients. But
in spite of the very great authority by which the
study of it is recommended, I never have been able
to believe that it has the value so often supposed.

A system of law at any time is the resultant of present needs and present notions of what is wise and right on the one hand, and, on the other, of rules handed down from earlier states of society and embodying needs and notions which more or less have passed away.

To get to the bottom of any system, therefore, a good deal of history has to be studied, and this is true of the law under which we live now. But our law has reached broader and more profound generalizations than the Roman law, and at the same time far surpasses it in the detail with which it has been worked out.

One who is master of our own will master any civilized body of law with ease. But while he is engaged in mastering one, I doubt the wisdom of adding to his difficulties by the attempt to learn another system which is even more in need than ours of historical explanation at every step, a large part of which is obsolete, and a part of which is hard to understand even in the best modern books. I cannot help suspecting that the advantages attributed to his study of it by the Lord Chief Justice were due to Sir Henry Maine more than to the Roman law.

The main roots of our law are Frankish, not Roman, and many ideas which formerly were supposed, and in the common books still are supposed, to have come from Rome are now traced to the *Lex Salica* and the folk-law which left its mark in the *Germania* of Tacitus. The last will is almost the only conception of first-rate importance which has a Roman origin, so far as I know.

Of course I recognize that a man hardly can be called accomplished in his profession who knows nothing of Roman law, and more particularly of the great Germans who have taught it in this century, but I am speaking of how to learn law for practice.

The study of jurisprudence is a different matter. When properly taught, jurisprudence means simply the broadest generalization of the principles and the deepest analysis of the ideas at the bottom of an actual system. It is the same process, carried further, by which the law is carried out from particular cases into general rules. A young man who has understood John Austin's tedious and often mistaken book has taken a real step forward, while Sir Henry Maine makes him feel as if his whole road were strewn with diamonds.

The means of thoroughly understanding the law now within every one's reach are very different from those with which we had to content ourselves when I was a student. Studied as it may be studied and as there are now many encouragements to study it, Burke no longer would fear, I think, that it would sharpen the mind by narrowing it.

One of the courses to be pursued is the anatomy of legal ideas worked out by the English school of jurisprudence; another is the embryology of the same conceptions to be found in history as the Germans have taught it to the world.

With regard to the chances of success, I remember

that the late Lord Justice Bowen once told me, when he was at the bar and already successful, that he thought that beside patience and talent a man must have luck.   But, so far as I have noticed, luck generally comes to patience and talent, if coupled with love of the thing, as the Lord Chief Justice so truly adds.

In this country there seems to be as good a chance to succeed at the bar as in other callings, and I should not think that much depended on luck for a man of the right sort.   Sometimes, too, the law has been the starting-point for a business career, and always it has offered an opening into politics.

For the last quarter of a century a large part of our best talent has gone into business rather than into politics, doubtless because it was more needed there and therefore the rewards were higher.   It has been more important that the country should be developed than that it should be governed by the greatest skill.   But there can be no doubt that we need all the ability we can get in our government at the present time and that we shall want, if we can get them, trained lawyers as well as economists in our legislatures.

But here again the situation is different from that in England; and political life generally means giving up the law for the time and rather a falling off in legal capacity, although I should not advise any one to sleep on that consideration if he should be trying a case against Senator Hoar.

In one of the most beautiful pieces of English in

the world, the essay called *The Lantern-Bearers,* Mr. Robert Louis Stevenson shows us how in their hearts all men are idealists. The only criticism which I should make upon his adorable essay is that his examples find their ideals outside their daily pursuits. George Herbert's

> "Who sweeps a room as for Thy laws,
> Makes that and th' action fine,"

has an intellectual as well as a moral meaning. If the world is a subject for rational thought it is all of one piece; the same laws are found everywhere, and everything is connected with everything else; and if this is so, there is nothing mean, and nothing in which may not be seen the universal law.

The difference between gossip and philosophy lies only in one's way of taking a fact. The law may lead to high things those who stay in it as well as those who pass beyond but not above it to other forms of command.

A REJOINDER

BY THE LORD CHIEF JUSTICE OF ENGLAND

I HAVE read the comments on "The Bar as a Profession," by Mr. Justice Holmes, with interest and with some surprise. With much that the learned judge says I find myself in agreement. On two main points I find myself differing from him. In the first place I regard university training as much more important than the learned judge appears to do. Robust minds can do much to make good the want of it, but to make an accomplished lawyer in the sense in which Chief Justice Marshall, Lord Mansfield and Sir William Grant, amongst others, answered that description, I regard university culture as almost indispensable.

My surprise in the next place arises from the depreciatory view which Mr. Justice Holmes seems to take of the value of the study of Roman law. Under that head I of course include not only the *Corpus Juris,* but also that body of text law, mainly German, which deals not only with the historical and scientific side of Roman law, but which, by modernizing it, has rejected much of the early Roman law now obsolete.

No one can read the judgments of your great Chief Justice Marshall or the writings of Story or of Kent without seeing how much, in arrangement and in breadth of view, they owe to the study of Roman law.

Mr. Justice Holmes speaks truly and with just pride of the system of legal education in the United States. It is in my opinion far superior to that existing in these islands. Its superiority I think mainly consists in its systematic teaching of the historical and scientific aspects of law before the actual, practical, workaday law is dealt with.

To the absence of this system I largely attribute the facts — which I deplore — that with but few exceptions our legal treatises are analyses of decided cases, our legal arguments at the bar are a nice discrimination of those cases, and the deliverances from the judges but little more than able efforts to establish analogies or differences between the case in hand and reported authority. I think also the form if not the substance of legislation is injuriously affected by the same cause.

If this state of things is to be remedied, it can only be by early training in law, historically and systematically taught, and I can imagine no such teaching from which the Roman law can be excluded. I need hardly say that in any study of comparative law the Roman system must find a prominent place.

The learned judge speaks of the broader and more profound generalizations reached in our time. May I suggest to him that even now, after the lapse of centuries, the *De regulis juris* still speaks with a living voice? Again, I cannot agree that the main roots of our law are Frankish — they are mainly of native growth — and still less that the "last will" is almost the only conception of first-rate importance which originates in the Roman law. But I would prefer to suggest other authority than my own in favor of the views I propound.

It happens that I have recently had to read the report known as that of the Gresham Commission (1894), before which were examined a number of distinguished men on the subject of the establishment of a legal faculty in connection with a teaching university in London. Amongst these were Lord Coleridge, Lord Bowen, Prof. J. Bryce, M. P., Lord Davey, Professor Westlake, and last, but by no means least, Prof. E. H. Emmott of the Johns Hopkins University, Baltimore. Each of these high authorities was emphatic as to the importance of the study of Roman law in any high system of legal training.

In *The Bar as a Profession*, I have suggested a high ideal of the accomplished lawyer — one who may make a great advocate, a great judge, a great writer, or a great legislator, or all of these. I do not deny that without the liberal equipment which I would desire, men of ability may make large incomes and even have distinguished careers at the bar, but I maintain that their careers would have been still more distinguished, their marks on their generation graven still deeper, and their contributions to the wisdom of the world still weightier, had they possessed it.

A POSTSCRIPT

BY MR. JUSTICE HOLMES

I HAVE read the second article of the Lord Chief Justice, but I see no reason to change the opinions which I have expressed. I will only add a few words of explanation.

I trust that it will be understood that I did not undervalue the moral or even the intellectual advantages of a university education, but that I am speaking of its importance for what I may call a fighting success.

In saying that the main roots of our law are Frankish I mean to deny the notion, which has been held, that they are Roman, rather than accurately to discriminate the particular folk-law to which we are most indebted. I do not think, however, that any of the most important conceptions of private law are of native origin in England.

For further expression of my views I should have to refer to my book on *The Common Law* and to an article on "Early English Equity" in the *Law Quarterly Review*. The leading ideas there advanced appear to me to have been followed in the main by the latest and most accomplished historians of English law, Sir F. Pollock and Mr. Maitland.

BROWN UNIVERSITY — COMMENCE-
MENT 1897 *

A UNIVERSITY is a place from which men start for the Eternal City. In the university are pictured the ideals which abide in the City of God. Many roads lead to that haven, and those who are here have traveled by different paths towards the goal. I do not know what better the travelers can do at a gathering like this, where for a moment the university becomes conscious of itself and of its meaning, than to report to those about to start something of their experiences and to give a hint of what is to be expected on the way .

My way has been by the ocean of the law. On that I have learned a part of the great lesson, the lesson not of law but of life. There were few of the charts and lights for which one longed when I began. One found oneself plunged in a thick fog of details — in a black and frozen night, in which were no flowers, no spring, no easy joys. Voices of authority warned that in the crush of that ice any craft might sink. One heard Burke saying that law sharpens the mind by narrowing it. One heard in Thackeray of a lawyer bending all the powers of a great mind to a mean profession. One saw that

* Hitherto unprinted.

164

artists and poets shrank from it as from an alien
world.   One doubted oneself how it could be worthy
of the interest of an intelligent mind.   And yet
one said to oneself, law is human — it is a part
of man, and of one world with all the rest.   There
must be a drift, if one will go prepared and have
patience, which will bring one out to daylight and
a worthy end.   You all have read or heard the
story of Nansen and see the parallel which I use.
Most men of the college-bred type in some form or
other have to go through that experience of sailing
for the ice and letting themselves be frozen in.   In
the first stage one has companions, cold and black
though it be, and if he sticks to it, he finds at last
that there is a drift as was foretold.   When he has
found that he has learned the first part of his lesson,
that one is safe in trusting to courage and to time.
But he has not yet learned all.   So far his trials
have been those of his companions.   But if he is a
man of high ambitions he must leave even his fellow-
adventurers and go forth into a deeper solitude and
greater trials.   He must start for the pole.   In plain
words he must face the loneliness of original work.
No one can cut out new paths in company.   He does
that alone.

When he has done that and has turned misgiving
into success he is master of himself and knows the
secret of achievement.   He has learned the second
part of his lesson and is ready for the consummation
of the whole.   For he has gained another knowledge
more fruitful than success.   He knows now what he

had divined at the outset, that one part of the universe yields the same teaching as any other if only it is mastered, that the difference between the great way of taking things and the small — between philosophy and gossip — is only the difference between realizing the part as a part of a whole and looking at it in its isolation as if it really stood apart. The consummation to which I referred comes when he applies this knowledge to himself. He may put it in the theological form of justification by faith or in the philosophical one of the continuity of the universe. I care not very much for the form if in some way he has learned that he cannot set himself over against the universe as a rival god, to criticize it, or to shake his fist at the skies, but that his meaning is its meaning, his only worth is as a part of it, as a humble instrument of the universal power. It seems to me that this is the key to intellectual salvation, as the key to happiness is to accept a like faith in one's heart, and to be not merely a necessary but a willing instrument in working out the inscrutable end.

THE PATH OF THE LAW *

WHEN we study law we are not studying a mystery but a well-known profession. We are studying what we shall want in order to appear before judges, or to advise people in such a way as to keep them out of court. The reason why it is a profession, why people will pay lawyers to argue for them or to advise them, is that in societies like ours the command of the public force is intrusted to the judges in certain cases, and the whole power of the state will be put forth, if necessary, to carry out their judgments and decrees. People want to know under what circumstances and how far they will run the risk of coming against what is so much stronger than themselves, and hence it becomes a business to find out when this danger is to be feared. The object of our study, then, is prediction, the prediction of the incidence of the public force through the instrumentality of the courts.

The means of the study are a body of reports, of treatises, and of statutes, in this country and in England, extending back for six hundred years, and now increasing annually by hundreds. In these

* An Address delivered by Mr. Justice Holmes, of the Supreme Judicial Court of Massachusetts, at the dedication of the new hall of the Boston University School of Law, on January 8, 1897. Copyrighted by O. W. Holmes, 1897. *Harvard Law Review*, Vol. X., 457.

sibylline leaves are gathered the scattered prophecies of the past upon the cases in which the axe will fall. These are what properly have been called the oracles of the law. Far the most important and pretty nearly the whole meaning of every new effort of legal thought is to make these prophecies more precise, and to generalize them into a thoroughly connected system. The process is one, from a lawyer's statement of a case, eliminating as it does all the dramatic elements with which his client's story has clothed it, and retaining only the facts of legal import, up to the final analyses and abstract universals of theoretic jurisprudence. The reason why a lawyer does not mention that his client wore a white hat when he made a contract, while Mrs. Quickly would be sure to dwell upon it along with the parcel gilt goblet and the sea-coal fire, is that he foresees that the public force will act in the same way whatever his client had upon his head. It is to make the prophecies easier to be remembered and to be understood that the teachings of the decisions of the past are put into general propositions and gathered into text-books, or that statutes are passed in a general form. The primary rights and duties with which jurisprudence busies itself again are nothing but prophecies. One of the many evil effects of the confusion between legal and moral ideas, about which I shall have something to say in a moment, is that theory is apt to get the cart before the horse, and to consider the right or the duty as something existing apart from and independent of the consequences of its breach, to which certain sanctions are added afterward. But, as I shall try to show, a legal duty so called is nothing but a prediction that if a man does or omits certain things he will be made to suffer in this or that way by judgment of the court; and so of a legal right.

The number of our predictions when generalized and reduced to a system is not unmanageably large. They present themselves as a finite body of dogma which may be mastered within a reasonable time. It is a great mistake to be frightened by the ever-increasing number of reports. The reports of a given jurisdiction in the course of a generation take up pretty much the whole body of the law, and restate it from the present point of view. We could reconstruct the corpus from them if all that went before were burned. The use of the earlier reports is mainly historical, a use about which I shall have something to say before I have finished.

I wish, if I can, to lay down some first principles for the study of this body of dogma or systematized prediction which we call the law, for men who want to use it as the instrument of their business to enable them to prophesy in their turn, and, as bearing upon the study, I wish to point out an ideal which as yet our law has not attained.

The first thing for a business-like understanding of the matter is to understand its limits, and therefore I think it desirable at once to point out and dispel a confusion between morality and law, which sometimes rises to the height of conscious theory, and more often and indeed constantly is making trouble in detail without reaching the point of consciousness. You can see very plainly that a bad man has as much reason as a good one for wishing to avoid an encounter with the public force, and therefore you can see the practical importance of the distinction between morality and law. A man who cares nothing for an ethical rule which is believed and practised by his neighbors is likely nevertheless to care a good deal to avoid being made to pay money, and will want to keep out of jail if he can.

I take it for granted that no hearer of mine will misinterpret what I have to say as the language of cynicism. The law is the witness and external deposit of our moral life. Its history is the history of the moral development of the race. The practice of it, in spite of popular jests, tends to make good citizens and good men. When I emphasize the difference between law and morals I do so with reference to a single end, that of learning and understanding the law. For that purpose you must definitely master its specific marks, and it is for that I ask you for the moment to imagine yourselves indifferent to other and greater things.

I do not say that there is not a wider point of view from which the distinction between law and morals becomes of secondary or no importance, as all mathematical distinctions vanish in presence of the infinite. But I do say that that distinction is of the first importance for the object which we are here to consider — a right study and mastery of the law as a business with well understood limits, a body of dogma enclosed within definite lines. I have just shown the practical reason for saying so. If you want to know the law and nothing else, you must look at it as a bad man, who cares only for the material consequences which such knowledge enables him to predict, not as a good one, who finds his reasons for conduct, whether inside the law or outside of it, in the vaguer sanctions of conscience. The theoretical importance of the distinction is no less, if you would reason on your subject aright. The law is full of phraseology drawn from morals, and by the mere force of language continually invites us to pass from one domain to the other without perceiving it, as we are sure to do unless we have the boundary constantly before our minds. The law talks about rights, and duties, and malice, and intent, and negligence, and so forth, and nothing is easier, or, I may say, more common in legal reasoning, than to take these words in their moral sense, at some stage of the argument, and so to drop into fallacy. For instance, when we speak of the rights of man in a moral sense, we mean to mark the limits of interference with individual freedom which we think are prescribed by conscience, or by our ideal, however reached. Yet it is certain that many laws have been enforced in the past, and it is likely that some are enforced now, which are condemned by the most enlightened opinion of the time, or which at all events pass the limit of interference as many consciences would draw it. Manifestly, therefore, nothing but confusion of thought can result from assuming that the rights of man in a moral sense are equally rights in the sense of the Constitution and the law. No doubt simple and extreme cases can be put of imaginable laws which the statute-making power would not dare to enact, even in the absence of written constitutional prohibitions, because the community would rise in rebellion and fight; and this gives some plausibility to the proposition that the law, if not a part of morality, is limited by it. But this limit of power is not coextensive with any system of morals. For the most part it falls far within the lines of any such system, and in some cases may extend beyond them, for reasons drawn from the habits of a particular people at a particular time. I once heard the late Professor Agassiz say that a German population would rise if you added two cents to the price of a glass of beer. A statute in such a case would be empty words, not because it was wrong, but because it could not be enforced. No one will deny that wrong statutes can be and are enforced, and we should not all agree as to which were the wrong ones.

The confusion with which I am dealing besets confessedly legal conceptions. Take the fundamental question, What constitutes the law? You will find some text writers telling you that it is something different from what is decided by the courts of Massachusetts or England, that it is a system of reason, that it is a deduction from principles of ethics or admitted axioms or what not, which may or may not coincide with the decisions. But if we take the view of our friend the bad man we shall find that he does not care two straws for the axioms or deductions, but that he does want to know what the Massachusetts or English courts are likely to do in fact. I am much of his mind. The prophecies of what the courts will do in fact, and nothing more pretentious, are what I mean by the law.

Take again a notion which as popularly under-stood is the widest conception which the law con-tains — the notion of legal duty, to which already I have referred. We fill the word with all the con-tent which we draw from morals. But what does it mean to a bad man? Mainly, and in the first place, a prophecy that if he does certain things he will be subjected to disagreeable consequences by way of imprisonment or compulsory payment of money. But from his point of view, what is the difference between being fined and being taxed a certain sum for doing a certain thing? That his point of view is the test of legal principles is shown by the many discussions which have arisen in the courts on the very quesetion whether a given statu-tory liability is a penalty or a tax. On the answer to this question depends the decision whether conduct is legally wrong or right, and also whether a man is under compulsion or free. Leaving the criminal law on one side, what is the difference between the liability under the mill acts or statutes authorizing a taking by eminent domain and the liability for what we call a wrongful conversion of property where restoration is out of the question. In both cases the party taking another man's property has to pay its fair value as assessed by a jury, and no more. What significance is there in calling one taking right and another wrong from the point of view of the law? It does not matter, so far as the given consequence, the compulsory payment, is concerned, whether the act to which it is attached is described in terms of praise or in terms of blame, or whether the law purports to prohibit it or to allow it. If it matters at all, still speaking from the bad man's point of view, it must be because in one case and not in the other some further disadvantages, or at least some further consequences, are attached to the act by the law. The only other disadvantages thus attached to it which I ever have been able to think of are to be found in two somewhat insignificant legal doctrines, both of which might be abolished without disturbance. One is, that a contract to do a prohibited act is unlawful, and the other, that, if one of two or more joint wrongdoers has to pay all the damages, he cannot recover contribution from his fellows. And that I believe is all. You see how the vague circumference of the notion of duty shrinks and at the same time grows more precise when we wash it with cynical acid and expel everything except the object of our study, the operations of the law.

Nowhere is the confusion between legal and moral ideas more manifest than in the law of contract. Among other things, here again the so called primary rights and duties are invested with a mystic significance beyond what can be assigned and explained.

The duty to keep a contract at common law means a prediction that you must pay damages if you do not keep it — and nothing else. If you commit a tort, you are liable to pay a compensatory sum. If you commit a contract, you are liable to pay a compensatory sum unless the promised event comes to pass, and that is all the difference. But such a mode of looking at the matter stinks in the nostrils of those who think it advantageous to get as much ethics into the law as they can. It was good enough for Lord Coke, however, and here, as in many other cases, I am content to abide with him. In *Bromage v. Genning*,[1] a prohibition was sought in the King's Bench against a suit in the marches of Wales for the specific performance of a covenant to grant a lease, and Coke said that it would subvert the intention of the covenantor, since he intends it to be at his election either to lose the damages or to make the lease. Sergeant Harris for the plaintiff confessed that he moved the matter against his conscience, and a prohibition was granted. This goes further than we should go now, but it shows what I venture to say has been the common law point of view from the beginning, although Mr. Harriman, in his very able little book upon Contracts has been misled, as I humbly think, to a different conclusion.

I have spoken only of the common law, because there are some cases in which a logical justification can be found for speaking of civil liabilities as imposing duties in an intelligible sense. These are

[1] Roll. Rep. 368.

the relatively few in which equity will grant an injunction, and will enforce it by putting the defendant in prison or otherwise punishing him unless he complies with the order of the court. But I hardly think it advisable to shape general theory from the exception, and I think it would be better to cease troubling ourselves about primary rights and sanctions altogether, than to describe our prophecies concerning the liabilities commonly imposed by the law in those inappropriate terms.

I mentioned, as other examples of the use by the law of words drawn from morals, malice, intent, and negligence. It is enough to take malice as it is used in the law of civil liability for wrongs — what we lawyers call the law of torts — to show that it means something different in law from what it means in morals, and also to show how the difference has been obscured by giving to principles which have little or nothing to do with each other the same name. Three hundred years ago a parson preached a sermon and told a story out of Fox's *Book of Martyrs* of a man who had assisted at the torture of one of the saints, and afterward died, suffering compensatory inward torment. It happened that Fox was wrong. The man was alive and chanced to hear the sermon, and thereupon he sued the parson. Chief Justice Wray instructed the jury that the defendant was not liable, because the story was told innocently, without malice. He took malice in the moral sense, as importing a malevolent motive. But nowadays no one doubts that a man may be liable, without any malevolent

motive at all, for false statements manifestly cal-
culated to inflict temporal damage. In stating the
case in pleading, we still should call the defendant's
conduct malicious; but, in my opinion at least, the
word means nothing about motives, or even about
the defendant's attitude toward the future, but only
signifies that the tendency of his conduct under the
known circumstances was very plainly to cause the
plaintiff temporal harm.[2]

In the law of contract the use of moral phraseology has led to equal confusion, as I have shown
in part already, but only in part. Morals deal with
the actual internal state of the individual's mind,
what he actually intends. From the time of the
Romans down to now, this mode of dealing has
affected the language of the law as to contract, and
the language used has reacted upon the thought. We
talk about a contract as a meeting of the minds
of the parties, and thence it is inferred in various
cases that there is no contract because their minds
have not met; that is, because they have intended
different things or because one party has not known
of the assent of the other. Yet nothing is more
certain than that parties may be bound by a contract
to things which neither of them intended, and when
one does not know of the other's assent. Suppose
a contract is executed in due form and in writing
to deliver a lecture, mentioning no time. One of
the parties thinks that the promise will be construed
to mean at once, within a week. The other thinks

2 See Hanson v. Globe Newspaper Co., 159 Mass. 293, 302.

that it means when he is ready. The court says that it means within a reasonable time. The parties are bound by the contract as it is interpreted by the court, yet neither of them meant what the court declares that they have said. In my opinion no one will understand the true theory of contract or be able even to discuss some fundamental questions intelligently until he has understood that all contracts are formal, that the making of a contract depends not on the agreement of two minds in one intention, but on the agreement of two sets of external signs — not on the parties' having *meant* the same thing but on their having *said* the same thing. Furthermore, as the signs may be addressed to one sense or another — to sight or to hearing — on the nature of the sign will depend the moment when the contract is made. If the sign is tangible, for instance, a letter, the contract is made when the letter of acceptance is delivered. If it is necessary that the minds of the parties meet, there will be no contract until the acceptance can be read — none, for example, if the acceptance be snatched from the hand of the offerer by a third person.

This is not the time to work out a theory in detail, or to answer many obvious doubts and questions which are suggested by these general views. I know of none which are not easy to answer, but what I am trying to do now is only by a series of hints to throw some light on the narrow path of legal doctrine, and upon two pitfalls which, as it seems to me, lie perilously near to it. Of the first of these

I have said enough. I hope that my illustrations have shown the danger, both to speculation and to practice, of confounding morality with law, and the trap which legal language lays for us on that side of our way. For my own part, I often doubt whether it would not be a gain if every word of moral significance could be banished from the law altogether, and other words adopted which should convey legal ideas uncolored by anything outside the law. We should lose the fossil records of a good deal of history and the majesty got from ethical associations, but by ridding ourselves of an unnecessary confusion we should gain very much in the clearness of our thought.

So much for the limits of the law. The next thing which I wish to consider is what are the forces which determine its content and its growth. You may assume, with Hobbes and Bentham and Austin, that all law emanates from the sovereign, even when the first human beings to enunciate it are the judges, or you may think that law is the voice of the Zeitgeist, or what you like. It is all one to my present purpose. Even if every decision required the sanction of an emperor with despotic power and a whimsical turn of mind, we should be interested none the less, still with a view to prediction, in discovering some order, some rational explanation, and some principle of growth for the rules which he laid down. In every system there are such explanations and principles to be found. It is with regard to them that a second fallacy comes in, which I think it important to expose.

The fallacy to which I refer is the notion that the only force at work in the development of the law is logic. In the broadest sense, indeed, that notion would be true. The postulate on which we think about the universe is that there is a fixed quantitative relation between every phenomenon and its antecedents and consequents. If there is such a thing as a phenomenon without these fixed quantitative relations, it is a miracle. It is outside the law of cause and effect, and as such transcends our power of thought, or at least is something to or from which we cannot reason. The condition of our thinking about the universe is that it is capable of being thought about rationally, or, in other words, that every part of it is effect and cause in the same sense in which those parts are with which we are most familiar. So in the broadest sense it is true that the law is a logical development, like everything else. The danger of which I speak is not the admission that the principles governing other phenomena also govern the law, but the notion that a given system, ours, for instance, can be worked out like mathematics from some general axioms of conduct. This is the natural error of the schools, but it is not confined to them. I once heard a very eminent judge say that he never let a decision go until he was absolutely sure that it was right. So judicial dissent often is blamed, as if it meant simply that one side or the óther were not doing their sums right, and, if they would take more trouble, agreement inevitably would come.

This mode of thinking is entirely natural. The training of lawyers is a training in logic. The processes of analogy, discrimination, and deduction are those in which they are most at home. The language of judicial decision is mainly the language of logic. And the logical method and form flatter that longing for certainty and for repose which is in every human mind. But certainty generally is illusion, and repose is not the destiny of man. Behind the logical form lies a judgment as to the relative worth and importance of competing legislative grounds, often an inarticulate and unconscious judgment, it is true, and yet the very root and nerve of the whole proceeding. You can give any conclusion a logical form. You always can imply a condition in a contract. But why do you imply it? It is because of some belief as to the practice of the community or of a class, or because of some opinion as to policy, or, in short, because of some attitude of yours upon a matter not capable of exact quantitative measurement, and therefore not capable of founding exact logical conclusions. Such matters really are battle grounds where the means do not exist for determinations that shall be good for all time, and where the decision can do no more than embody the preference of a given body in a given time and place. We do not realize how large a part of our law is open to reconsideration upon a slight change in the habit of the public mind. No concrete proposition is self evident, no matter how ready we may be to accept it, not even Mr. Herbert Spencer's

"Every man has a right to do what he wills, provided he interferes not with a like right on the part of his neighbors."

Why is a false and injurious statement privileged, if it is made honestly in giving information about a servant. It is because it has been thought more important that information should be given freely, than that a man should be protected from what under other circumstances would be an actionable wrong. Why is a man at liberty to set up a business which he knows will ruin his neighbor? It is because the public good is supposed to be best subserved by free competition. Obviously such judgments of relative importance may vary in different times and places. Why does a judge instruct a jury that an employer is not liable to an employee for an injury received in the course of his employment unless he is negligent, and why do the jury generally find for the plaintiff if the case is allowed to go to them? It is because the traditional policy of our law is to confine liability to cases where a prudent man might have foreseen the injury, or at least the danger, while the inclination of a very large part of the community is to make certain classes of persons insure the safety of those with whom they deal. Since the last words were written, I have seen the requirement of such insurance put forth as part of the programme of one of the best known labor organizations. There is a concealed, half conscious battle on the question of legislative policy, and if any one thinks that it can be settled deductively, or once for all, I only can say that I think he is theoretically wrong, and that I am certain that his conclusion will not be accepted in practice *semper ubique et ab omnibus*.

Indeed, I think that even now our theory upon this matter is open to reconsideration, although I am not prepared to say how I should decide if a reconsideration were proposed. Our law of torts comes from the old days of isolated, ungeneralized wrongs, assaults, slanders, and the like, where the damages might be taken to lie where they fell by legal judgment. But the torts with which our courts are kept busy to-day are mainly the incidents of certain well known businesses. They are injuries to person or property by railroads, factories, and the like. The liability for them is estimated, and sooner or later goes into the price paid by the public. The public really pays the damages, and the question of liability, if pressed far enough, is really the question how far it is desirable that the public should insure the safety of those whose work it uses. It might be said that in such cases the chance of a jury finding for the defendant is merely a chance, once in a while rather arbitrarily interrupting the regular course of recovery, most likely in the case of an unusually conscientious plaintiff, and therefore better done away with. On the other hand, the economic value even of a life to the community can be estimated, and no recovery, it may be said, ought to go beyond that amount. It is conceivable that some day in certain cases we may find ourselves imitating, on a higher plane, the tariff for life and limb which we see in the *Leges Barbarorum*.

I think that the judges themselves have failed adequately to recognize their duty of weighing considerations of social advantage. The duty is inevitable, and the result of the often proclaimed judicial aversion to deal with such considerations is simply to leave the very ground and foundation of judgments inarticulate, and often unconscious, as I have said. When socialism first began to be talked about, the comfortable classes of the community were a good deal frightened. I suspect that this fear has influenced judicial action both here and in England, yet it is certain that it is not a conscious factor in the decisions to which I refer. I think that something similar has led people who no longer hope to control the legislatures to look to the courts as expounders of the Constitutions, and that in some courts new principles have been discovered outside the bodies of those instruments, which may be generalized into acceptance of the economic doctrines which prevailed about fifty years ago, and a wholesale prohibition of what a tribunal of lawyers does not think about right. I cannot but believe that if the training of lawyers led them habitually to consider more definitely and explicitly the social advantage on which the rule they lay down must be justified, they sometimes would hesitate where now they are confident, and see that really they were taking sides upon debatable and often burning questions.

So much for the fallacy of logical form. Now let

us consider the present condition of the law as a subject for study, and the ideal toward which it tends. We still are far from the point of view which I desire to see reached. No one has reached it or can reach it as yet. We are only at the beginning of a philosophical reaction, and of a reconsideration of the worth of doctrines which for the most part still are taken for granted without any deliberate, conscious, and systematic questioning of their grounds. The development of our law has gone on for nearly a thousand years, like the development of a plant, each generation taking the inevitable next step, mind, like matter, simply obeying a law of spontaneous growth. It is perfectly natural and right that it should have been so. Imitation is a necessity of human nature, as has been illustrated by a remarkable French writer, M. Tarde, in an admirable book, *Les Lois de l'Imitation*. Most of the things we do, we do for no better reason than that our fathers have done them or that our neighbors do them, and the same is true of a larger part than we suspect of what we think. The reason is a good one, because our short life gives us no time for a better, but it is not the best. It does not follow, because we all are compelled to take on faith at second hand most of the rules on which we base our action and our thought, that each of us may not try to set some corner of his world in the order of reason, or that all of us collectively should not aspire to carry reason as far as it will go throughout the whole domain. In regard to the law, it is true, no doubt, that an evolutionist will hesitate to affirm universal validity for his social ideals, or for the principles which he thinks should be embodied in legislation. He is content if he can prove them best for here and now. He may be ready to admit that he knows nothing about an absolute best in the cosmos, and even that he knows next to nothing about a permanent best for men. Still it is true that a body of law is more rational and more civilized when every rule it contains is referred articulately and definitely to an end which it subserves, and when the grounds for desiring that end are stated or are ready to be stated in words.

At present, in very many cases, if we want to know why a rule of law has taken its particular shape, and more or less if we want to know why it exists at all, we go to tradition. We follow it into the Year Books, and perhaps beyond them to the customs of the Salian Franks, and somewhere in the past, in the German forests, in the needs of Norman kings, in the assumptions of a dominant class, in the absence of generalized ideas, we find out the practical motive for what now best is justified by the mere fact of its acceptance and that men are accustomed to it. The rational study of law is still to a large extent the study of history. History must be a part of the study, because without it we cannot know the precise scope of rules which it is our business to know. It is a part of the rational study, because it is the first step toward an enlightened scepticism, that is, towards a deliberate reconsidera-

tion of the worth of those rules. When you get the
dragon out of his cave on to the plain and in the
daylight, you can count his teeth and claws, and
see just what is his strength. But to get him out
is only the first step. The next is either to kill him,
or to tame him and make him a useful animal. For
the rational study of the law the black-letter man
may be the man of the present, but the man of the
future is the man of statistics and the master of
economics. It is revolting to have no better reason
for a rule of law than that so it was laid down in
the time of Henry IV. It is still more revolting
if the grounds upon which it was laid down have
vanished long since, and the rule simply persists from
blind imitation of the past. I am thinking of the
technical rule as to trespass *ab initio,* as it is called,
which I attempted to explain in a recent Massachusetts case. [3]

Let me take an illustration, which can be stated
in a few words, to show how the social end which
is aimed at by a rule of law is obscured and only
partially attained in consequence of the fact that
the rule owes its form to a gradual historical development, instead of being reshaped as a whole, with
conscious articulate reference to the end in view.
We think it desirable to prevent one man's property
being misappropriated by another, and so we make
larceny a crime. The evil is the same whether the
misappropriation is made by a man into whose hands
the owner has put the property, or by one who wrong-

[3] Commonwealth *v.* Rubin, 165 Mass. 453.

fully takes it away.   But primitive law in its weakness did not get much beyond an effort to prevent violence, and very naturally made a wrongful taking, a trespass, part of its definition of the crime.   In modern times the judges enlarged the definition a little by holding that, if the wrong-doer gets possession by a trick or device, the crime is committed. This really was giving up the requirement of a trespass, and it would have been more logical, as well as truer to the present object of the law, to abandon the requirement altogether.   That, however, would have seemed too bold, and was left to statute. Statutes were passed making embezzlement a crime. But the force of tradition caused the crime of embezzlement to be regarded as so far distinct from larceny that to this day, in some jurisdictions at least, a slip corner is kept open for thieves to contend, if indicted for larceny, that they should have been indicted for embezzlement, and if indicted for embezzlement, that they should have been indicted for larceny, and to escape on that ground.

Far more fundamental questions still await a better answer than that we do as our fathers have done. What have we better than a blind guess to show that the criminal law in its present form does more good than harm?   I do not stop to refer to the effect which it has had in degrading prisoners and in plunging them further into crime, or to the question whether fine and imprisonment do not fall more heavily on a criminal's wife and children than on himself.   I have in mind more far-reaching questions. Does punishment deter? Do we deal with criminals on proper principals? A modern school of Continental criminalists plumes itself on the formula, first suggested, it is said, by Gall, that we must consider the criminal rather than the crime. The formula does not carry us very far, but the inquiries which have been started look toward an answer of my questions based on science for the first time. If the typical criminal is a degenerate, bound to swindle or to murder by as deep seated an organic necessity as that which makes the rattlesnake bite, it is idle to talk of deterring him by the classical method of imprisonment. He must be got rid of; he cannot be improved, or frightened out of his structural reaction. If, on the other hand, crime, like normal human conduct, is mainly a matter of imitation, punishment fairly may be expected to help to keep it out of fashion. The study of criminals has been thought by some well known men of science to sustain the former hypothesis. The statistics of the relative increase of crime in crowded places like large cities, where example has the greatest chance to work, and in less populated parts, where the contagion spreads more slowly, have been used with great force in favor of the latter view. But there is weighty authority for the belief that, however this may be, "not the nature of the crime, but the dangerousness of the criminal, constitutes the only reasonable legal criterion to guide the inevitable social reaction against the criminal." [4]

4 Havelock Ellis, *The Criminal*, 41, citing Garofalo. See also Ferri, *Sociologie Criminelle, passim.* Compare Tarde, *La Philosophie Pénale.*

The impediments to rational generalization, which I illustrated from the law of larceny, are shown in the other branches of the law, as well as in that of crime. Take the law of tort or civil liability for damages apart from contract and the like. Is there any general theory of such liability, or are the cases in which it exists simply to be enumerated, and to be explained each on its special ground, as is easy to believe from the fact that the right of action for certain well known classes of wrongs like trespass or slander has its special history for each class? I think that there is a general theory to be discovered, although resting in tendency rather than established and accepted. I think that the law regards the infliction of temporal damage by a responsible person as actionable, if under the circumstances known to him the danger of his act is manifest according to common experience, or according to his own experience if it is more than common, except in cases where upon special grounds of policy the law refuses to protect the plaintiff or grants a privilege to the defendant.[5] I think that commonly malice, intent, and negligence mean only that the danger was manifest to a greater or less degree, under the circumstances known to the actor, although in some cases of privilege malice may mean an actual malevolent motive,

---

[5] An example of the law's refusing to protect the plaintiff is when he is interrupted by a stranger in the use of a valuable way, which he has travelled adversely for a week less than the period of prescription. A week later he will have gained a right, but now he is only a trespasser. Example of privilege I have given already. One of the best is competition in business.

and such a motive may take away a permission knowingly to inflict harm, which otherwise would be
granted on this or that ground of dominant public
good. But when I stated my view to a very eminent English judge the other day, he said: "You are
discussing what the law ought to be; as the law is,
you must show a right. A man is not liable for
negligence unless he is subject to a duty." If our
difference was more than a difference in words, or
with regard to the proportion between the exceptions
and the rule, then, in his opinion, liability for an
act cannot be referred to the manifest tendency of
the act to cause temporal damage in general as a
sufficient explanation, but must be referred to the
special nature of the damage, or must be derived
from some special circumstances outside of the tendency of the act, for which no generalized explanation exists. I think that such a view is wrong, but
it is familiar, and I dare say generally is accepted in
England.

Everywhere the basis of principle is tradition, to
such an extent that we even are in danger of making
the rôle of history more important than it is. The
other day Professor Ames wrote a learned article
to show, among other things, that the common law
did not recognize the defence of fraud in actions
upon specialties, and the moral might seem to be
that the personal character of that defence is due
to its equitable origin. But if, as I have said, all
contracts are formal, the difference is not merely
historical, but theoretic, between defects of form

which prevent a contract from being made, and mistaken motives which manifestly could not be considered in any system that we should call rational except against one who was privy to those motives. It is not confined to specialties, but is of universal application. I ought to add that I do not suppose that Mr. Ames would disagree with what I suggest.

However, if we consider the law of contract, we find it full of history. The distinctions between debt, covenant, and assumpsit are merely historical. The classification of certain obligations to pay money, imposed by the law irrespective of any bargain as quasi contracts, is merely historical. The doctrine of consideration is merely historical. The effect given to a seal is to be explained by history alone. Consideration is a mere form. Is it a useful form? If so, why should it not be required in all contracts? A seal is a mere form, and is vanishing in the scroll and in enactments that a consideration must be given, seal or no seal. Why should any merely historical distinction be allowed to affect the rights and obligations of business men?

Since I wrote this discourse I have come on a very good example of the way in which tradition not only overrides rational policy, but overrides it after first having been misunderstood and having been given a new and broader scope than it had when it had a meaning. It is the settled law of England that a material alteration of a written contract by a party avoids it as against him. The doctrine is contrary to the general tendency of the law.

We do not tell a jury that if a man ever has lied in one particular he is to be presumed to lie in all. Even if a man has tried to defraud, it seems no sufficient reason for preventing him from proving the truth. Objections of like nature in general go to the weight, not to the admissibility, of evidence. Moreover, this rule is irrespective of fraud, and is not confined to evidence. It is not merely that you cannot use the writing, but that the contract is at an end. What does this mean? The existence of a written contract depends on the fact that the offerer and offeree have interchanged their written expressions, not on the continued existence of those expressions. But in the case of a bond, the primitive notion was different. The contract was inseparable from the parchment. If a stranger destroyed it, or tore off the seal, or altered it, the obligee could not recover, however free from fault, because the defendant's contract, that is, the actual tangible bond which he had sealed, could not be produced in the form in which it bound him. About a hundred years ago Lord Kenyon undertook to use his reason on this tradition, as he sometimes did to the detriment of the law, and, not understanding it, said he could see no reason why what was true of a bond should not be true of other contracts. His decision happened to be right, as it concerned a promissory note, where again the common law regarded the contract as inseparable from the paper on which it was written, but the reasoning was general, and soon was extended to other written contracts, and various absurd and unreal grounds of policy were invented to account for the enlarged rule.

I trust that no one will understand me to be speaking with disrespect of the law, because I criticise it so freely. I venerate the law, and especially our system of law, as one of the vastest products of the human mind. No one knows better than I do the countless number of great intellects that have spent themselves in making some addition or improvement, the greatest of which is trifling when compared with the mighty whole. It has the final title to respect that it exists, that it is not a Hegelian dream, but a part of the lives of men. But one may criticise even what one reveres. Law is the business to which my life is devoted, and I should show less than devotion if I did not do what in me lies to improve it, and, when I perceive what seems to me the ideal of its future, if I hesitated to point it out and to press toward it with all my heart.

Perhaps I have said enough to show the part which the study of history necessarily plays in the intelligent study of the law as it is to-day. In the teaching of this school and at Cambridge it is in no danger of being undervalued. Mr. Bigelow here and Mr. Ames and Mr. Thayer there have made important contributions which will not be forgotten, and in England the recent history of early English law by Sir Frederick Pollock and Mr. Maitland has lent the subject an almost deceptive charm. We must beware of the pitfall of antiquarianism, and must remember that for our purposes our only interest in the past is for the light it throws upon the present. I look forward to a time when the part played by history in the explanation of dogma shall be very small, and instead of ingenious research we shall spend our energy on a study of the ends sought to be attained and the reasons for desiring them. As a step toward that ideal it seems to me that every lawyer ought to seek an understanding of economics. The present divorce between the schools of political economy and law seems to me an evidence of how much progress in philosophical study still remains to be made. In the present state of political economy, indeed, we come again upon history on a larger scale, but there we are called on to consider and weigh the ends of legislation, the means of attaining them, and the cost. We learn that for everything we have we give up something else, and we are taught to set the advantage we gain against the other advantage we lose, and to know what we are doing when we elect.

There is another study which sometimes is undervalued by the practical minded, for which I wish to say a good word, although I think a good deal of pretty poor stuff goes under that name. I mean the study of what is called jurisprudence. Jurisprudence, as I look at it, is simply law in its most generalized part. Every effort to reduce a case to a rule is an effort of jurisprudence, although the name as used in English is confined to the broadest rules and most fundamental conceptions. One mark of a great lawyer is that he sees the application of the broadest rules. There is a story of a Vermont justice of the peace before whom a suit was brought by one farmer against another for breaking a churn. The justice took time to consider, and then said that he had looked through the statutes and could find nothing about churns, and gave judgment for the defendant. The same state of mind is shown in all our common digests and text-books. Applications of rudimentary rules of contract or tort are tucked away under the head of Railroads or Telegraphs or go to swell treatises on historical subdivisions, such as Shipping or Equity, or are gathered under an arbitrary title which is thought likely to appeal to the practical mind, such as Mercantile Law. If a man goes into law it pays to be a master of it, and to be a master of it means to look straight through all the dramatic incidents and to discern the true basis for prophecy. Therefore, it is well to have an accurate notion of what you mean by law, by a right, by a duty, by malice, intent, and negligence, by ownership, by possession, and so forth. I have in my mind cases in which the highest courts seem to me to have floundered because they had no clear ideas on some of these themes. I have illustrated their importance already. If a further illustration is wished, it may be found by reading the Appendix to Sir James Stephen's *Criminal Law* on the subject of possession, and then turning to Pollock and Wright's enlightened book. Sir James Stephen is not the only writer whose attempts to analyze legal ideas have been confused by striving for a useless quintessence of all sys-

tems, instead of an accurate anatomy of one. The
trouble with Austin was that he did not know enough
English law. But still it is a practical advantage to
master Austin, and his predecessors, Hobbes and
Bentham, and his worthy successors, Holland and
Pollock. Sir Frederick Pollock's recent little book
is touched with the felicity which marks all his works,
and is wholly free from the perverting influence of
Roman models.

The advice of the elders to young men is very
apt to be as unreal as a list of the hundred best
books. At least in my day I had my share of such
counsels, and high among the unrealities I place the
recommendation to study the Roman law. I assume
that such advice means more than collecting a few
Latin maxims with which to ornament the discourse
— the purpose for which Lord Coke recommended
Bracton. If that is all that is wanted, the title *De
Regulis Juris Antiqui* can be read in an hour. I assume that, if it is well to study the Roman Law, it is
well to study it as a working system. That means
mastering a set of technicalities more difficult and
less understood than our own, and studying another
course of history by which even more than our own
the Roman law must be explained. If any one
doubts me, let him read Keller's *Der Römische
Civil Process und die Actionen,* a treatise on the
praetor's edict, Muirhead's most interesting *Historical Introduction to the Private Law of Rome,*
and, to give him the best chance, Sohm's admirable
Institutes. No. The way to gain a liberal view of

your subject is not to read something else, but to get to the bottom of the subject itself. The means of doing that are, in the first place, to follow the existing body of dogma into its highest generalizations by the help of jurisprudence; next, to discover from history how it has come to be what it is; and, finally, so far as you can, to consider the ends which the several rules seek to accomplish, the reasons why those ends are desired, what is given up to gain them, and whether they are worth the price.

We have too little theory in the law rather than too much, especially on this final branch of study. When I was speaking of history, I mentioned larceny as an example to show how the law suffered from not having embodied in a clear form a rule which will accomplish its manifest purpose. In that case the trouble was due to the survival of forms coming from a time when a more limited purpose was entertained. Let me now give an example to show the practical importance, for the decision of actual cases, of understanding the reasons of the law, by taking an example from rules which, so far as I know, never have been explained or theorized about in any adequate way. I refer to statutes of limitation and the law of prescription. The end of such rules is obvious, but what is the justification for depriving a man of his rights, a pure evil as far as it goes, in consequence of the lapse of time? Sometimes the loss of evidence is referred to, but that is a secondary matter. Sometimes the desirability of peace, but why is peace more desirable after twenty years than

before? It is increasingly likely to come without
the aid of legislation. Sometimes it is said that, if
a man neglects to enforce his rights, he cannot complain if, after a while, the law follows his example.
Now if this is all that can be said about it, you
probably will decide a case I am going to put, for
the plaintiff; if you take the view which I shall suggest, you possibly will decide it for the defendant.
A man is sued for trespass upon land, and justifies
under a right of way. He proves that he has used
the way openly and adversely for twenty years, but
it turns out that the plaintiff had granted a license
to a person whom he reasonably supposed to be the
defendant's agent, although not so in fact, and therefore had assumed that the use of the way was per-
missive, in which case no right would be gained.
Has the defendant gained a right or not? If his
gaining it stands on the fault and neglect of the
landowner in the ordinary sense, as seems commonly
to be supposed, there has been no such neglect, and
the right of way has not been acquired. But if I
were the defendant's counsel, I should suggest that
the foundation of the acquisition of rights by lapse
of time is to be looked for in the position of the person who gains them, not in that of the loser. Sir
Henry Maine has made it fashionable to connect the
archaic notion of property with prescription. But
the connection is further back than the first recorded
history. It is in the nature of man's mind. A thing
which you have enjoyed and used as your own for a
long time, whether property or an opinion, takes

root in your being and cannot be torn away without your resenting the act and trying to defend yourself, however you came by it. The law can ask no better justification than the deepest instincts of man. It is only by way of reply to the suggestion that you are disappointing the former owner, that you refer to his neglect having allowed the gradual dissociation between himself and what he claims, and the gradual association of it with another. If he knows that another is doing acts which on their face show that he is on the way toward establishing such an association, I should argue that in justice to that other he was bound at his peril to find out whether the other was acting under his permission, to see that he was warned, and if necessary, stopped.

I have been speaking about the study of the law, and I have said next to nothing of what commonly is talked about in that connection — text-books and the case system, and all the machinery with which a student comes most immediately in contact. Nor shall I say anything about them. Theory is my subject, not practical details. The modes of teaching have been improved since my time, no doubt, but ability and industry will master the raw material with any mode. Theory is the most important part of the dogma of the law, as the architect is the most important man who takes part in the building of a house. The most important improvements of the last twenty-five years are improvements in theory. It is not to be feared as unpractical, for, to the competent, it simply means going to the bottom of the subject. For the incompetent, it sometimes is true, as has been said, that an interest in general ideas means an absence of particular knowledge. I remember in army days reading of a youth who, being examined for the lowest grade and being asked a question about squadron drill, answered that he never had considered the evolutions of less than ten thousand men. But the weak and foolish must be left to their folly. The danger is that the able and practical minded should look with indifference or distrust upon ideas the connection of which with their business is remote. I heard a story, the other day, of a man who had a valet to whom he paid high wages, subject to deduction for faults. One of his deductions was, "For lack of imagination, five dollars." The lack is not confined to valets. The object of ambition, power, generally presents itself nowadays in the form of money alone. Money is the most immediate form, and is a proper object of desire. "The fortune," said Rachel, "is the measure of the intelligence." That is a good text to waken people out of a fool's paradise. But, as Hegel says,[6] "It is in the end not the appetite, but the opinion, which has to be satisfied." To an imagination of any scope the most far-reaching form of power is not money, it is the command of ideas. If you want great examples, read Mr. Leslie Stephen's *History of English Thought in the Eighteenth Century,* and see how a hundred years after his death the abstract speculations of Descartes had become a practical force con-

6 Phil. des Rechts, § 190.

trolling the conduct of men. Read the works of the great German jurists, and see how much more the world is governed to-day by Kant than by Bonaparte. We cannot all be Descartes or Kant, but we all want happiness. And happiness, I am sure from having known many successful men, cannot be won simply by being counsel for great corporations and having an income of fifty thousand dollars. An intellect great enough to win the prize needs other food besides success. The remoter and more general aspects of the law are those which give it universal interest. It is through them that you not only become a great master in your calling, but connect your subject with the universe and catch an echo of the infinite, a glimpse of its unfathomable process, a hint of the universal law.

THE THEORY OF LEGAL INTERPRETATION*

THE paper upon the "Principles of Legal Interpretation," by Mr. F. Vaughan Hawkins, reprinted in Professor Thayer's recently published and excellent *Preliminary Treatise on Evidence,* induces me to suggest what seems to me the theory of our rules of interpretation — a theory which I think supports Lord Wensleydale and the others whom Mr. Hawkins quotes and disapproves, if I correctly understand their meaning and his.

It is true that in theory any document purporting to be serious and to have some legal effect has one meaning and no other, because the known object is to achieve some definite result. It is not true that in practice (and I know no reason why theory should disagree with the facts) a given word or even a given collocation of words has one meaning and no other. A word generally has several meanings, even in the dictionary. You have to consider the sentence in which it stands to decide which of those meanings it bears in the particular case, and very likely will see that it there has a shade of significance more refined than any given in the word-book. But in this first step, at least, you are not troubling yourself

* *Harvard Law Review,* Vol. XII., 417 (1899).

about the idiosyncrasies of the writer, you are considering simply the general usages of speech. So
when you let whatever galvanic current may come
from the rest of the instrument run through the particular sentence, you still are doing the same thing.
How is it when you admit evidence of circumstances
and read the document in the light of them? Is this
trying to discover the particular intent of the individual, to get into his mind and to bend what he said
to what he wanted? No one would contend that
such a process should be carried very far, but, as
it seems to me, we do not take a step in that direction. It is not a question of tact in drawing a line.
We are after a different thing. What happens is
this. Even the whole document is found to have
a certain play in the joints when its words are
translated into things by parol evidence, as they have
to be. It does not disclose one meaning conclusively
according to the laws of language. Thereupon we
ask, not what this man meant, but what those words
would mean in the mouth of a normal speaker of English, using them in the circumstances in which they
were used, and it is to the end of answering this last
question that we let in evidence as to what the circumstances were. But the normal speaker of English is merely a special variety, a literary form, so
to speak, of our old friend the prudent man. He
is external to the particular writer, and a reference
to him as the criterion is simply another instance of
the externality of the law.

But then it is said, and this is thought to be the

crux: In the case of a gift of Blackacre to John Smith, when the donor owned two Blackacres and the directory reveals two John Smiths, you may give direct evidence of the donor's intention, and it is only an anomaly that you cannot give the same evidence in every case. I think, on the contrary, that the exceptional rule is a proof of the instinctive insight of the judges who established it. I refer again to the theory of our language. By the theory of our language, while other words may mean different things, a proper name means one person or thing and no other. If language perfectly performed its function, as Bentham wanted to make it, it would point out the person or thing in every case. But under our random system it sometimes happens that your name is *idem sonans* with mine, and it may be the same even in spelling. But it never means you or me indifferently. In theory of speech your name means you and my name means me, and the two names are different. They are different words. *Licet idem sit nomen, tamen diversum est propter diversitatem personae.*[1] In such a case we let in evidence of intention not to help out what theory recognizes as an uncertainty of speech, and to read what the writer meant into what he has tried but failed to say, but, recognizing that he has spoken with theoretic certainty, we inquire what he meant in order to find out what he has said. It is on this ground that there is no contract when the proper name used by one party means one ship, and that used by the other

[1] Bract. 190a.

means another.[2] The mere difference of intent as such is immaterial. In the use of common names and words a plea of different meaning from that adopted by the court would be bad, but here the parties have said different things and never have expressed a contract. If the donor, instead of saying "Blackacre," had said "my gold watch" and had owned more than one, inasmuch as the words, though singular, purport to describe any such watch belonging to the speaker, I suppose that no evidence of intention would be admitted. But I dare say that evidence of circumstances sufficient to show that the normal speaker of English would have meant a particular watch by the same words would be let in.

I have stated what I suppose to be our general theory of construction. It remains to say a few words to justify it. Of course, the purpose of written instruments is to express some intention or state of mind of those who write them, and it is desirable to make that purpose effectual, so far as may be, if instruments are to be used. The question is how far the law ought to go in aid of the writers. In the case of contracts, to begin with them, it is obvious that they express the wishes not of one person but of two, and those two adversaries. If it turns out that one meant one thing and the other another, speaking generally, the only choice possible for the

---

[2] Raffles v. Wichelhaus, 2 H. & C. 906. See Mead v. Phenix Insurance Co., 158 Mass. 124; Hanson v. Globe Newspaper Co., 159 Mass. 293, 305.

legislator is either to hold both parties to the judge's interpretation of the words in the sense which I have explained, or to allow the contract to be avoided because there has been no meeting of minds. The latter course not only would greatly enhance the difficulty of enforcing contracts against losing parties, but would run against a plain principle of justice. For each party to a contract has notice that the other will understand his words according to the usage of the normal speaker of English under the circumstances, and therefore cannot complain if his words are taken in that sense.[8]

Different rules conceivably might be laid down for the construction of different kinds of writing. In the case of a statute, to turn from contracts to the opposite extreme, it would be possible to say that as we are dealing with the commands of the sovereign the only thing to do is to find out what the sovereign wants. If supreme power resided in the person of a despot who would cut off your hand or your head if you went wrong, probably one would take every available means to find out what was wanted. Yet in fact we do not deal differently with a statute from our way of dealing with a contract. We do not inquire what the legislature meant; we ask only what the statute means. In this country, at least, for constitutional reasons, if for no other, if the same legislature that passed it should declare at a later

---

[8] In Nash v. Minnesota Title Insurance and Trust Company, 163 Mass. 574, I thought that this principle should be carried further than the majority of the court were willing to go.

date a statute to have a meaning which in the opinion
of the court the words did not bear, I suppose that
the declaratory act would have no effect upon intervening transactions unless in a place and case where
retrospective legislation was allowed.   As retrospective legislation it would not work by way of construction except in form.

So in the case of a will.   It is true that the testator is a despot, within limits, over his property, but
he is required by statute to express his commands in
writing, and that means that his words must be
sufficient for the purpose when taken in the sense in
which they would be used by the normal speaker of
English under his circumstances.

I may add that I think we should carry the external
principle of construction even further than I have
indicated.   I do not suppose that you could prove,
for purposes of construction as distinguished from
avoidance, an oral declaration or even an agreement
that words in a dispositive instrument making sense
as they stand should have a different meaning from
the common one; for instance, that the parties to a
contract orally agreed that when they wrote five hundred feet it should mean one hundred inches, or at
Bunker Hill Monument should signify Old South
Church.[4]   On the other hand, when you have the
security of a local or class custom or habit of speech,
it may be presumed that the writer conforms to the
usage of his place or class when that is what a normal
person in his situation would do.   But these cases

---

[4] Goode v. Riley, 153 Mass. 585, 586.

are remote from the point of theory upon which I started to speak.

It may be, after all, that the matter is one in which the important thing, the law, is settled, and different people will account for it by such theory as pleases them best, as in the ancient controversy whether the finder of a thing which had been thrown away by the owner got a title in privity by gift, or a new title by abandonment. That he got a title no one denied. But although practical men generally prefer to leave their major premises inarticulate, yet even for practical purposes theory generally turns out the most important thing in the end. I am far from saying that it might not make a difference in the old question to which I have referred.

LAW IN SCIENCE AND SCIENCE IN LAW *

THE law of fashion is a law of life. The crest of the wave of human interest is always moving, and it is enough to know that the depth was greatest in respect of a certain feature or style in literature or music or painting a hundred years ago to be sure that at that point it no longer is so profound. I should draw the conclusion that artists and poets, instead of troubling themselves about the eternal, had better be satisfied if they can stir the feelings of a generation, but that is not my theme. It is more to my point to mention that what I have said about art is true within the limits of the possible in matters of the intellect. What do we mean when we talk about explaining a thing? A hundred years ago men explained any part of the universe by showing its fitness for certain ends, and demonstrating what they conceived to be its final cause according to a providential scheme. In our less theological and more scientific day, we explain an object by tracing the order and process of its growth and development from a starting point assumed as given.

This process of historical explanation has been

* An Address delivered by Mr. Justice Holmes before the New York State Bar Association on January 17, 1899. — *Harvard Law Review*, Vol. XII., 443.

applied to the matter of our profession, especially
of recent years, with great success, and with so much
eagerness, and with such a feeling that when you had
the true historic dogma you had the last word not
only in the present but for the immediate future,
that I have felt warranted heretofore in throwing out
the caution that continuity with the past is only a
necessity and not a duty. As soon as a legislature
is able to imagine abolishing the requirement of a
consideration for a simple contract, it is at perfect
liberty to abolish it, if it thinks it wise to do so,
without the slightest regard to continuity with the
past. That continuity simply limits the possibilities
of our imagination, and settles the terms in which
we shall be compelled to think.

Historical explanation has two directions or aspects, one practical and the other abstractly scientific.
I by no means share that morality which finds in a
remoter practice the justification of philosophy and
science. I do not believe that we must justify our
pursuits by the motive of social well-being. If we
have satisfied ourselves that our pursuits are good for
society, or at least not bad for it, I think that
science, like art, may be pursued for the pleasure of
the pursuit and of its fruits, as an end in itself.
I somewhat sympathize with the Cambridge mathe-
matician's praise of his theorem, "The best of it all
is that it can never by any possibility be made of the
slightest use to anybody for anything." I think it
one of the glories of man that he does not sow seed,
and weave cloth, and produce all the other economic

means simply to sustain and multiply other sowers and weavers that they in their turn may multiply, and so *ad infinitum,* but that on the contrary he devotes a certain part of his economic means to uneconomic ends — ends, too, which he finds in himself and not elsewhere. After the production of food and cloth has gone on a certain time, he stops producing and goes to the play, or he paints a picture, or asks unanswerable questions about the universe, and thus delightfully consumes a part of the world's food and clothing, while he idles away the only hours that fully account for themselves.

Thinking in this way, you readily will understand that I do not consider the student of the history of legal doctrine bound to have a practical end in view. It is perfectly proper to regard and study the law simply as a great anthropological document. It is proper to resort to it to discover what ideals of society have been strong enough to reach that final form of expression, or what have been the changes in dominant ideals from century to century. It is proper to study it as an exercise in the morphology and transformation of human ideas. The study pursued for such ends becomes science in the strictest sense. Who could fail to be interested in the transition through the priest's test of truth,[1] the miracle of the ordeal, and the soldier's, the battle of the duel, to the democratic verdict of the jury! Perhaps I might add, in view of the great increase of jury-waived cases, a later transition yet — to the commer-

[1] I do not forget that the church abolished the ordeal.

cial and rational test of the judgment of a man trained to decide.

It is still only the minority who recognize how the change of emphasis which I have called the law of fashion has prevailed even in the realm of morals. The other day I was looking over Bradford's history — the book which Mr. Bayard brought as a gift from Lambeth to the Massachusetts State House — and I was struck to see recounted the execution of a man with horrible solemnities for an offence which still, to be sure, stands on the statute book as a serious crime, but which no longer is often heard of in court, which many would regard as best punished simply by the disgust of normal men, and which a few think of only as a physiological aberration, of interest mainly to the pathologist. I found in the same volume the ministers consulted as the final expounders of the law, and learnedly demonstrating that what now we should consider as needing no other repression than a doctor's advice, was a crime punishable with death and to be ferreted out by searching the conscience of the accused, although after discussion it was thought that torture should be reserved for state occasions.

To take a less odious as well as less violent contrast, when we read in the old books that it is the duty of one exercising a common calling to do his work upon demand and to do it with reasonable skill, we see that the gentleman is in the saddle and means to have the common people kept up to the mark for his convenience. We recognize the imperative tone which in our day has changed sides, and is oftener to be heard from the hotel clerk than from the guest.

I spoke of the scientific study of the morphology and transformation of human ideas in the law, and perhaps the notion did not strike all of you as familiar. I am not aware that the study ever has been systematically pursued, but I have given some examples as I have come upon them in my work, and perhaps I may mention some now by way of illustration, which, so far as I know, have not been followed out by other writers. In the Lex Salica[2] — the law of the Salian Franks — you find going back to the fifth century a very mysterious person, later[3] named the salmannus — the sale-man — a third person who was called in to aid in completing the transfer of property in certain cases. The donor handed to him a symbolic staff which he in due season handed over in solemn form to the donee. If we may trust M. Dareste, and take our information at second hand, a copious source of error, it would look as if a similar use of a third person was known to the Egyptians and other early peoples. But what is certain is that we see the same form used down to modern times in England for the transfer of copyhold. I dare say that many of you were puzzled, as I was when I was a law student, at the strange handing over of a staff to the lord or steward of the manor as a first step toward conveying copyhold land to somebody else. It really is nothing but a survival of the old form

[2] Merkel, ch. 46.
[3] A.D. 1108, Beseler, 263, n.

of the Salic law, as M. Vinogradoff at last has noticed, in his work on Villainage in England. There you have the Salic device in its original shape. But it is the transformations which it has undergone to which I wish to call your attention. The surrender to the steward is expressed to be to the use of the purchaser or donee. Now, although Mr. Kenelm Digby in his *History of the Law of Real Property* warns us that this has nothing to do with the doctrine of uses, I venture to think that, helped by the work of learned Germans as to the development of the saleman on the continent, I have shown heretofore that the saleman became in England the better known feoffee to uses, and thus that the connection between him and the steward of the manor when he receives the surrender of a copyhold is clear. But the executor originally was nothing but a feoffee to uses. The heir was the man who paid his ancestor's debts and took his property. The executor did not step into the heir's shoes, and come fully to represent the person of the testator as to personal property and liabilities until after Bracton wrote his great treatise on the Laws of England. Surely a flower is not more unlike a leaf, or a segment of a skull more unlike a vertebra, than the executor as we know him is remote from his prototype, the saleman of the Salic law. I confess that such a development as that fills me with interest, not only for itself, but as an illustration of what you see all through the law — the paucity of original ideas in man, and the slow, coasting way in which he works along from rudimentary beginnings to the complex and artificial conceptions of civilized life. It is like the niggardly uninventiveness of nature in its other manifestations, with its few smells or colors or types, its short list of elements, working along in the same slow way from compound to compound until the dramatic impressiveness of the most intricate compositions, which we call organic life, makes them seem different in kind from the elements out of which they are made, when set opposite to them in direct contrast.

In a book which I printed a good many years ago I tried to establish another example of the development and transformation of ideas. The early law embodied hatred for any immediate source of hurt, which comes from the association of ideas and imperfect analysis, in the form of proceedings against animals and inanimate objects, and of the *noxae deditio* by which the owner of the offending thing surrendered it and was free from any further liability. I tried to show that from this primitive source came, in part at least, our modern responsibility of an owner for his animals and of a master for his servants acting within the scope of their employment, the limited liability of shipowners under the law which allows them to surrender their vessel and free themselves, and that curious law of deodand, under which a steam engine was declared forfeited by the Court of Exchequer in 1842.[4] I shall have to suggest later that it played a part also in the development of contract.

[4] Regina *v.* Eastern Counties Railway Company, 10 M. & W. 59.

Examples like these lead us beyond the transformations of an idea to the broader field of the
development of our more general legal conceptions.
We have evolution in this sphere of conscious thought
and action no less than in lower organic stages, but
an evolution which must be studied in its own field.
I venture to think that the study is not yet finished.
Take for instance the origin of contract. A single
view has prevailed with slight modifications since
Sohm published *Das Recht der Eheschliessung* in
1875. But fashion is potent in science as well as
elsewhere, and it does not follow because Sohm
smashed his predecessor that there may not arise
a later champion who will make some impact upon
him. Sohm, following a thought first suggested, I
believe, by Savigny, and made familiar by Maine in
his *Ancient Law*, sees the beginning of contract in
an interrupted sale. This is expressed in later law
by our common law debt, founded upon a *quid pro
quo* received by the debtor from the creditor. Out
of this, by a process differently conceived by different
writers, arises the formal contract, the *fides facta* of
the Salic law, the covenant familiar to us. And this
dichotomy exhausts the matter. I do not say that
this may not be proved to be the final and correct
account, but there are some considerations which I
should like to suggest in a summary way. We are
not bound to assume with Sohm that his Frankish
ancestors had a theory in their heads which, even if
a trifle inarticulate, was the majestic peer of all that
was done at Rome. The result of that assumption

is to lead to the further one, tacitly made, but felt to be there, that there must have been some theory of contract from the beginning, if only you can find what it was. It seems to me well to remember that men begin with no theory at all, and with no such generalization as contract. They begin with particular cases, and even when they have generalized they are often a long way from the final generalizations of a later time. Down into this century consideration was described by enumeration, as you may see in Tidd's *Practice*, or Blackstone,[5] and only of late years has it been reduced to the universal expression of detriment to the promises. So, bailment was bailment and nothing further until modern times. It was not contract. And so warranty was warranty, a duty imposed by law upon the vendor, and nothing more.[6] A trust still is only a trust, although according to the orthodox it creates merely a personal obligation.

Well, I have called attention elsewhere to the fact that giving hostages may be followed back to the beginning of our legal history, as far back as sales, that is, and that out of the hostage grew the surety, quite independently of the development of debt or formal contract. If the obligation of the surety, who, by a paradox explained by his origin, appears often in early law without a principal contractor, as the only party bound, had furnished the

---

[5] 1 Tidd, Ch. 1.; 2 Bl. Comm. 444, 445.

[6] Glanv. X, C. 16; Bracton, 151; 1 Löning, Vertragsbruch, § 14, p. 103; cf. Sohm, Inst. Rom. Law, § 46, § 11, n. 7.

analogy for other undertakings, we never should have had the doctrine of consideration. If other undertakings were to be governed by the analogy of the law developed out of sales, sureties must either have received a *quid pro quo* or have made a covenant. There was a clash between the competing ideas, and just as commerce was prevailing over war the children of the sale drove the child of the hostage from the field. In the time of Edward III. it was decided that a surety was not bound without a covenant, except in certain cities where local custom maintained the ancient law. Warranty of land came to require, and thus to be, a covenant in the same way, although the warranty of title upon a sale of chattels still retains its old characteristics, except that it now is thought of as a contract.[7]

But the hostage was not the only competitor for domination. The oath also goes back as far as the history of our race.[8] It started from a different point, and, leaving the possible difference of sanction on one side, it might have been made to cover the whole field of promises. The breach of their promissory oath by witnesses still is punished as perjury, and formerly there were severe penalties for the jury if convicted of a similar offence by attaint.[9] The solemnity was used for many other purposes, and, if the church had had its way, the

7 Y. B. 13 & 14 Ed. III, 80.

8 Caesar, B. G., IV, 11; Ammianus Marcellinus, XVII, 1, 13, *jurantes conceptis ritu patrio verbis.*

9 Bracton, 292b.

oath, helped by its cousin the plighting of troth, would have been very likely to succeed. In the time of Henry III., faith, oath, and writing, that is, the covenant, were the popular familiar forms of promise. The plighting of a man's faith or troth, still known to us in the marriage ceremony, was in common use, and the courts of the church claimed jurisdiction over it as well as over the oath. I have called attention elsewhere to a hint of inclination on the part of the early clerical chancellors to continue the clerical jurisdiction in another court, and to enforce the ancient form of obligation. Professor Ames has controverted my suggestion, but I cannot but think it of significance that down to later times we still find the ecclesiastical tribunals punishing breach of faith or of promissory oaths with spiritual penalties. When we know that a certain form of undertaking was in general use, and that it was enforced by the clergy in their own courts, a very little evidence is enough to make us believe that in a new court, also presided over by a clergyman and with no substantive law of its own, the idea of enforcing it well might have been entertained, especially in view of the restrictions which the civil power put upon the church. But oath and plighting of troth did not survive in the secular forum except as an occasional solemnity, and I have mentioned them only to show a lively example of the struggle for life among competing ideas, and of the ultimate victory and survival of the strongest. After victory the law of covenant and debt went on, and consolidated and developed their empire in a way that is familiar to you all, until they in their turn lost something of their power and prestige in consequence of the rise of a new rival, Assumpsit.

There were other seeds which dropped by the wayside in early law, and which were germs of relations that might now be termed contractual, such as the blood covenant, by which people bound themselves together or made themselves of one substance by drinking the blood or eating the flesh of a newly killed animal. Such was the fiction of family relationship, by which, for instance, the Aedui symbolized their alliance with the Romans.[10] I may notice in this connection that I suspect that the *mundium* or early German guardianship was the origin of our modern bail, while, as I have said, the surety came from a different source. I mention these only to bring still closer home the struggle for existence between competing ideas and forms to which I have referred. In some instances the vanquished competitor has perished. In some it has put on the livery of its conqueror, and has become in form and external appearance merely a case of covenant or assumpsit.

Another important matter is the way in which the various obligations were made binding after they were recognized. A breach of oath of course brought with it the displeasure of the gods. In other cases, as might be expected, we find hints that liabilities of a more primitive sort were extended to the new

10 Strabo, IV., 32.

candidates for legal recognition. In the Roman law a failure to pay the price of a purchase seems to have suggested the analogy of theft. All over the world slavery for debt is found, and this seems not to have stood on the purely practical considerations which first would occur to us, but upon a notion akin to the noxal surrender of the offending body for a tort. There is a mass of evidence that various early contracts in the systems of law from which our own is descended carried with them the notion of pledging the person of the contracting party — a notion which we see in its extreme form in the seizure or division of the dead body of the debtor,[11] and which seems to come out in the maxim *Debita inhaerent ossibus debitoris.*

I am not going to trace the development of every branch of our law in succession, but if we turn to the law of torts we find there, perhaps even more noticeably than in the law of contracts, another evolutionary process which Mr. Herbert Spencer has made familiar to us by the name of Integration. The first stage of torts embraces little if anything beyond those simple acts of violence where the appeals of death, of wounding or maiming, of arson and the like had taken the place of self-help, to be succeeded by the modification known as the action of trespass. But when the action on the case let libel and slander and all the other wrongs which are known to the

---

[11] See, e.g., *Three Metrical Romances,* Camden Soc. 1842, introd. p. xxvi, and cantos XII and XXII; Boccaccio, Bohn's tr., p. 444 n., referring to an old English ballad.

modern law into the civil courts, for centuries each
of the recognized torts had its special history, its
own precedents, and no one dreamed, so far as I
know, that the different cases of liability were, or
ought to be, governed by the same principles throughout. As is said in the preface to Mr. Jaggard's
book, "the use of a book on Torts, as a distinct
subject, was a few years ago a matter of ridicule."
You may see the change which has taken place by
comparing *Hilliard on Torts*, which proceeds by
enumeration in successive chapters through assault
and battery, libel and slander, nuisance, trespass,
conversion, etc., with Sir Frederick Pollock's *Introduction*, in which he says that the purpose of his
book "is to show that there really is a Law of Torts,
not merely a number of rules of law about various
kinds of torts — that this is a true living branch
of the Common Law, not a collection of heteroge-
neous instances." It would be bold, perhaps, to
say that the integration was complete, that it did
not rest partly in tendency. The recent much discussed case of Allen *v.* Flood, in the House of Lords,
seems to me to indicate that, in the view of the
older generation even of able and learned men, the
foundation of liability still is somewhat in the air,
and that tradition and enumeration are the best
guides to this day. But I have no doubt that the
generalizing principle will prevail, as generalization
so often prevails, even in advance of evidence, because of the ease of mind and comfort which it brings.

Any one who thinks about the world as I do does

not need proof that the scientific study of any part of it has an interest which is the same in kind as that of any other part. If the examples which I have given fail to make the interest plain, there is no use in my adding to them, and so. I shall pass to another part of my subject. But first let me add a word. The man of science in the law is not merely a bookworm. To a microscopic eye for detail he must unite an insight which tells him what details are significant. Not every maker of exact investigation counts, but only he who directs his investigation to a crucial point. But I doubt if there is any more exalted form of life than that of a great abstract thinker, wrapt in the successful study of problems to which he devotes himself, for an end which is neither unselfish nor selfish in the common sense of those words, but is simply to feed the deepest hunger and to use the greatest gifts of his soul.

But after all the place for a man who is complete in all his powers is in the fight. The professor, the man of letters, gives up one-half of life that his protected talent may grow and flower in peace. But to make up your mind at your peril upon a living question, for purposes of action, calls upon your whole nature. I trust that I have shown that I appreciate what I thus far have spoken of as if it were the only form of the scientific study of law, but of course I think, as other people do, that the main ends of the subject are practical, and from a practical point of view, history, with which I have been dealing thus far, is only a means, and one of the least of the means, of mastering a tool. From a practical point of view, as I have illustrated upon another occasion, its use is mainly negative and skeptical. It may help us to know the true limit of a doctrine, but its chief good is to burst inflated explanations. Every one instinctively recognizes that in these days the justification of a law for us cannot be found in the fact that our fathers always have followed it. It must be found in some help which the law brings toward reaching a social end which the governing power of the community has made up its mind that it wants. And when a lawyer sees a rule of law in force he is very apt to invent, if he does not find, some ground of policy for its base. But in fact some rules are mere survivals. Many might as well be different, and history is the means by which we measure the power which the past has had to govern the present in spite of ourselves, so to speak, by imposing traditions which no longer meet their original end. History sets us free and enables us to make up our minds dispassionately whether the survival which we are enforcing answers any new purpose when it has ceased to answer the old. Notwithstanding the contrasts which I have been making, the practical study of the law ought also to be scientific. The true science of the law does not consist mainly in a theological working out of dogma or a logical development as in mathematics, or only in a study of it as an anthropological document from the outside; an even more important part consists in the establishment of its postulates from within upon

accurately measured social desires instead of tradition. It is this latter part to which I now am turning, and I begin with one or two instances of the
help of history in clearing away rubbish — instances
of detail from my own experience.

Last autumn our court had to consider the grounds
upon which evidence of fresh complaint by a rav-
ished woman is admitted as part of the government's
case in an indictment for rape. All agree that it is
an exception to the ordinary rules of evidence to
allow a witness to be corroborated by proof that he
has said the same thing elsewhere when not under
oath, except possibly by way of rebuttal under extraordinary circumstances. But there is the exception, almost as well settled as the rule, and courts and
lawyers finding the law to be established proceed to
account for it by consulting their wits. We are told
that the outrage is so great that there is a natural
presumption that a virtuous woman would disclose
it at the first suitable opportunity. I confess that
I should think this was about the last crime in which
such a presumption could be made, and that it was
far more likely that a man who had had his pocket
picked or who had been the victim of an attempt to
murder would speak of it, than that a sensitive
woman would disclose such a horror. If we look
into history no further than Hale's *Pleas of the
Crown*, where we find the doctrine, we get the real
reason and the simple truth. In an appeal of rape
the first step was for the woman to raise hue and
cry. Lord Hale, after stating that fact, goes on to

say that upon an indictment for the same offence the woman can testify, and that her testimony will be corroborated if she made fresh complaint and pursued the offender. That is the hue and cry over again. At that time there were few rules of evidence. Later our laws of evidence were systematized and developed. But the authority of Lord Hale has caused his dictum to survive as law in the particular case, while the principle upon which it would have to be justified has been destroyed. The exception in other words is a pure survival, having nothing or very little to back it except that the practice is established.[12]

In a somewhat earlier case [13] I tried to show that the doctrine of trespass *ab initio* in like manner was the survival in a particular class of cases of a primitive rule of evidence, which established intent by a presumption of law from subsequent conduct, after the rule had gone to pieces and had been forgotten as a whole. Since that decision Professor Ames has made some suggestions which may or may not modify or enlarge the view which I took, but which equally leave the doctrine a survival, the reasons for which long have disappeared.

In Brower *v.* Fisher,[14] the defendant, a deaf and dumb person, had conveyed to the plaintiff real and personal property, and had got a judgment against the plaintiff for the price. The plaintiff brought a

12 Commonwealth *v.* Cleary, 172 Mass. 172.
18 Commonwealth *v.* Rubin, 165 Mass. 453.
14 4 Johns. Ch. 441.

bill to find out whether the conveyance was legal, and got an injunction *pendente lite* to stay execution on the judgment. On the plaintiff's petition a commission of lunacy was issued to inquire whether the defendant was *compos mentis*. It was found that he was so unless the fact that he was born deaf and dumb made him otherwise. Thereupon Chancellor Kent dismissed the bill but held the inquiry so reasonable that he imposed no costs. The old books of England fully justified his view; and why? History again gives us the true reason. The Roman law held very properly that the dumb, and by extension the deaf, could not make the contract called *stipulatio* because the essence of that contract was a formal question and answer which the dumb could not utter and the deaf could not hear. Bracton copies the Roman law and repeats the true reason, that they could not express assent, *consentire;* but shows that he had missed the meaning of *stipulari* by suggesting that perhaps it might be done by gestures or writing. Fleta copied Bracton, but seemed to think that the trouble was inability to bring the consenting mind, and whereas the Roman law explained that the rule did not apply to one who was only hard of hearing — *qui tardius exaudit* — Fleta seems to have supposed that this pointed to a difference between a man born deaf and dumb and one who became so later in life.[15] In Perkins's *Profitable Book,* this is improved upon by requiring that the man should be born blind, deaf, and dumb,

---

[15] But see C. 6, 22, 10.

and then the reason is developed that "a man that is born blind, deaf, and dumb can have no understanding, so that he cannot make a gift or a grant." [16] In a case before Vice-Chancellor Wood [17] good sense prevailed, and it was laid down that there is no exception to the presumption of sanity in the case of a deaf and dumb person.

Other cases of what I have called inflated and unreal explanations, which collapse at the touch of history, are the liability of a master for the torts of his servant in the course of his employment, to which I have referred earlier, and which thus far never, in my opinion, has been put upon a rational footing; and the liability of a common carrier, which, as I conceive, is another distorted survival from the absolute responsibility of bailees in early law, crossed with the liability of those exercising a common calling to which I have referred. These examples are sufficient, I hope, to illustrate my meaning, and to point out the danger of inventing reasons offhand for whatever we find established in the law. They lead me to some other general considerations in which history plays no part, or a minor part, but in which my object is to show the true process of law-making, and the real meaning of a decision upon a doubtful case and thus, as in what I have said before, to help in substituting a scientific foundation for empty words.

I pass from unreal explanations to unreal formulas and inadequate generalizations, and I will take up

16 Pl. 25; Co. Lit. 42b.
17 Harrod v. Harrod, 1 K. & J. 4, 9.

one or two with especial reference to the problems with which we have to deal at the present time. The first illustration which occurs to me, especially in view of what I have been saying, is suggested by another example of the power of fashion. I am immensely struck with the blind imitativeness of man when I see how a doctrine, a discrimination, even a phrase, will run in a year or two over the whole English-speaking world. Lately have we not all been bored to death with *volenti non fit injuria,* and with Lord Justice Bowen's remark that it is *volenti* and not *scienti?* I congratulate any State in whose reports you do not see the maxim and its qualification repeated. I blush to say that I have been as guilty as the rest. Do we not hear every day of taking the risk — an expression which we never heard used as it now is until within a very few years? Do we not hear constantly of invitation and trap — which came into vogue within the memory of many, if not most of those who are here? Heaven forbid that I should find fault with an expression because it is new, or with the last mentioned expressions on any ground! Judges commonly are elderly men, and are more likely to hate at sight any analysis to which they are not accustomed, and which disturbs repose of mind, than to fall in love with novelties. Every living sentence which shows a mind at work for itself is to be welcomed. It is not the first use but the tiresome repetition of inadequate catch words which I am observing — phrases which originally were contributions, but which, by their very felicity, delay further analysis for fifty years. That comes from the same source as dislike of novelty — intellectual indolence or weakness — a slackening in the eternal pursuit of the more exact.

The growth of education is an increase in the knowledge of measure. To use words familiar to logic and to science, it is a substitution of quantitative for qualitative judgments. The difference between the criticism of a work of art by a man of perception without technical training and that by a critic of the studio will illustrate what I mean. The first, on seeing a statue, will say, "It is grotesque," a judgment of quality merely; the second will say, "That statue is so many heads high, instead of the normal so many heads." His judgment is one of quantity. On hearing a passage of Beethoven's Ninth Symphony the first will say, "What a gorgeous sudden outburst of sunshine!" the second, "Yes, great idea to bring in his major third just there, wasn't it?" Well, in the law we only occasionally can reach an absolutely final and quantitative determination, because the worth of the competing social ends which respectively solicit a judgment for the plaintiff or the defendant cannot be reduced to number and accurately fixed. The worth, that is, the intensity of the competing desires, varies with the varying ideals of the time, and, if the desires were constant, we could not get beyond a relative decision that one was greater and one was less. But it is of the essence of improvement that we should be as accurate as we can. Now to recur to such expressions as taking the risk and *volenti non fit injuria*, which are very well for once in the sprightly mouth which first applies them, the objection to the repetition of them as accepted legal formulas is that they do not represent a final analysis, but dodge difficulty and responsibility with a rhetorical phrase. When we say that a workman takes a certain risk as incident to his employment, we mean that on some general grounds of policy blindly felt or articulately present to our mind, we read into his contract a term of which he never thought; and the real question in every case is, What are the grounds, and how far do they extend? The question put in that form becomes at once and plainly a question for scientific determination, that is, for quantitative comparison by means of whatever measure we command. When we speak of taking the risk apart from contract, I believe that we merely are expressing what the law means by negligence, when for some reason or other we wish to express it in a conciliatory form.

In our approach towards exactness we constantly tend to work out definite lines or equators to mark distinctions which we first notice as a difference of poles. It is evident in the beginning that there must be differences in the legal position of infants and adults. In the end we establish twenty-one as the dividing point. There is a difference manifest at the outset between night and day. The statutes of Massachusetts fix the dividing points at one hour after sunset and one hour before sunrise, ascertained according to mean time. When he has discovered that a difference is a difference of degree, that distinguished extremes have between them a penumbra in which one gradually shades into the other, a tyro thinks to puzzle you by asking where you are going to draw the line, and an advocate of more experience will show the arbitrariness of the line proposed by putting cases very near to it on one side or the other. But the theory of the law is that such lines exist, because the theory of the law as to any possible conduct is that it is either lawful or unlawful. As that difference has no gradation about it, when applied to shades of conduct that are very near each other it has an arbitrary look. We like to disguise the arbitrariness, we like to save ourselves the trouble of nice and doubtful discriminations. In some regions of conduct of a special sort we have to be informed of facts which we do not know before we can draw our lines intelligently, and so, as we get near the dividing point, we call in the jury. From saying that we will leave a question to the jury to saying that it is a question of fact is but a step, and the result is that at this day it has come to be a widespread doctrine that negligence not only is a question for the jury but is a question of fact. I have heard it urged with great vehemence by counsel, and calmly maintained by professors that, in addition to their wrongs to labor, courts were encroaching upon the province of the jury when they directed a verdict in a negligence case, even in the unobtrusive form of a ruling that there was no evidence of neglect.

I venture to think, on the other hand, now, as

I thought twenty years ago, before I went upon the bench, that every time that a judge declines to rule whether certain conduct is negligent or not he avows his inability to state the law, and that the meaning of leaving nice questions to the jury is that while if a question of law is pretty clear we can decide it, as it is our duty to do, if it is difficult it can be decided better by twelve men at random from the street. If a man fires a gun over a prairie that looks empty to the horizon, or crosses a railroad which he can see is clear for a thousand yards each way, he is not negligent, that is, he is free from legal liability in the first case, he has not prevented his recovery by his own conduct, if he is run over, in the second, as matter of law. If he fires a gun into a crowded street, or tries to cross a track ten feet in front of an express train in full sight running sixty miles an hour, he is liable, or he cannot recover, again as matter of law, supposing these to be all the facts in the case. What new question of fact is introduced if the place of firing is something half way between a prairie and a crowded street, or if the express train is two hundred, one hundred, or fifty yards away?   I do not wish to repeat arguments which I published long ago, and which have been more or less quoted in leading text-books. I only wish to insist that false reasons and false analogies shall not be relied upon for daily practice. It is so easy to accept the phrase "there is no evidence of negligence," and thence to infer, as the English House of Lords has inferred, as Professor Thayer infers in his admirable *Preliminary Treatise on Evidence* which has appeared since these words were written, that the question is the same in kind as any other question whether there is evidence of a fact.

When we rule on evidence of negligence we are ruling on a standard of conduct, a standard which we hold the parties bound to know beforehand, and which in theory is always the same upon the same facts and not a matter dependent upon the whim of the particular jury or the eloquence of the particular advocate. And I may be permitted to observe that, referring once more to history, similar questions originally were, and to some extent still are, dealt with as questions of law. It was and is so on the question of probable cause in malicious prosecution.[18] It was so on the question of necessaries for an infant.[19] It was so in questions of what is reasonable,[20] as — a reasonable fine,[21] convenient time,[22] seasonable time,[23] reasonable time,[24] reasonable notice of dishonor.[25] It is so in regard to the remoteness

---

[18] Knight *v.* Jermin, Cro. Eliz. 134; S.C. *nom.* Knight *v.* German, Cro. Eliz. 70; Paine *v.* Rochester, Cro. Eliz. 871; Chambers *v.* Taylor, Cro. Eliz. 900.

[19] Mackarell *v.* Bachelor, Cro. Eliz. 583. As to married women see Manby *v.* Scott, 1 Siderfin, 109, 2 Sm. L.C.

[20] Caterall *v.* Marshall, 1 Mod. 70.

[21] Hobart *v.* Hammond, 4 Co. Rep. 27b.

[22] Stodder *v.* Harvey, Cro. Jac. 204.

[23] Bell *v.* Wardell, Willes, 202, A.D. 1740.

[24] Butler *v.* Play, 1 Mod. 27.

[25] Tindal *v.* Brown, 1 T.R. 167, A.D. 1786. In this case an exact line has been worked out for commercial paper, and an arbitrary rule established.

of damage in an action of contract.[26]   Originally in malicious prosecution, probable cause, instead of being negatived in the declaration, was pleaded by the defendant, and the court passed upon the sufficiency of the cause alleged.   In the famous case of Weaver v. Ward,[27] the same course was suggested as proper for negligence.   I quote: "as if the defendant had said that the plaintiff ran across his piece when it was discharging, or had set forth the case with the circumstances, so as it had appeared to the court that it had been inevitable, and that the defendant had committed no negligence to give occasion to the hurt."   But about the middle of the last century, when the rule of conduct was complicated with practical details the court began to leave some of these questions to the jury.   Nevertheless, Mr. Starkie, a man of intellect, who was not imposed upon by phrases, very nearly saw the ground upon which it was done, and puts it on the purely practical distinction that when the circumstances are too special and complicated for a general rule to be laid down the jury may be called in.   But it is obvious that a standard of conduct does not cease to be law because the facts to which that standard applies are not likely often to be repeated.

I do not believe that the jury have any historic or *a priori* right to decide any standard of conduct.

[26] Hobbs v. London & Southwestern Railway, L.R. 10 Q.B. 111, 122; Hammond & Co. v. Bussey, 20 Q.B.D. 79, 89; Johnston v. Faxon, 172 Mass., 466.
[27] Hobart, 134.

I think that the logic of the contrary view would be
that every decision upon such a question by the court
is an invasion of their province, and that all the law
properly is in their breasts. I refer to the subject,
however, merely as another matter in which phrases
have taken the place of real reasons, and to do my
part toward asserting a certain freedom of approach
in dealing with negligence cases, not because I wish
to quarrel with the existing and settled practice. I
think that practice may be a good one, as it certainly
is convenient, for Mr. Starkie's reason. There are
many cases where no one could lay down a standard
of conduct intelligently without hearing evidence
upon that, as well as concerning what the conduct
was. And although it does not follow that such
evidence is for the jury, any more than the question
of fact whether a legislature passed a certain statute,
still they are a convenient tribunal, and if the evidence to establish a rule of law is to be left to them,
it seems natural to leave the conclusion from the
evidence to them as well. I confess that in my experience I have not found juries specially inspired for
the discovery of truth. I have not noticed that they
could see further into things or form a saner judgment than a sensible and well trained judge. I have
not found them freer from prejudice than an ordinary judge would be. Indeed one reason why I
believe in our practice of leaving questions of negligence to them is what is precisely one of their gravest
defects from the point of view of their theoretical
function: that they will introduce into their verdict

a certain amount — a very large amount, so far as I have observed — of popular prejudice, and thus keep the administration of the law in accord with the wishes and feelings of the community. Possibly such a justification is a little like that which an eminent English barrister gave me many years ago for the distinction between barristers and solicitors. It was in substance that if law was to be practised somebody had to be damned, and he preferred that it should be somebody else.

My object is not so much to point out what seem to me to be fallacies in particular cases as to enforce by various examples and in various applications the need of scrutinizing the reasons for the rules which we follow, and of not being contented with hollow forms of words merely because they have been used very often and have been repeated from one end of the Union to the other. We must think things not words, or at least we must constantly translate our words into the facts for which they stand, if we are to keep to the real and the true. I sometimes tell students that the law schools pursue an inspirational combined with a logical method, that is, the postulates are taken for granted upon authority without inquiry into their worth, and then logic is used as the only tool to develop the results. It is a necessary method for the purpose of teaching dogma. But inasmuch as the real justification of a rule of law, if there be one, is that it helps to bring about a social end which we desire, it is no less necessary that those who make and develop the law should have those ends articulately in their minds. I do not expect or think it desirable that the judges should undertake to renovate the law. That is not their province. Indeed precisely because I believe that the world would be just as well off if it lived under laws that differed from ours in many ways, and because I believe that the claim of our especial code to respect is simply that it exists, that it is the one to which we have become accustomed, and not that it represents an eternal principle, I am slow to consent to overruling a precedent, and think that our important duty is to see that the judicial duel shall be fought out in the accustomed way. But I think it most important to remember whenever a doubtful case arises, with certain analogies on one side and other analogies on the other, that what really is before us is a conflict between two social desires, each of which seeks to extend its dominion over the case, and which cannot both have their way. The social question is which desire is stronger at the point of conflict. The judicial one may be narrower, because one or the other desire may have been expressed in previous decisions to such an extent that logic requires us to assume it to preponderate in the one before us. But if that be clearly so, the case is not a doubtful one. Where there is doubt the simple tool of logic does not suffice, and even if it is disguised and unconscious, the judges are called on to exercise the sovereign prerogative of choice.

I have given an example of what seems to me the

uninstructive and indolent use of phrases to save the trouble of thinking closely, in the expression "taking the risk," and of what I think a misleading use in calling every question left to the jury a question of fact. Let me give one of over-generalization, or rather of the danger of reasoning from generalizations unless you have the particulars which they embrace in mind. A generalization is empty so far as it is general. Its value depends on the number of particulars which it calls up to the speaker and the hearer. Hence the futility of arguments on economic questions by any one whose memory is not stored with economic facts. Allen v. Flood was decided lately by the English House of Lords upon a case of maliciously inducing workmen to leave the plaintiff's employ. It is made harder to say what the precise issue before the House was, by the fact that except in fragmentary quotations it does not appear what the jury were told would amount to a malicious interference. I infer that they were instructed as in Temperton v. Russell,[28] in such a way that their finding meant little more than that the defendant had acted with knowledge and understanding of the harm which he would inflict if successful. Or if I should add an intent to harm the plaintiff without reference to any immediate advantage to the defendant, still I do not understand that finding meant that the defendant's act was done from disinterestedly malevolent motives, and not from a wish to better the defendant's union in a battle of the mar-

[28] 1893, 1 Q.B. 715.

ket. Taking the point decided to be what I suppose it to be, this case confirms opinions which I have had occasion to express judicially, and commands my hearty assent. But in the elaborate, although to my notion inadequate, discussion which took place, eminent judges intimated that anything which a man has a right to do he has a right to do whatever his motives, and this has been hailed as a triumph of the principle of external standards in the law, a principle which I have done my best to advocate as well as to name. Now here the reasoning starts from the vague generalization Right, and one asks himself at once whether it is definite enough to stand the strain. If the scope of the right is already determined as absolute and irrespective of motive, *cadit quaestio*, there is nothing to argue about. So if all rights have that scope. But if different rights are of different extent, if they stand on different grounds of policy and have different histories, it does not follow that because one right is absolute, another is — and if you simply say all rights shall be so, that is only a pontifical or imperial way of forbidding discussion. The right to sell property is about as absolute as any I can think of, although, under statutes at least, even that may be affected by motive, as in the case of an intent to prefer creditors. But the privilege of a master to state his servant's character to one who is thinking of employing him is also a right within its limits. Is it equally extensive? I suppose it would extend to mistaken statements volunteered in good faith out of love for the possible employer. Would it extend to such statements volunteered simply out of hate for the man? To my mind here, again, generalities are worse than useless, and the only way to solve the problem presented is to weigh the reasons for the particular right claimed and those for the competing right to be free from slander as well as one can, and to decide which set preponderates. Any solution in general terms seems to me to mark a want of analytic power.

Gentlemen, I have tried to show by examples something of the interest of science as applied to the law, and to point out some possible improvement in our way of approaching practical questions in the same sphere. To the latter attempt, no doubt, many will hardly be ready to yield me their assent. But in that field, as in the other, I have had in mind an ultimate dependence upon science because it is finally for science to determine, so far as it can, the relative worth of our different social ends, and, as I have tried to hint, it is our estimate of the proportion between these, now often blind and unconscious, that leads us to insist upon and to enlarge the sphere of one principle and to allow another gradually to dwindle into atrophy. Very likely it may be that with all the help that statistics and every modern appliance can bring us there never will be a commonwealth in which science is everywhere supreme. But it is an ideal, and without ideals what is life worth? They furnish us our perspectives and open glimpses of the infinite. It often is a merit of an ideal to be unattainable. Its being so keeps forever before

us something more to be done, and saves us from
the ennui of a monotonous perfection. At the least
it glorifies dull details, and uplifts and sustains weary
years of toil with George Herbert's often quoted
but ever-inspiring verse:

> "Who sweeps a room as for Thy laws,
> Makes that and the action fine."

SPEECH

GENTLEMEN OF THE SUFFOLK BAR:

THE kindness of this reception almost unmans me, and it shakes me the more when taken with a kind of seriousness which the moment has for me. As with a drowning man, the past is telescoped into a minute, and the stages are all here at once in my mind. The day before yesterday I was at the law school, fresh from the army, arguing cases in a little club with Goulding and Beaman and Peter Olney, and laying the dust of pleading by certain sprinklings which Huntington Jackson, another ex-soldier, and I managed to contrive together. A little later in the day, in Bob Morse's office, I saw a real writ, acquired a practical conviction of the difference between assumpsit and trover, and marvelled open-mouthed at the swift certainty with which a master of his business turned it off.

Yesterday I was at the law school again, in the chair instead of on the benches, when my dear partner, Shattuck, came out and told me that in one hour the Governor would submit my name to the council for a judgeship, if notified of my assent. It was a

* From *Speeches* (1913), Little, Brown & Co.

stroke of lightning which changed the whole course
of my life.

And the day before yesterday, gentlemen, was
thirty-five years, and yesterday was more than eighteen years, ago. I have gone on feeling young, but
I have noticed that I met fewer of the old to whom
to show my deference, and recently I was startled
by being told that ours is an old bench. Well, I
accept the fact, although I find it hard to realize,
and I ask myself, what is there to show for this half
lifetime that has passed? I look into my book in
which I keep a docket of the decisions of the full
court which fall to me to write, and find about a
thousand cases. A thousand cases, many of them
upon trifling or transitory matters, to represent
nearly half a lifetime! A thousand cases, when one
would have liked to study to the bottom and to say
his say on every question which the law ever has presented, and then to go on and invent new problems
which should be the test of doctrine, and then to
generalize it all and write it in continuous, logical,
philosophic exposition, setting forth the whole corpus
with its roots in history and its justifications of ex-
pedience real or supposed!

Alas, gentlemen, that is life. I often imagine
Shakespeare or Napoleon summing himself up and
thinking: "Yes, I have written five thousand lines of
solid gold and a good deal of padding — I, who would
have covered the milky way with words that out-
shone the stars!" "Yes, I beat the Austrians in
Italy and elsewhere: I made a few brilliant cam-

paigns, and I ended in middle life in a *cul-de-sac* —
I, who had dreamed of a world monarchy and Asiatic
power." We cannot live our dreams. We are lucky
enough if we can give a sample of our best, and if
in our hearts we can feel that it has been nobly done.

Some changes come about in the process, changes
not necessarily so much in the nature as in the
emphasis of our interest. I do not mean in our wish
to make a living and to succeed — of course, we all
want those things — but I mean in our ulterior intellectual or spiritual interest, in the ideal part, without which we are but snails or tigers.

One begins with a search for a general point of
view. After a time he finds one, and then for a while
he is absorbed in testing it, in trying to satisfy himself whether it is true. But after many experiments
or investigations all have come out one way, and his
theory is confirmed and settled in his mind, he knows
in advance that the next case will be but another
verification, and the stimulus of anxious curiosity is
gone. He realizes that his branch of knowledge only
presents more illustrations of the universal principle;
he sees it all as another case of the same old *ennui,*
or the same sublime mystery — for it does not matter
what epithets you apply to the whole of things, they
are merely judgments of yourself. At this stage the
pleasure is no less, perhaps, but it is the pure pleasure
of doing the work, irrespective of further aims, and
when you reach that stage you reach, as it seems to
me, the triune formula of the joy, the duty, and the
end of life.

It was of this that Malebranche was thinking when he said that, if God held in one hand truth, and in the other the pursuit of truth, he would say: "Lord, the truth is for thee alone; give me the pursuit." The joy of life is to put out one's power in some natural and useful or harmless way. There is no other. And the real misery is not to do this. The hell of the old world's literature is to be taxed beyond one's powers. This country has expressed in story — I suppose because it has experienced it in life — a deeper abyss, of intellectual asphyxia or vital *ennui*, when powers conscious of themselves are denied their chance.

The rule of joy and the law of duty seem to me all one. I confess that altruistic and cynically selfish talk seem to me about equally unreal. With all humility, I think "Whatsoever thy hand findeth to do, do it with thy might" infinitely more important than the vain attempt to love one's neighbor as one's self. If you want to hit a bird on the wing, you must have all your will in a focus, you must not be thinking about yourself, and, equally, you must not be thinking about your neighbor; you must be living in your eye on that bird. Every achievement is a bird on the wing.

The joy, the duty, and, I venture to add, the end of life. I speak only of this world, of course, and of the teachings of this world. I do not seek to trench upon the province of spiritual guides. But from the point of view of the world the end of life is life. Life is action, the use of one's powers. As to use them to their height is our joy and duty, so it is the one end the justifies itself. Until lately the best thing that I was able to think of in favor of civilization, apart from blind acceptance of the order of the universe, was that it made possible the artist, the poet, the philosopher, and the man of science. But I think that is not the greatest thing. Now I believe that the greatest thing is a matter that comes directly home to us all. When it is said that we are too much occupied with the means of living to live, I answer that the chief worth of civilization is just that it makes the means of living more complex; that it calls for great and combined intellectual efforts, instead of simple, uncoördinated ones, in order that the crowd may be fed and clothed and housed and moved from place to place. Because more complex and intense intellectual efforts mean a fuller and richer life. They mean more life. Life is an end in itself, and the only question as to whether it is worth living is whether you have enough of it.

I will add but a word. We all are very near despair. The sheathing that floats us over its waves is compounded of hope, faith in the unexplainable worth and sure issue of effort, and the deep, sub-conscious content which comes from the exercise of our powers. In the words of a touching negro song —

> Sometimes I's up, sometimes I's down,
> Sometimes I's almost to the groun';

but these thoughts have carried me, as I hope they will carry the young men who hear me, through long years of doubt, self-distrust, and solitude. They do now, for, although it might seem that the day of trial was over, in fact it is renewed each day. The kindness which you have shown me makes me bold in happy moments to believe that the long and passionate struggle has not been quite in vain.

MONTESQUIEU *

"THERE is no new thing under the sun." It is the judgment of a man of the world, and from his point of view it is true enough. The things which he sees in one country he sees in another, and he is slightly bored from the beginning. But the judgment is quite untrue from the point of view of science or philosophy. From the time of Pericles to now, during the whole period that counts in the intellectual history of the race, the science or philosophy of one century has been different from that of the one before, and in some sense further along. By a corollary easy to work out, we have the paradox that the books which are always modern, the thoughts which are as stinging to-day as they were in their cool youth, are the books and thoughts of the men of the world. Ecclesiastes, Horace, and Rochefoucauld give us as much pleasure as they gave to Hebrew or Roman or the subject of Louis XIV. In this sense it is the second rate that lasts. But the greatest works of intellect soon lose all but their historic significance. The science of one generation is refuted or outgeneralized by the science of the next; the philosophy of one century is taken up or transcended by the philosophy of a later one; and so Plato, St. Augustine, and Descartes, and we almost may say Kant and

* Introduction to a reprint of the *Esprit des Lois.* (1900.)

Hegel, are not much more read than Hippocrates or Cuvier or Bichat.

Montesquieu was a man of science and at the same time a man of the world. As a man of science he wrote an epoch-making book. And just because and in so far as his book was a work of science and epoch-making, it is as dead as the classics. The later investigations which it did so much to start have taken up what was true in it and have refuted what needed refutation, and without the need of controversy they have killed many pale shoots of fancy and insufficient knowledge simply by letting in light and air. For a beginner to read Montesquieu with the expectation that there he is to find his understanding of the laws of social being, would be as ingenuous as to read Plato at eighteen expecting to find in him the answers to the riddles of life when they begin to perplex and sadden the mind of youth. He would learn a good deal more from Lecky. Montesquieu is buried under his own triumphs, to use his own words with a different application.

But Montesquieu also was a man of the world and a man of *esprit*. That wit which deals with the daily aspect of life and offers trenchant solutions in two or three lines is a dangerous gift. It hardly is compatible with great art, and Flaubert is not without reason when he rails at it in his letters. It is no less dangerous to great thinking, to that profound and sustained insight which distrusts the dilemma as an instrument of logic, and discerns that a thing may be neither A nor not A, but the perpendicular, or, more plainly, that the truth may escape from the limitations of a given plane of thought to a higher one. Montesquieu said that Voltaire had too much *esprit* to understand him. Nevertheless, Montesquieu had enough of it to have sustained the *Saturday Review* when Maine and Fitzjames Stephen or Venables were its contributors, and as a man of wit he still is fresh and pleasant reading. When one runs through the *Lettres Persanes* one feels as he does after reading Swift's *Polite Conversation*, struck with a wondering shame at the number of things he has been capable of feeling pleased with himself for saying, when they had been noted as familiar two hundred years before. He is in the realm of the ever old which also is the ever new, those middle axioms of experience which have been made from the beginning of society, but which give each generation a fresh pleasure as they are realized again in actual life. There is a good deal more than this, because Montesquieu was a good deal more than a man of the world, but there is this also in which we escape from the preliminary dulness of things really great.

We find the same thing in the *Esprit des Lois*, and one might read that work happily enough simply as literature. One may read it also as a first step in studies intended to be carried further and into later days. But to read it as it should be read, to appreciate the great and many-sided genius of the author and his place in the canonical succession of the high priests of thought, one must come back to it in the

fulness of knowledge and the ripeness of age. To
read the great works of the past with intelligent
appreciation, is one of the last achievements of a
studious life. But I will postpone what more I
have to say of this book until we come to it in
following the course of the author's career.

Charles de Secondat, Baron de la Brède, was born
at the Château de la Brède, near Bordeaux, on January 18, 1689. His family had gained distinction both
by the sword and in the law. His father was a magistrate, and intended that he should be one. His
mother was pious, and no doubt hoped that he might
be like her. Neither wish was entirely fulfilled.

At the moment of his birth a beggar presented himself at the château, and was retained that he might
be god-father to the young noble, and so remind him
all his life that the poor were his brothers. He was
nursed by peasants, and he kept through life a
touch of Gascon speech, and, the Frenchmen say,
something of the Gascon in his style. His early
education was by churchmen, but at twenty he
showed the tendency of his mind by composing an
essay to prove that the pagan did not deserve to be
eternally damned. The essay has not been preserved, but perhaps an echo of his reflections is to be
found in the thirty-fifth of the *Lettres Persanes*, in
which Usbek, who, not without dispute, has been
taken for the author, asks the "sublime dervish"
Gemchid whether he thinks that the Christians are
to be damned forever for not having embraced the
true religion of which they never have heard.

He studied law. "When I left college," he said, "they put law books into my hands. I tried to find their inner meaning" (*J'en cherchais l'esprit*). The *Esprit des Lois* was the outcome, but not the immediate outcome, of his studies. The immediate result was that, at twenty-five, on February 24, 1714, he was admitted to the Parlement de Bordeaux as conseiller. On July 13, 1716, he succeeded to the office (*président à mortier*) and fortune of an uncle, on condition of assuming the name of Montesquieu. Meantime he had married, and he had a son this same year, and later two daughters. As a magistrate he seems to have been not without weight. In 1722 he was intrusted with the shaping of a remonstrance to the king against a tax on wines, which for the time was successful. As a husband he was not wanting in decorum. But neither magistracy nor marriage seems to have filled his life.

He made a reasonable amount of love in his day, I infer not wholly before 1715. Whether or not he would have said that the society of women makes us "subtle and insincere," he did say that it spoils our morals and forms our taste. I suspect also that it added a poignancy to his phrase when he came to write, as it certainly gave him a freedom and alertness of interest in dealing with matters of sex. He took his passions easily. As soon as he ceased to believe that a woman loved him, he broke with her at once, he says, and elsewhere he tells us in more general terms that he never had a sorrow which an hour's reading would not dispel. At times his detachment seems to have been too visible, as one lady reproached him with writing his book in society. Perhaps it was timidity, which he says was a plague of his life. So much for his relations, domestic and otherwise, with women. As to the magistracy, he resigned his place in 1726. He found procedure hard to master, and it disgusted him to see men upon whose talents he justly looked down excelling in a matter that was too much for him.

About the same time that he succeeded his uncle he joined a society in Bordeaux, in which for a while he devoted himself to science. He made some experiments, wrote some scientific memoirs, planned a physical history of the earth, and sent out circulars of inquiry in 1719, but happily it all came to nothing, and this failure, combined with the shortness of his outward and the reach of his inward sight, helped to fix his attention upon his kind. He had the "disease of book-making," and as early as 1721 he published his *Lettres Persanes*. The putting of the criticism of his own times into the mouth of an intelligent foreigner, and all the Oriental coloring, seem a trifle faded nowadays. But these are merely the frame or excuse for a series of essays — somewhat like those in the nearly contemporary *Spectator* — on social subjects and subjects of social interest, running all the way from God to the Fashions.

In almost every letter there are things which have been quoted so often that one is afraid to repeat them. In one he makes a few reflections upon suicide that are hard to answer, and which had a practical aim, in view of the monstrous condition of the law. In another he is equally outspoken with regard to divorce, and says, not without some truth, that wishing to tighten the knot the law has untied it, and instead of uniting hearts, as it proposed, has separated them forever. Before Adam Smith he remarks the activity of dissenting sects, and he points out with unorthodox candor their service in reforming the abuses of the established faith.

In the person of Usbek he says: "Everything interests me, everything excites my wonder. I am like a child whose immature organs are keenly struck by the most insignificant objects." Montesquieu proves it in these letters. Alongside of such grave discussions as the foregoing he has portraits, or rather types, that still live. The *parvenu* tax farmer, the father confessor, the old soldier who can not hope for preferment "because we" (very sensibly) "believe that a man who has not the qualities of a general at thirty never will have them," the *homme à bonnes fortunes* who has hair, little wit, and so much impertinence, the poet (Montesquieu despised the poets, at least those whom he saw) — the poet, with grimaces and language different from the others, who would stand a beating better than the least criticism, the grand seigneur who personates himself. "He took a pinch of snuff so haughtily, he wiped his nose so pitilessly, he spit with so much phlegm, he fondled his dogs in a way so insulting to men, that I could not weary of wondering." The *décisionnaire:* "In a quarter of an hour he decided three questions of morals, four problems of history, and five points of physics. . . . They dropped the sciences and talked of the news of the day. . . . I thought that I would catch him, and spoke of Persia. But I hardly had said four words when he contradicted me twice. . . . Ah! *bon Dieu!* said I to myself, what sort of man is this? Soon he will know the streets of Ispahan better than I."

The letter on fashion ought to be quoted entire. When he says in the next one that what is foreign always seems ridiculous to the French, of course he is only noticing an instance of the universal law, but he makes us remember that Little Pedlington is everywhere, and that this day there is no more marked Little Pedlingtonian than the Parisian boulevardier man of letters. It is true that Montesquieu limits his remarks to trifles. They readily will admit that other people are wiser, he says, if you grant them that they are better dressed. His talk about the Spaniards is equally good. The Spaniards whom they do not burn, he says, seem so attached to the Inquisition that it would be ill-natured to deprive them of it. But at the end he gives them their revenge. He imagines a Spaniard in Paris and makes him say that they have a house there in which they shut up a few madmen in order to persuade the world that the rest are not mad. After things of this sort, two pages further on we read that the most perfect government is that which attains its ends with the least cost, so that the one which leads men in the way most according to their inclination is best. What have two hundred years added? What proximate test of excellence can be found except correspondence to the actual equilibrium of force in the community — that is, conformity to the wishes of the dominant power? Of course, such conformity may lead to destruction, and it is desirable that the dominant power should be wise. But wise or not, the proximate test of a good government is that the dominant power has its way.

There are considerations upon colonies, upon population, upon monarchy, a striking prophecy that the Protestant countries will grow richer and more powerful and the Catholic countries weaker. There is, in short, a scattering criticism of pretty nearly everything in the social order, of a sceptically radical kind, but always moderate and rational, with hints and germs of his future work, interspersed with many little sayings not too bright or good for human nature's daily food, and with some which are famous, such as, "It sometimes is necessary to change certain laws, but the case is rare, and when it occurs one should touch them only with a trembling hand"; or, "Nature always acts slowly and, so to speak, sparingly; her operations are never violent." This last is said by Sorel to be the whole philosophy of the *Esprit des Lois,* and suggests a more extensive philosophy still, which no doubt was more or less in the air, which found expression a little later in Linnaeus's *Natura non facit saltus,* and which nowadays in its more developed form we call evolution.

The *Lettres Persanes* came out anonymously, os-

tensibly from Amsterdam, when Montesquieu was
little more than thirty, and ran through four editions
in the first year. The name of the author became
known to everybody. He went to Paris, and there
frequented the society of men and women whose
names to us of this country and time are but foam
from the sea of oblivion, but who were the best of
their day. There, to please the ladies, or a lady,
he wrote in 1725 the *Temple de Gnide* and *Cephise
et l'Amour,* which need not delay us. He says that
only well-curled and well-powdered heads will understand them. At the beginning of 1728 he was
elected to the Academy, which he, like other Frenchmen, had made sport of but desired to enter. He
had been elected before, but had been refused by
the king. This time he had better luck. Voltaire
and D'Alembert tell a tale of how it was managed.
Entrance to the Academy is apt to be an occasion
for the display of malice on the one side or the other;
the address of welcome twitted him with having no
recognized works to justify the election, under the
form of a compliment on the certainty that the public would give him the credit of clever anonymous
ones. For this or other reasons he did not go much
to the Academy, and he soon set out upon a tour of
Europe. He went to Vienna, and there met the
Prince Eugene. He applied for a post as a diplomat,
and again, luckily for the world, he failed. He
visited Hungary, then Venice, where he met the
famous John Law and became a friend of Lord
Chesterfield; then Switzerland and Holland by way

of the Rhine. From Holland he went with Lord Chesterfield to England, where he remained for nearly two years, returning in August, 1731, to La Brède, his family, and his writing.

In 1734 he published his *Considérations sur les causes de la grandeur des Romains et de leur décadence*. He was drawing nearer to his great work; from sporadic *aperçus* he was turning to systematic exposition. It often is said, and with a good deal of truth, that men reach their highest mark between thirty and forty. Perhaps the statement seems more significant than it really is, because men generally have settled down to their permanent occupation by thirty, and in the course of the next ten years are likely to have found such leading and dominant conceptions as they are going to find; the rest of life is working out details. Montesquieu and Kant either are exceptions to the rule or illustrate the qualification just suggested. In their earlier life as you look back at it you see the *Critique* and the *Esprit des Lois* coming, but the fruit did not ripen fully until they were in the neighborhood of sixty. In 1734 Montesquieu was already forty-five.

Roman history has been rewritten since his day by Niebuhr and his successors. But Montesquieu gives us the key to his mode of thought and to all fruitful thought upon historic subjects when he says that "there are general causes, moral or physical, at work in every monarchy, which elevate and maintain it or work its downfall; all accidents are the result of causes; and if the chance of a battle — that is, a special cause — has ruined a state, there was a general cause at work which made that state ready to perish by a single battle. In a word, the main current carries with it all the special accidents."

Montesquieu the ladies' man, Montesquieu the student of science, Montesquieu the lover of travel both real and fictitious, Montesquieu the learned in the classics and admirer of that conventional antiquity that passed so long for the real thing in France — all these Montesquieus unite in the *Esprit des Lois,* as is pointed out most happily by Faguet, whose many-sided and delicate appreciation of the author I read just as I was writing this sentence. The book, he says, is called *Esprit des Lois;* it should have been called simply *Montesquieu.* Perhaps the fact is due in part to the subject's not having become a specialty. In the same way Adam Smith's *Wealth of Nations* has many interesting and penetrating remarks that, alas! hardly would be allowed in a modern political economy, even if the writer had the wit to make them. At all events, after his Roman history, the rest of Montesquieu's life may be summed up as the production of this volume. In the preface he calls it the labor of twenty years. It appeared in 1748. When it was done his hair had whitened over the last books, and his eyes had grown dim. "It seems to me," he said, "that the light left to me is but the dawn of the day on which my eyes shall close forever." He published a defence of the work in 1750, attended to the sale of wine from his vineyards, noticed with pleasure that the sale seemed to have been increased in England by the publication of his book, and died in Paris on February 10, 1755, watched, if not like Arthur by weeping queens, at least by the Duchess d'Aiguillon and a houseful of loving and admiring friends. According to Maupertuis, he was well proportioned, careless in dress, modest in demeanor, candid in speech, simple in his mode of life, and welcomed in society with universal joy. The medallion gives him a distinguished face.

It would be out of place to offer an analysis of a book which is before the reader, and it would take a larger book to contain all the thoughts which it suggests. The chapters on the feudal law are so far separable from the rest that it had been thought a mistake of Montesquieu to add them. The modern student naturally would turn to Roth or whatever still later man may displace Roth. With regard to the main body of the work, one might say that it expressed a theory of the continuity of the phenomenal universe at a time when, through no fault of the author, its facts were largely miraculous. He was not able to see history as an evolution, he looked at all events as if they were contemporaneous. Montesquieu's Rome was the Rome of fable uncritically accepted. His anthropology was anecdotic. His notion of a democracy suggests a Latin town meeting rather than the later developements in the United States and France. He made the world realize the influence of the climate and physical environment — which in our day furnished the already forgotten Buckle a suggestive chapter — but had not the data to be more than a precursor.

His England — the England of the threefold division of power into legislative, executive and judicial — was a fiction invented by him, a fiction which misled Blackstone and Delolme. Hear Bagehot in his work upon the subject: "The efficient secret of the English Constitution may be described as the close union, the nearly complete fusion of the executive and legislative powers." And again: "The American Constitution was made upon a most careful argument, and most of that argument assumes the king to be the administrator of the English Constitution, and an unhereditary substitute for him — viz., a president — to be peremptorily necessary. Living across the Atlantic, and misled by accepted doctrines, the acute framers of the Federal Constitution, even after the keenest attention, did not perceive the Prime Minister to be the principal executive of the British Constitution, and the sovereign a cog in the mechanism."

It is worth remarking that, notwithstanding his deep sense of the inevitableness of the workings of the world, Montesquieu had a possibly exaggerated belief in the power of legislation, and an equally strong conviction of the reality of abstract justice. But it is vain to attempt to criticise the book in detail. Indeed, it is more important to understand its relation to what had been done before than to criticise. There is not space even to point out how many seeds it sowed. Montesquieu is a precursor, to repeat the

word, in so many ways. He was a precursor of political economy. He was the precursor of Beccaria
in the criminal law. He was the precursor of Burke
when Burke seems a hundred years ahead of his time.
The Frenchmen tell us that he was the precursor of
Rousseau. He was an authority for the writers of
The Federalist. He influenced, and to a great
extent started scientific theory in its study of societies, and he hardly less influenced practice in legislation, from Russia to the United States. His book
had a dazzling success at the moment, and since then
probably has done as much to remodel the world
as any product of the eighteenth century, which
burned so many forests and sowed so many fields.

And this was the work of a lonely scholar sitting
in a library. Like Descartes or Kant, he commanded the future from his study more than
Napoleon from his throne. At the same time he
affects no august sovereignty, but even gives us one
or two discreet personal touches full of a sort of
pathetic charm — the *"Italiam! Italiam!"* when the
long day's work was done and the author saw his
goal before darkness closed upon him; the suppressed
invocation at the beginning of Book XX; the proud
epigraph, *"Prolem sine matre creatam";* and above
all the preface, that immortal cheer to other lonely
spirits. It is the great sigh of a great man when he
has done a great thing. The last words of that are
the words with which this introduction should end.
"If this work meets with success, I shall owe it
largely to the majesty of my subject. However, I

do not think that I have been wholly wanting in genius. When I have seen what so many great men in France, England, and Germany have written before me, I have been lost in admiration, but I have not lost my courage. 'And I too am a painter,' I have said with Correggio."

JOHN MARSHALL *

IN ANSWER TO A MOTION THAT THE COURT ADJOURN,
ON FEBRUARY 4, 1901, THE ONE HUNDREDTH
ANNIVERSARY OF THE DAY ON WHICH
MARSHALL TOOK HIS SEAT AS
CHIEF JUSTICE.

As we walk down Court Street in the midst of a jostling crowd, intent like us upon to-day and its affairs, our eyes are like to fall upon the small, dark building that stands at the head of State Street, and, like an ominous reef, divides the stream of business in its course to .the gray cliffs that tower beyond. And, whoever we may be, we may chance to pause and forget our hurry for a moment, as we remember that the first waves that foretold the coming storm of the Revolution broke around that reef. But, if we are lawyers, our memories and our reverence grow more profound. In the Old State House, we remember, James Otis argued the case of the writs of assistance, and in that argument laid one of the foundations for American constitutional law. Just as that little building is not diminished, but rather is enhanced and glorified, by the vast structures which somehow it turns into a background, so the begin-

* From *Speeches* (1913), Little, Brown & Co.

nings of our national life, whether in battle or in law, lose none of their greatness by contrast with all the mighty things of later date, beside which, by every law of number and measure, they ought to seem so small. To us who took part in the Civil War, the greatest battle of the Revolution seems little more than a reconnoissance in force, and Lexington and Concord were mere skirmishes that would not find mention in the newspapers. Yet veterans who have known battle on a modern scale, are not less aware of the spiritual significance of those little fights, I venture to say, than the enlightened children of commerce who tell us that soon war is to be no more.

If I were to think of John Marshall simply by number and measure in the abstract, I might hesitate in my superlatives, just as I should hesitate over the battle of the Brandywine if I thought of it apart from its place in the line of historic cause. But such thinking is empty in the same proportion that it is abstract. It is most idle to take a man apart from the circumstances which, in fact, were his. To be sure, it is easier in fancy to separate a person from his riches than from his character. But it is just as futile. Remove a square inch of mucous membrane, and the tenor will sing no more. Remove a little cube from the brain, and the orator will be speechless; or another, and the brave, generous and profound spirit becomes a timid and querulous trifler. A great man represents a great ganglion in the nerves of society, or, to vary the figure, a strategic point in the campaign of history, and part of his greatness consists in his being *there*. I no more can separate John Marshall from the fortunate circumstance that the appointment of Chief Justice fell to John Adams, instead of to Jefferson a month later, and so gave it to a Federalist and loose constructionist to start the working of the Constitution, than I can separate the black line through which he sent his electric fire at Fort Wagner from Colonel Shaw. When we celebrate Marshall we celebrate at the same time and indivisibly the inevitable fact that the oneness of the nation and the supremacy of the national Constitution were declared to govern the dealings of man with man by the judgments and decrees of the most august of courts.

I do not mean, of course, that personal estimates are useless or teach us nothing. No doubt to-day there will be heard from able and competent persons such estimates of Marshall. But I will not trench upon their field of work. It would be out of place when I am called on only to express the answer to a motion addressed to the court and when many of those who are here are to listen this afternoon to the accomplished teacher who has had every occasion to make a personal study of the judge, and again this evening to a gentleman who shares by birth the traditions of the man. My own impressions are only those that I have gathered in the common course of legal education and practice. In them I am conscious, perhaps, of some little revolt from our purely local or national estimates, and of a wish to see things and people judged by more cosmopolitan standards.

A man is bound to be parochial in his practice — to give his life, and if necessary his death, for the place where he has his roots. But his thinking should be cosmopolitan and detached. He should be able to criticise what he reveres and loves.

The Federalist, when I read it many years ago, seemed to me a truly original and wonderful production for the time. I do not trust even that judgment unrevised when I remember that *The Federalist* and its authors struck a distinguished English friend of mine as finite; and I should feel a greater doubt whether, after Hamilton and the Constitution itself, Marshall's work proved more than a strong intellect, a good style, personal ascendancy in his court, courage, justice and the convictions of his party. My keenest interest is excited, not by what are called great questions and great cases, but by little decisions which the common run of selectors would pass by because they did not deal with the Constitution or a telephone company, yet which have in them the germ of some wider theory, and therefore of some profound interstitial change in the very tissue of the law. The men whom I should be tempted to commemorate would be the originators of transforming thought. They often are half obscure, because what the world pays for is judgment, not the original mind.

But what I have said does not mean that I shall join in this celebration or in granting the motion before the court in any half-hearted way. Not only do I recur to what I said in the beginning, and remembering that you cannot separate a man from his

place, remember also that there fell to Marshall perhaps the greatest place that ever was filled by a
judge; but when I consider his might, his justice, and
his wisdom, I do fully believe that if American law
were to be represented by a single figure, sceptic and
worshipper alike would agree without dispute that
the figure could be one alone, and that one, John
Marshall.

A few words more and I have done. We live by
symbols, and what shall be symbolized by any image
of the sight depends upon the mind of him who sees
it. The setting aside of this day in honor of a great
judge may stand to a Virginian for the glory of his
glorious State; to a patriot for the fact that time has
been on Marshall's side, and that the theory for
which Hamilton argued, and he decided, and Webster
spoke, and Grant fought, and Lincoln died, is now
our corner-stone. To the more abstract but farther-
reaching contemplation of the lawyer, it stands for
the rise of a new body of jurisprudence, by which
guiding principles are raised above the reach of
statute and State, and judges are entrusted with a
solemn and hitherto unheard-of authority and duty.
To one who lives in what may seem to him a solitude
of thought, this day — as it marks the triumph of a
man whom some Presidents of his time bade carry
out his judgments as he could — this day marks the
fact that all thought is social, is on its way to action;
that, to borrow the expression of a French writer,
every idea tends to become first a catechism and then
a code; and that according to its worth his unhelped

meditation may one day mount a throne, and without armies, or even with them, may shoot across the world the electric despotism of an unresisted power. It is all a symbol, if you like, but so is the flag. The flag is but a bit of bunting to one who insists on prose. Yet, thanks to Marshall and to the men of his generation — and for this above all we celebrate him and them — its red is our lifeblood, its stars our world, its blue our heaven. It owns our land. At will it throws away our lives.

The motion of the bar is granted, and the court will now adjourn.

ADDRESS OF CHIEF JUSTICE HOLMES

At the Dedication of the Northwestern University
Law School Building, Chicago, October 20, 1902.

MR. PRESIDENT AND GENTLEMEN:

NATURE has but one judgment on wrong conduct
— if you can call that a judgment which seemingly
has no reference to conduct as such — the judgment
of death.   That is the judgment or the consequence
which follows uneconomical expenditure if carried far
enough.   If you waste too much food you starve;
too much fuel, you freeze; too much nerve tissue,
you collapse.   And so it might seem that the law
of life is the law of the herd; that man should produce food and raiment in order that he might produce
yet other food and other raiment to the end of time.
Yet who does not rebel at that conclusion?   Accept-
ing the premises, I nevertheless almost am prepared
to say that every joy that gives to life its inspiration
consists in an excursion toward death, although wisely
stopping short of its goal.   Art, philosophy, charity,
the search for the north pole, the delirium of every
great moment in man's experience — all alike mean
uneconomic expenditure — mean waste — mean a
step toward death.   The justification of art is not
that it offers prizes to those who succeed in the
economic struggle, to those who in an economic sense
have produced the most, and that thus by indirection

it increases the supply of wine and oil. The justification is in art itself, whatever its economic effect. It gratifies an appetite which in some noble spirits is stronger than the appetite for food. The principle might be pressed even further and be found to furnish art with one of its laws. For it might be said, as I often have said, and as I have been gratified to find elaborated by that true poet Coventry Patmore, that one of the grounds of aesthetic pleasure is waste. I need not refer to Charles Lamb's well-known comments on the fallacy that enough is as good as a feast. Who does not know how his delight has been increased to find some treasure of carving upon a mediaeval cathedral in a back alley — to see that the artist has been generous as well as great, and has not confined his best to the places where it could be seen to most advantage? Who does not recognize the superior charm of a square-hewed beam over a joist set on edge which would be enough for the work? To leave art, who does not feel that Nansen's account of his search for the pole rather loses than gains in ideal satisfaction by the pretense of a few trifling acquisitions for science? If I wished to make you smile I might even ask whether life did not gain an enrichment from neglected opportunities which would be missed in the snug filling out of every chance. But I am not here to press a paradox. I only mean to insist on the importance of the uneconomic to man as he actually feels to-day. You may philosophize about the honors of leisure as a survival; you may, if you like, describe in the same way, as I have heard them described, the ideals which burn in the center of our hearts. None the less they are there. They are categorical imperatives. They hold their own against hunger and thirst; they scorn to be classed as mere indirect supports of our bodily needs, which rather they defy; and our friends the economists would do well to take account of them, as some great writers like M. Tarde would take account of them, if they are to deal with man as he is. No doubt already you have perceived the reason why I have insisted upon this double view of life. The special value of a university is that it moves in the twofold direction of man's desires which I have described. I have listened with interest to able business men when they argued and testified that a university training made men fitter to succeed in their practical struggles. I am far from denying it. No doubt such a training gives men a larger mastery of the laws of nature under which they must work, a wider outlook over the world of science and of fact. If it could give to every student a scientific point of view, if education could make men realize that you can not produce something out of nothing and make them promptly detect the pretense of doing so with which at present the talk of every day is filled, I should think it had more than paid for itself. Still more should I think so if it could send men into the world with a good rudimentary knowledge of the laws of their environment. I can not believe that anything else would be so likely to secure prosperity as the universal acceptance of scientific premises in every department of thought. But beside prosperity there is to be considered happiness, which is not the same thing. The chance of a university to enlarge men's power of happiness is at least not less than its chance to enlarge their capacity for gain. I own that with regard to this, as with regard to every other aspiration of man, the most important question seems to me to be, what are his inborn qualities?

Mr. Ruskin's first rule for learning to draw, you will remember, was, Be born with genius. It is the first rule for everything else. If a man is adequate in native force, he probably will be happy in the deepest sense, whatever his fate. But we must not undervalue effort, even if it is the lesser half. And the opening which a university is sure to offer to all the idealizing tendencies — which, I am not afraid to say, it ought to offer to the romantic side of life — makes it above all other institutions the conservator of the vestal fire. Our tastes are finalities, and it has been recognized since the days of Rome that there is not much use in disputing about them. If some professor should proclaim that what he wanted was a strictly economic world, I should see no more use in debating with him than I do in arguing with those who despise the ideals which we owe to war. But most men at present are on the university side. They want to be told stories and to go to the play. They want to understand and, if they can, to paint pictures, and to write poems, whether the food product is greater in the long run because of them or not.

They want to press philosophy to the uttermost edge of the articulate, and to try forever after some spiritual ray outside the spectrum that will bring a message to them from behind phenomena. They love the gallant adventure which yields no visible return. I think it the glory of that university which I know best, that under whatever reserves of manner they may hide it, its graduates have the romantic passion in their hearts.

But, gentlemen, there is one department of your institution to which I must be permitted specially to refer — the department to which I am nearest by profession, and to which I owe the honor of being here. I mean, of course, the department of law. Let me say one word about that before I sit down. It was affirmed, I believe, by a man not without deserved honor in his generation — the late Chief Justice Cooley — that the law was and ought to be commonplace. No doubt the remark has its truth. It is better that the law should be commonplace than that it should be eccentric. No doubt, too, in any aspect it would seem commonplace to a mind that understood everything. But that is the weakness of all truth. If instead of the joy of eternal pursuit you imagine yourself to have mastered it as a complete whole, you would find yourself reduced to the alternative either of finding the remotest achievement of quaternions or ontology — the whole frame of the universe, in short — a bore, or of dilating with undying joy over the proposition that twice two is four. It seems to me that for men as they are, the law may keep its every-day character and yet be an object of understanding wonder and a field for the lightning of genius.   One reason why it gives me pleasure to be here today and to express my good wishes for the future and my appreciation of the past of your law school, is that it is here and in places like it that such wonder is kindled and that from it may fly sparks that shall set free in some genius his explosive message.

I am not dealing in generalities.   I mean more than good will to a law school, simply because it is a law school.   Indeed, I almost fear that the intellectual ferment of the better schools may be too potent an attraction to young men and seduce into the profession many who would be better elsewhere.   But I am thinking of this law school and no other.   I never have had an opportunity to give public expression to my sense of the value of the work of your accomplished dean.[1]   I have come in for my share of criticism from him, as also I have had from him words which have given me new courage on a lonely road.   But my appreciation of what I have seen from his hands is untouched by personal relations.   It is solely because I think that it is the duty of those who know to recognize the unadvertised first rate, that I wish now to express my respect for his great learning and originality and for the volume and delicacy of his production, which seem to me to deserve more distinct and public notice than, so far as I am aware, they have received.   I feel quite sure,

[1] Professor John H. Wigmore.

from his printed work, that his teaching will satisfy the two-fold desire of man; that it will be enlightened with intelligent economic views and give men what they want to know when they go out to fight, but that also it will send them forth with a pennon as well as with a sword, to keep before their eyes in the long battle the little flutter that means ideals, honor, yes, even romance, in all the dull details.

ECONOMIC ELEMENTS *

I ENTERTAIN some opinions concerning the issues raised by your questions, and though not strictly responsive, I will state them.

The real problem is not who owns, but who consumes, the annual product. The identification of these two very different questions is the source of many fallacies, and misleads many workingmen. The real evil of fifty-thousand-dollar balls and other manifestations of private splendor is that they tend to confirm this confusion in the minds of the ignorant by an appeal to their imagination, and make them think that the Vanderbilts and Rockefellers swallow their incomes like Cleopatra's dissolved pearl. The same conception is at the bottom of Henry George's *Progress and Poverty*. He thinks he has finished the discussion when he shows the tendency of wealth to be owned by the landlords. He does not consider what the landlords do with it.

I conceive that economically it does not matter whether you call Rockefeller or the United States owner of all the wheat in the United States, if that wheat is annually consumed by the body of the people; except that Rockefeller, under the illusion of self-seeking or in the conscious pursuit of power,

* A letter written in response to questions and not intended for print, but reprinted here, as it was published in a magazine (1904).

will be likely to bring to bear a more poignant scrutiny of the future in order to get a greater return for the next year.

If then, as I believe, the ability of the ablest men under the present régime is directed to getting the largest markets and the largest returns, such ability is directed to the economically desirable end.

I have vainly urged our various statisticians to exhibit in the well-known form the proportions of the products consumed by the many and those consumed by the few, expressed in labor hours or in any other convenient way. This would show whether private ownership was abused for the production of an undue proportion of luxuries for the few. I do not believe the luxuries would be one per cent.

It follows from what I have said that the objections to unlimited private ownership are sentimental or political, not economic. Of course, as the size of a private fortune increases, the interest of the public in the administration of it increases. If a man owned one-half of the wheat in the country and announced his intention to burn it, such abuse of ownership would not be permitted. The crowd would kill him sooner than stand it.

But it seems to me that if every desirable object were in the hands of a monopolist, intent on getting all he could for it (subject to the limitation that it must be consumed, and that it might not be wantonly destroyed, as, of course, it would not be), the value of the several objects would be settled by the intensity of the desires for them respectively, and they would be consumed by those who were able to get them and that would be the ideal result.

The first question put,* if I may be permitted to say so, seems to me rather fanciful. I see no way of answering it intelligently, and if I am right, it appears to imply an acceptance of what I have already tried to show to be a fallacy or confusion.

So far as I can answer it, what I should say would be this: All that any man contributes to the world is the intelligence which directs a change in the place of matter. A man does not create the thing he handles or the force he exerts. The force could be got cheaper if the directing intelligence were not needed. The whole progress of the world in a material way is to put the need of intelligence further back. It is obvious that the intelligence of an architect contributes more to the change of form which takes place in a house than that of all the laboring hands. How can any one measure the scope and value of remote causes of change? How can I compare the present effect on the lives of men of the speculations of Kant and of the empire of Napoleon? I should not think it absurd to assert that the former counted for the more, though, of course, it is impossible to prove it. My practical answer is that a great fortune does not mean a corresponding consumption, but a power of command; that some one must exercise that command, and that I know of no way of finding the fit man so good as the fact of winning it in the competition of the market.

* Whether a man can render services entitling him to a fortune as great as some of ours in America.

I already have intimated my opinion that the owner of a great fortune has public functions, and therefore, subject to legal questions which I am not considering, should be subject to some negative restraint. Among others, I should like to see him prohibited from giving great sums to charities which could not be clearly justified as long-sighted public investments.

The only other question on which I desire to say a word is the nature of taxes in this connection. Taxes, when thought out in things and results, mean an abstraction of a part of the annual product for government purposes, and cannot mean anything else. Whatever form they take in their imposition they must be borne by the consumer, that is, mainly by the working-men and fighting-men of the community. It is well that they should have this fact brought home to them, and not too much disguised by the form in which the taxes are imposed.

ON F. W. MAITLAND'S DEATH *

ONE is almost ashamed to praise a dead master for what he did in a field where he was acknowledged to be supreme. When his work is finished it is too late for praise to give the encouragement which all need, and of which the successful get too little. Still, there is a pleasure in bearing one's testimony even at that late time, and thus in justifying the imagination of posthumous power on which all idealists and men not seeking the immediate rewards of success must live. That imagination, if Mr. Maitland was not, as I fear, too modest to get much joy from it, will be realized, I am sure. His profound knowledge of the sources of English law equipped him, as perhaps no other was equipped, to illustrate and explain the present. His knowledge was only a tool to his good sense. His good sense and insight were illuminated and made vivid by his power of statement and gift of narrative, so that any reasonably prepared reader of his writings, even those dealing with what one would have expected to be dry details, is sure to become interested, absorbed, and charmed. His last work, the *Life of Sir Leslie Stephen,* was a no less successful excursion into new fields, and showed the same gifts, coupled with an

* *Law Quarterly Review* (1907).

unconscious spirituality, which did not surprise, but which found freer scope for expression there. To elaborate an estimate of Mr. Maitland's achievements would require time which my occupations do not permit me to give. But I would not willingly miss the chance to say what I believe about him, and to lay a wreath, if only of dry leaves, upon his grave.

HOLDSWORTH'S ENGLISH LAW *

THE study of English law has been slow to feel
the impulse of science. But during the last thirty
years, alongside of the practitioners to whom the law
is a ragbag from which they pick out the piece and
color that they want, there have been some students
who have striven to make their knowledge organic.
A brilliant result of that effort was Pollock and Maitland's history. Mr. Holdsworth is giving us another.
The first dealt mainly with the embryology of the subject. The present work intends to deal with it in its
maturity as well; and the two volumes just published
trace its development through the Year Books to the
point where we begin to recognize its adult form. A
development is hard to describe. Mr. Holdsworth is
to be complimented on the skill with which he has
done it, although it would be difficult to give an account of his book, precisely because of his skill. One
is made to feel the complex antecedents — Saxon tradition, Norman practice, the Roman law, the character of kings, the rise of Parliament, the varying
economic needs and aims — out of which the plant
has grown, and one is made to see the growth. The
reading leaves the conviction that one has received

* A History of English Law. By W. S. Holdsworth, D.C.L.
London: Methuen & Co., 1909. 8vo. Vol. II., xxxi, and 572 pp.; Vol.
III., xxxviii, and 532 pp. Law Quarterly Review (1909).

the most important of object lessons in the birth and life of ideas. The difficulty in remembering the details is the difficulty of marking the steps of an organic process. One sees that the embryo has taken form, gained size and coherence, more readily than one marks the moments of the change.

The line between antiquarianism and knowledge of practical importance is kept with tact. Enough is told to gratify disinterested philosophic curiosity, yet not more than should be read by any one who desires to understand his art. No doubt Mr. Holdsworth is right in saying that "We cannot date the beginnings of the common law much earlier than the first half of the twelfth century." For that reason he properly does not spend much time on what he calls Anglo-Saxon antiquities, but what he says tells, and makes a proper beginning. The Church and the Roman law are other secondary influences, and those again are delicately and judiciously expounded. They are shown strengthening the royal power; impelling the first attempt at systematizing the new corpus that is to be; tending to qualify the old principle of liability (stated somewhat strongly perhaps in the proposition that a man acted at his peril); introducing the last will and also the book for land grants, which fostered free alienation; suggesting new remedies and the *exceptio* in pleading; and in short, in various ways by their foreign atmosphere forcing the growth of the native plant, especially through their influence on the King's Court. Much, perhaps most, of what we are told has been told before, and the author is frank in his reference to previous work, but it is told here in continuous form, with proportion, and so as to bring out the story of the birth and life of the common law.

Attention has been called before now to the struggle for life carried on among ideas; to the result that some perish and others put on the livery of the conqueror; and to the fact that law only ends with a theory, but begins with a concrete case. But so far as I know these considerations have not been much attended to heretofore. Mr. Holdsworth illustrates them with more or less definite reference to this mode of approach. A slight example is that twenty-one, the time of coming of age for the knight, prevails over fifteen, the time for the socman. But the best instance is that of contract. We are shown how there are brought under that head matters that earlier were thought of in terms of grant, or like bailment formed a head by themselves. The surety, from a hostage, becomes a covenantor. We are given many illustrations of the persistence of the *fides facta* and the oath as older competitors of the real and formal contracts that finally got the power. Ecclesiastical penalties for perjury in the breach of a promissory oath continue to a late period,[1] and although the opinion has been controverted, I think that there are signs that ecclesiastical chancellors hesitated before they denied a remedy for breach of faith.

[1] In Chaucer's Frere's Tale the Archdeacon "dide execucioun In punisshinge of . . . diffamacioun . . . and of testaments, Of contractes, and of lakke of sacraments," etc.

While I am speaking of contract I may add that the progress from tort to assumpsit seems to me better told than it has been before. Perhaps there is some perpetuation of what seems to me the confusion between the fraud that is wrought if a man keeps an executed consideration and will not perform his promise, and the misfortune that may be caused by not keeping a promise for which no consideration has been given. The very meaning of the doctrine of consideration is that if a man relies upon a promise made without it, he does so at his peril. Unless action on the faith of the promise is the conventional inducement for the promise, it has no effect. By conventional inducement I mean, of course, that which is contemplated, as the ground for the promise, by the bargain, whatever may be the motive in fact. Unless my memory deceives me, the false doctrine sometimes has been treated as if it were the main ground out of which assumpsit grew.

If the development of ideas and their struggle for life are the interests of the day, the interest of the future, the final and most important question in the law is that of their worth. I mean their worth in a more far-reaching sense than that of expressing the *de facto* will of the community for the time. On this as yet no one has much to say. To answer it we should have in the first place to establish the ideals upon which our judgments of worth depend; and the statement of such ideals by different classes would differ, at least in form. But suppose that we had agreed that the end of law was, for instance, the survival of a certain type of man, still we should have made very little way toward the founding of a scientific code. Statistics would leave the effect of the criminal law open to doubt. Who can prove that the doctrine of master and servant, or the theory of consideration, helps to attain the ideal assumed? The attitude of the State toward marriage and divorce is governed more by church and tradition than by facts. Wherever we turn we find that what are called good laws are apt to be called so because men see that they promote a result that they fancy desirable, and do not see the bill that has to be paid in reactions that are relatively obscure. One fancies that one could invent a different code under which men would have been as well off as they are now, if they had happened to adopt it. But that *if* is a very great one. The tree has grown as we know it. The practical question is what is to be the next organic step. No doubt the history of the law encourages scepticism when one sees how a rule or a doctrine has grown up, or when one notices the *naïveté* with which social prejudices are taken for eternal principles. But it also leads to an unconvinced conservatism. For it points out that almost the only thing that can be assumed as certainly to be wished is that men should know the rules by which the game will be played. Doubt as to the value of some of those rules is no sufficient reason why they should not be followed by the courts. Legislation gives notice at least if it makes a change. And after all, those of us who believe with Mr. Lester Ward, the sociologist, in the superiority of the artificial to the natural, may see in what has been done some ground for believing that mankind yet may take its own destiny consciously and intelligently in hand.

Mr. Holdsworth is telling us a profoundly interesting story. It is one of the most important chapters in the greatest human document — the tale of what men have most believed and most wanted. It is told with learning and scientific instinct, and the book is to be recommended equally to philosophers who can understand it and to practical students of the law. Readers of M. Tarde will see that author's laws of imitation illustrated by the most striking example, and if they doubt how far it can be said that the principles of any system are eternal, will realize that imitation of the past, until we have a clear reason for change, no more needs justification than appetite. It is a form of the inevitable to be accepted until we have a clear vision of what different thing we want.

LAW AND THE COURT

SPEECH AT A DINNER OF THE HARVARD LAW SCHOOL
ASSOCIATION OF NEW YORK ON FEBRUARY
15, 1913 *

MR. CHAIRMAN AND GENTLEMEN:

VANITY is the most philosophical of those feelings
that we are taught to despise. For vanity recognizes
that if a man is in a minority of one we lock him up,
and therefore longs for an assurance from others
that one's work has not been in vain. If a man's
ambition is the thirst for a power that comes not from
office but from within, he never can be sure that any
happiness is not a fool's paradise — he never can be
sure that he sits on that other bench reserved for the
masters of those who know. Then too, at least
until one draws near to seventy, one is less likely to
hear the trumpets than the rolling fire of the front.
I have passed that age, but I still am on the firing
line, and it is only in rare moments like this that
there comes a pause and for half an hour one feels
a trembling hope. They are the rewards of a lifetime's work.

But let me turn to more palpable realities — to
that other visible Court to which for ten now accomplished years it has been my opportunity to be-

* From *Speeches* (1913), Little, Brown & Co.

long. We are very quiet there, but it is the quiet of a storm centre, as we all know. Science has taught the world scepticism and has made it legitimate to put everything to the test of proof. Many beautiful and noble reverences are impaired, but in these days no one can complain if any institution, system, or belief is called on to justify its continuance in life. Of course we are not excepted and have not escaped. Doubts are expressed that go to our very being. Not only are we told that when Marshall pronounced an Act of Congress unconstitutional he usurped a power that the Constitution did not give, but we are told that we are the representatives of a class — a tool of the money power. I get letters, not always anonymous, intimating that we are corrupt. Well, gentlemen, I admit that it makes my heart ache. It is very painful, when one spends all the energies of one's soul in trying to do good work, with no thought but that of solving a problem according to the rules by which one is bound, to know that many see sinister motives and would be glad of evidence that one was consciously bad. But we must take such things philosophically and try to see what we can learn from hatred and distrust and whether behind them there may not be some germ of inarticulate truth.

The attacks upon the Court are merely an expression of the unrest that seems to wonder vaguely whether law and order pay. When the ignorant are taught to doubt they do not know what they safely may believe. And it seems to me that at this time we need education in the obvious more than investi-

gation of the obscure. I do not see so much immediate use in committees on the high cost of living
and inquiries how far it is due to the increased production of gold, how far to the narrowing of cattle
ranges and the growth of population, how far to
the bugaboo, as I do in bringing home to people a
few social and economic truths. Most men think
dramatically, not quantitatively, a fact that the rich
would be wise to remember more than they do. We
are apt to contrast the palace with the hovel, the
dinner at Sherry's with the working man's pail, and
never ask how much or realize how little is withdrawn
to make the prizes of success (subordinate prizes —
since the only prize much cared for by the powerful
is power. The prize of the general is not a bigger
tent, but command). We are apt to think of ownership as a terminus, not as a gateway, and not to
realize that except the tax levied for personal consumption large ownership means investment, and
investment means the direction of labor towards the
production of the greatest returns — returns that so
far as they are great show by that very fact that they
are consumed by the many, not alone by the few.
If I may ride a hobby for an instant, I should say
we need to think things instead of words — to drop
ownership, money, etc., and to think of the stream
of products; of wheat and cloth and railway travel.
When we do, it is obvious that the many consume
them; that they now as truly have substantially all
there is, as if the title were in the United States; that
the great body of property is socially administered

now, and that the function of private ownership is to divine in advance the equilibrium of social desires — which socialism equally would have to divine, but which, under the illusion of self-seeking, is more poignantly and shrewdly foreseen.

I should like to see it brought home to the public that the question of fair prices is due to the fact that none of us can have as much as we want of all the things we want; that as less will be produced than the public wants, the question is how much of each product it will have and how much go without; that thus the final competition is between the objects of desire, and therefore between the producers of those objects; that when we oppose labor and capital, labor means the group that is selling its product and capital all the other groups that are buying it. The hated capitalist is simply the mediator, the prophet, the adjuster according to his divination of the future desire. If you could get that believed, the body of the people would have no doubt as to the worth of law.

That is my outside thought on the present discontents. As to the truth embodied in them, in part it cannot be helped. It cannot be helped, it is as it should be, that the law is behind the times. I told a labor leader once that what they asked was favor, and if a decision was against them they called it wicked. The same might be said of their opponents. It means that the law is growing. As law embodies beliefs that have triumphed in the battle of ideas and then have translated themselves into action, while there still is doubt, while opposite convictions still keep a battle front against each other, the time for law has not come; the notion destined to prevail is not yet entitled to the field. It is a misfortune if a judge reads his conscious or unconscious sympathy with one side or the other prematurely into the law, and forgets that what seem to him to be first principles are believed by half his fellow men to be wrong. I think that we have suffered from this misfortune, in State courts at least, and that this is another and very important truth to be extracted from the popular discontent. When twenty years ago a vague terror went over the earth and the word socialism began to be heard, I thought and still think that fear was translated into doctrines that had no proper place in the Constitution or the common law. Judges are apt to be naif, simple-minded men, and they need something of Mephistopheles. We too need education in the obvious — to learn to transcend our own convictions and to leave room for much that we hold dear to be done away with short of revolution by the orderly change of law.

I have no belief in panaceas and almost none in sudden ruin. I believe with Montesquieu that if the chance of a battle — I may add, the passage of a law — has ruined a state, there was a general cause at work that made the state ready to perish by a single battle or a law. Hence I am not much interested one way or the other in the nostrums now so strenuously urged. I do not think the United States would come to an end if we lost our power to declare an Act of Congress void. I do think the Union would be imperiled if we could not make that declaration as to the laws of the several States. For one in my place sees how often a local policy prevails with those who are not trained to national views and how often action is taken that embodies what the Commerce Clause was meant to end. But I am not aware that there is any serious desire to limit the Court's power in this regard. For most of the things that properly can be called evils in the present state of the law I think the main remedy, as for the evils of public opinion, is for us to grow more civilized.

If I am right it will be a slow business for our people to reach rational views, assuming that we are allowed to work peaceably to that end. But as I grow older I grow calm. If I feel what are perhaps an old man's apprehensions, that competition from new races will cut deeper than working men's disputes and will test whether we can hang together and can fight; if I fear that we are running through the world's resources at a pace that we cannot keep; I do not lose my hopes. I do not pin my dreams for the future to my country or even to my race. I think it probable that civilization somehow will last as long as I care to look ahead — perhaps with smaller numbers, but perhaps also bred to greatness and splendor by science. I think it not improbable that man, like the grub that prepares a chamber for the winged thing it never has seen but is to be — that man may have cosmic destinies that he does not understand. And so beyond the vision of battling races and an impoverished earth I catch a dreaming glimpse of peace.

The other day my dream was pictured to my mind. It was evening. I was walking homeward on Pennsylvania Avenue near the Treasury, and as I looked beyond Sherman's Statue to the west the sky was aflame with scarlet and crimson from the setting sun. But, like the note of downfall in Wagner's opera, below the sky line there came from little globes the pallid discord of the electric lights. And I thought to myself the Götterdämmerung will end, and from those globes clustered like evil eggs will come the new masters of the sky. It is like the time in which we live. But then I remembered the faith that I partly have expressed, faith in a universe not measured by our fears, a universe that has thought and more than thought inside of it, and as I gazed, after the sunset and above the electric lights there shone the stars.

INTRODUCTION TO THE GENERAL SURVEY

BY EUROPEAN AUTHORS IN THE CONTINENTAL LEGAL HISTORICAL SERIES *

The authors whose writings are offered in this volume and Series do not need introduction. They introduce the man who has the honor for a moment to associate his name with theirs. But a few words from a veteran may catch the attention of those who still are in the school of the soldier and have not seen their first fight.

The philosophers teach us that an idea is the first step toward an act. Beliefs, so far as they bear upon the attainment of a wish (as most beliefs do), lead in the first place to a social attitude, and later to combined social action, that is, to law. Hence, ever since it has existed, the law expressed what men most strongly have believed and desired. And, as the beliefs and desires of the Western world have changed and developed a good deal since the days of the Twelve Tables and the Law of the Salian Franks, I thought it dangerously near a platitude to say, a dozen years ago, that the law might be regarded as a great anthropological document. But, as a gentleman prominent at the bar of one of the States professed

* Little, Brown & Co., Boston. 1913.

difficulty in understanding what I meant, it is evident that the rudiments need eternal repetition. Any man who is interested in ideas needs only the suggestion that I have made to realize that the history of the law is the embryology of a most important set of ideas, and perhaps more than any other history tells the story of a race.

The trouble with general or literary historical works is that they deal with premises or conclusions that are both unquantified. We readily admit their assumption that such and such a previous fact tended to produce such and such a later one; but how much of the first would be necessary to produce how much of the last, and how much there actually was of either, we are not told. On the other hand, in the history of philosophy and economics we can say with more confidence that we trace cause and effect. The one shows the inward bond between the successive stages of the thought of man; the other the sequence of outward events that have governed his action and (some believe) really have determined his thought. At all events the latter fits the former as the outside of a cathedral fits the inside, — although there are gargoyles and Mephistopheles without and angels and saints within.

There is no place for the history of law in this metaphor; but, in plain prose, it is midway between the other two. As we follow it down from century to century, we see logic at work attempting to develop the concrete cases given in experience into universal rules, and the struggle for life between the attempted generalizations and other competing forms. We watch the metamorphosis of the simple into the complex. We see changes of environment producing new institutions, and new taking the place of old beliefs and wants. We observe the illustrations, as striking here as in poetry or music, of the universal change of emphasis that each century brings along. An argument that would have prevailed in Plowden's time, and perhaps, would have raised a difficulty to be got rid of in Lord Ellenborough's, now would be answered only with a smile.

The most obvious moral of what I have said is that the law will furnish philosophical food to philosophical minds. The surgeon of my regiment in the War of Secession used to divide the world into external and internal men. The distinction is as old as Plato. For I take it that what makes the Banquet immortal is not the divine gossip about Aristophanes and Alcibiades and Socrates, but that it and some of the Dialogues are the first articulate expression that has come down to us of what internal men believe, that ideas are more interesting than things. To the internal men, I need say no more to recommend the theme of this and the following volumes. But the profit is not confined to them. When a man has a working knowledge of his business, he can spend his leisure better than in reading all the reported cases he has time for. They are apt to be only the small change of legal thought. They represent the compromise of the moment between tradition and precedent on the one side and the free conception of the desirable on the other. It is worth while, even with the most mundane ideals, to get as big a grasp of one's subject as one can. And therefore it is worth while to do what we can to enlighten our notions of the desirable and to understand the precedents by which we are constrained. The history of the law stands alongside of sociology and economics as a necessary tool if one is to practise law in a large way.

If what I have said is granted, not much argument is needed to show that a survey of the general development of Continental law is necessary to understand our own. The relationship is too well established to need new proofs, — although I believe that there still are standard treatises that ascribe trusts to Rome and ignore the Salman. Indeed, I am not sure that the best way of proving the need of this Series would not be to present a series of Elegant Extracts from text-books and decisions.

I can but envy the felicity of the generation to whom it is made so easy to see their subject as a whole. When I began, the law presented itself as a ragbag of details. The best approach that I found to general views on the historical side was the first volume of Spence's *Equitable Jurisdiction,* and, on the practical, Walker's *American Law.* The only philosophy within reach was Austin's *Jurisprudence.* It was not without anguish that one asked oneself whether the subject was worthy of the interest of an intelligent man. One saw people whom one respected and admired leaving the study because they thought it narrowed the mind; for which they had the authority of Burke. It required blind faith — faith that could not yet find the formula of justification for itself. The works of foreign scholarship were then inaccessible. One had to spend long days of groping, with the inward fear that if one only knew where to look, one would find that one's difficulties and questions were fifty years behind the times. Now, a man can start with the knowledge that he starts fair — that the best results of Europe, as well as of this country and England, are before him. And those results are so illuminating that diligence alone is enough to give him an understanding of how the law came to be what it is, of its broadest generalizations, and (so far as any one yet can state them) of the reasons to be offered for continuing it in its present form or for desiring a change.

WASHINGTON, D.C., November 28, 1911.

IDEALS AND DOUBTS*

FOR the last thirty years we have been preoccupied with the embryology of legal ideas; and explanations, which, when I was in college, meant a reference to final causes, later came to mean tracing origin and growth. But fashion is as potent in the intellectual world as elsewhere, and there are signs of an inevitable reaction. The reaction, if there is one, seems to me an advance, for it is toward the ultimate question of worth. That is the text of an excellent article, "History versus Value," by Morris R. Cohen in the *Journal of Philosophy, Psychology and Scientific Methods*, and although perhaps rather in the form of conservation than of advance, of Del Vecchio's *Formal Bases of Law* in the Modern Legal Philosophical Series. To show that it has my sympathy I may refer to the *Law Quarterly Review*.[1] But perhaps it will not be out of place to express the caution with which I am compelled to approach any general recension from which the young hope so much.

The first inquiry is for the criterion. If I may do Del Vecchio the wrong of summing up in a sentence or two what from a hasty reading I gather to be his mode of reaching one, it is that of a Neo-Kan-

* *Illinois Law Review*, Vol. X (1915).
[1] 25 *Law Quarterly Review*, 412, 414, *October*, 1909. *Ante*, pp. 285–290.

tian idealist. Experience takes place and is organized in consciousness, by its machinery and according to its laws, such as the category of cause and effect. Therefore consciousness constructs the universe and as the fundamental fact is entitled to fundamental reverence. From this it is easy to proceed to the Kantian injunction to regard every human being as an end in himself and not as a means.

I confess that I rebel at once. If we want conscripts, we march them up to the front with bayonets in their rear to die for a cause in which perhaps they do not believe. The enemy we treat not even as a means but as an obstacle to be abolished, if so it may be. I feel no pangs of conscience over either step, and naturally am slow to accept a theory that seems to be contradicted by practices that I approve. In fact, it seems to me that the idealists give away their case when they write books. For it shows that they have done the great act of faith and decided that they are not God. If the world were my dream, I should be God in the only universe I know. But although I cannot prove that I am awake, I believe that my neighbors exist in the same sense that I do, and if I admit that, it is easy to admit also that I am in the universe, not it in me.

When I say that a thing is true, I mean that I cannot help believing it. I am stating an experience as to which there is no choice. But as there are many things that I cannot help doing that the universe can, I do not venture to assume that my inabilities in the way of thought are inabilities of the universe. I therefore define the truth as the system of my limitations, and leave absolute truth for those who are better equipped. With absolute truth I leave absolute ideals of conduct equally on one side.

But although one believes in what commonly, with some equivocation, is called necessity; that phenomena always are found to stand in quantitatively fixed relations to earlier phenomena; it does not follow that without such absolute ideals we have nothing to do but to sit still and let time run over us. As I wrote many years ago, the mode in which the inevitable comes to pass is through effort. Consciously or unconsciously we all strive to make the kind of a world that we like. And although with Spinoza we may regard criticism of the past as futile, there is every reason for doing all that we can to make a future such as we desire.

There is every reason also for trying to make our desires intelligent. The trouble is that our ideals for the most part are inarticulate, and that even if we have made them definite we have very little experimental knowledge of the way to bring them about. The social reformers of today seem to me so far to forget that we no more can get something for nothing by legislation than we can by mechanics as to be satisfied if the bill to be paid for their improvements is not presented in a lump sum. Interstitial detriments that may far outweigh the benefit promised are not bothered about. Probably I am too skeptical as to our ability to do more than shift disagreeable burdens from the shoulders of the stronger to those of the weaker. But I hold to a few articles of a creed that I do not expect to see popular in my day. I believe that the wholesale social regeneration which so many now seem to expect, if it can be helped by conscious, coördinated human effort, cannot be affected appreciably by tinkering with the institution of property, but only by taking in hand life and trying to build a race. That would be my starting point for an ideal for the law. The notion that with socialized property we should have women free and a piano for everybody seems to me an empty humbug.

To get a little nearer to the practical, our current ethics and our current satisfaction with conventional legal rules, it seems to me, can be purged to a certain extent without reference to what our final ideal may be. To rest upon a formula is a slumber that, prolonged, means death. Our system of morality is a body of imperfect social generalizations expressed in terms of emotion. To get at its truth, it is useful to omit the emotion and ask ourselves what those generalizations are and how far they are confirmed by fact accurately ascertained. So in regard to the formulas of the law, I have found it very instructive to consider what may be the postulates implied. They are generically two: that such and such a condition or result is desirable and that such and such means are appropriate to bring it about. In all debatable matters there are conflicting desires to be accomplished by inconsistent means, and the further question arises, which is entitled to prevail in the specific case? Upon such issues logic does not carry

us far, and the practical solution sometimes may
assume a somewhat cynical shape. But I have
found it a help to clear thinking to try to get behind
my conventional assumptions as a judge whose first
business is to see that the game is played according
to the rules whether I like them or not. To have
doubted one's own first principles is the mark of a
civilized man. To know what you want and why
you think that such a measure will help it is the first
but by no means the last step towards intelligent
legal reform. The other and more difficult one is
to realize what you must give up to get it, and to
consider whether you are ready to pay the price.

It is fashionable nowadays to emphasize the criterion of social welfare as against the individualistic
eighteenth century bills of rights. I may venture to
refer to a book of mine published thirty-four years
ago to show that it is no novelty.[2] The trouble with
some of those who hold to that modest platitude is
that they are apt to take the general premise as a
sufficient justification for specific measures. One
may accept the premise in good faith and yet dis-
believe all the popular conceptions of socialism, or
even doubt whether there is a panacea in giving
women votes. Personally I like to know what the
bill is going to be before I order a luxury. But it
is a pleasure to see more faith and enthusiasm in
the young men; and I thought that one of them made
a good answer to some of my skeptical talk when he
said, "You would base legislation upon regrets rather
than upon hopes."

[2] The Common Law, pp. 43, 44, 48.

BRACTON DE LEGIBUS ET CONSUETU-
DINIBUS ANGLIAE

Edited by George E. Woodbine, Yale University Press,
New Haven, 1915. Volume I.

ONE who in the last thirty-five years, not to speak
of more usual themes, has seen more of treaties with
North American Indians than of Bracton cannot
speak competently of the detail of this monumental
work.   Indeed the case probably is not unlike that
of the Greek Lexicon of the Roman and Byzantine
periods written by the late Professor Sophocles, of
which it was said that there was only one man in
Europe who could criticize it.   That one in this case
may be my friend Sir Frederick Pollock, but it certainly is not I.   But some things may be said.   The
history of the law is of much importance to the
understanding of the law, even apart from its significance in the more disinterested study of anthropology.   Bracton is a work of the very highest
value for the theme.   There is no edition that gives
us anything like an adequate approach to the unknown original, that lets us see the variations of the
better manuscripts, or that opens to us a solution of
the problems of the text.   The little but important
world that these questions interest has been praying

* *Yale Review*, 1915.

for years that someone might undertake Professor Woodbine's task.

Now the man has come. Backed by a generous gift of money he makes the more splendid one of his life. For he already has devoted years and expects to devote many more to bringing his work to an end. The first volume, now published, proves the thoroughness, the all but exhaustive collection of apparatus (that two manuscripts have been missed is no fault of his), and the critical aptitude that he commands. It contains a study of the pedigree of the texts with diagrams illustrating their probable relations to their source and to one another, and an analysis of the *addiciones*. It illustrates the infinity of detail that · the editor has scrutinized with microscopic eye. It shows the interest of the results to which his researches point. At this stage perhaps the only thing really proper to be dwelt upon is the nobility of spirit, the heroism of the scholar that the undertaking exhibits. Those who at any time have spent fewer months than Professor Woodbine already has spent years upon details, fired with the faith that one day they would disclose the organic line of life that made them great, those who remember Browning's picture of his imaginary hero of letters in "A Grammarian's Funeral," who

> Gave us the doctrine of the enclitic *De*,
> Dead from the waist down,

will salute with a soldier's respect for a soldier this real man who is achieving honor by sacrificing self as fully as did the Grammarian and to a greater end.

NATURAL LAW*

IT is not enough for the knight of romance that
you agree that his lady is a very nice girl — if you
do not admit that she is the best that God ever made
or will make, you must fight. There is in all men
a demand for the superlative, so much so that the
poor devil who has no other way of reaching it attains
it by getting drunk. It seems to me that this demand is at the bottom of the philosopher's effort
to prove that truth is absolute and of the jurist's
search for criteria of universal validity which he col-
lects under the head of natural law.

I used to say, when I was young, that truth was
the majority vote of that nation that could lick all
others. Certainly we may expect that the received
opinion about the present war will depend a good
deal upon which side wins (I hope with all my soul
it will be mine), and I think that the statement was
correct in so far as it implied that our test of truth
is a reference to either a present or an imagined
future majority in favor of our view. If, as I have
suggested elsewhere, the truth may be defined as the
system of my (intellectual) limitations,[1] what gives

---

* Suggested by reading Francois Geny, *Science et Technique en
Droit Positif Privé, Paris,* 1915. (*Harvard Law Review,* Vol. XXXII.)
(1918.)

[1] *Ante,* Ideals and Doubts.

it objectivity is the fact that I find my fellow man to a greater or less extent (never wholly) subject to the same *Can't Helps*. If I think that I am sitting at a table I find that the other persons present agree with me; so if I say that the sum of the angles of a triangle is equal to two right angles. If I am in a minority of one they send for a doctor or lock me up; and I am so far able to transcend the to me convincing testimony of my senses or my reason as to recognize that if I am alone probably something is wrong with my works.

Certitude is not the test of certainty. We have been cock-sure of many things that were not so. If I may quote myself again, property, friendship, and truth have a common root in time. One can not be wrenched from the rocky crevices into which one has grown for many years without feeling that one is attacked in one's life. What we most love and revere generally is determined by early associations. I love granite rocks and barberry bushes, no doubt because with them were my earliest joys that reach back through the past eternity of my life. But while one's experience thus makes certain preferences dogmatic for oneself, recognition of how they came to be so leaves one able to see that others, poor souls, may be equally dogmatic about something else. And this again means scepticism. Not that one's belief or love does not remain. Not that we would not fight and die for it if important — we all, whether we know it or not, are fighting to make the kind of a world that we should like — but that we have learned to recognize that others will fight and die to make a different world, with equal sincerity or belief. Deep-seated preferences can not be argued about — you can not argue a man into liking a glass of beer — and therefore, when differences are sufficiently far reaching, we try to kill the other man rather than let him have his way. But that is perfectly consistent with admitting that, so far as appears, his grounds are just as good as ours.

The jurists who believe in natural law seem to me to be in that naïve state of mind that accepts what has been familiar and accepted by them and their neighbors as something that must be accepted by all men everywhere. No doubt it is true that, so far as we can see ahead, some arrangements and the rudiments of familiar institutions seem to be necessary elements in any society that may spring from our own and that would seem to us to be civilized — some form of permanent association between the sexes — some residue of property individually owned — some mode of binding oneself to specified future conduct — at the bottom of all, some protection for the person. But without speculating whether a group is imaginable in which all but the last of these might disappear and the last be subject to qualifications that most of us would abhor, the question remains as to the *Ought* of natural law.

It is true that beliefs and wishes have a transcendental basis in the sense that their foundation is arbitrary. You can not help entertaining and feeling them, and there is an end of it. As an arbitrary

fact people wish to live, and we say with various degrees of certainty that they can do so only on certain
conditions. To do it they must eat and drink.
That necessity is absolute. It is a necessity of less
degree but practically general that they should live
in society. If they live in society, so far as we can
see, there are further conditions. Reason working
on experience does tell us, no doubt, that if our wish
to live continues, we can do it only on those terms.
But that seems to me the whole of the matter. I see
no *a priori* duty to live with others and in that way,
but simply a statement of what I must do if I wish
to remain alive. If I do live with others they tell me
that I must do and abstain from doing various things
or they will put the screws on to me. I believe that
they will, and being of the same mind as to their
conduct I not only accept the rules but come in time
to accept them with sympathy and emotional affirma-
tion and begin to talk about duties and rights. But
for legal purposes a right is only the hypostasis of a
prophecy — the imagination of a substance support-
ing the fact that the public force will be brought to
bear upon those who do things said to contravene it
— just as we talk of the force of gravitation account-
ing for the conduct of bodies in space. One phrase
adds no more than the other to what we know without it. No doubt behind these legal rights is the
fighting will of the subject to maintain them, and the
spread of his emotions to the general rules by which
they are maintained; but that does not seem to
me the same thing as the supposed *a priori* discern-

ment of a duty or the assertion of a preëxisting right. A dog will fight for his bone.

The most fundamental of the supposed preëxisting rights — the right to life — is sacrificed without a scruple not only in war, but whenever the interest of society, that is, of the predominant power in the community, is thought to demand it. Whether that interest is the interest of mankind in the long run no one can tell, and as, in any event, to those who do not think with Kant and Hegel it is only an interest, the sanctity disappears. I remember a very tender-hearted judge being of opinion that closing a hatch to stop a fire and the destruction of a cargo was justified even if it was known that doing so would stifle a man below. It is idle to illustrate further, because to those who agree with me I am uttering commonplaces and to those who disagree I am ignoring the necessary foundations of thought. The *a priori* men generally call the dissentients superficial. But I do agree with them in believing that one's attitude on these matters is closely connected with one's general attitude toward the universe. Proximately, as has been suggested, it is determined largely by early associations and temperament, coupled with the desire to have an absolute guide. Men to a great extent believe what they want to — although I see in that no basis for a philosophy that tells us what we should want to want.

Now when we come to our attitude toward the universe I do not see any rational ground for demanding the superlative — for being dissatisfied unless we are assured that our truth is cosmic truth, if there is such a thing — that the ultimates of a little creature on this little earth are the last word of the unimaginable whole. If a man sees no reason for believing that significance, consciousness and ideals are more than marks of the finite, that does not justify what has been familiar in French sceptics; getting upon a pedestal and professing to look with haughty scorn upon a world in ruins. The real conclusion is that the part can not swallow the whole — that our categories are not, or may not be, adequate to formulate what we cannot know. If we believe that we come out of the universe, not it out of us, we must admit that we do not know what we are talking about when we speak of brute matter. We do know that a certain complex of energies can wag its tail and another can make syllogisms. These are among the powers of the unknown, and if, as may be, it has still greater powers that we can not understand, as Fabre in his studies of instinct would have us believe, studies that gave Bergson one of the strongest strands for his philosophy and enabled Maeterlinck to make us fancy for a moment that we heard a clang from behind phenomena — if this be true, why should we not be content? Why should we employ the energy that is furnished to us by the cosmos to defy it and shake our fist at the sky? It seems to me silly.

That the universe has in it more than we understand, that the private soldiers have not been told the plan of campaign, or even that there is one, rather than some vaster unthinkable to which every predicate is an impertinence, has no bearing upon our conduct. We still shall fight — all of us because we want to live, some, at least, because we want to realize our spontaneity and prove our powers, for the joy of it, and we may leave to the unknown the supposed final valuation of that which in any event has value to us. It is enough for us that the universe has produced us and has within it, as less than it, all that we believe and love. If we think of our existence not as that of a little god outside, but as that of a ganglion within, we have the infinite behind us. It gives us our only but our adequate significance. A grain of sand has the same, but what competent person supposes that he understands a grain of sand? That is as much beyond our grasp as man. If our imagination is strong enough to accept the vision of ourselves as parts inseverable from the rest, and to extend our final interest beyond the boundary of our skins, it justifies the sacrifice even of our lives for ends outside of ourselves. The motive, to be sure, is the common wants and ideals that we find in man. Philosophy does not furnish motives, but it shows men that they are not fools for doing what they already want to do. It opens to the forlorn hopes on which we throw ourselves away, the vista of the farthest stretch of human thought, the chords of a harmony that breathes from the unknown.

August, 1918.

www.ingramcontent.com/pod-product-compliance
Lightning Source LLC
Chambersburg PA
CBHW031236090426
42742CB00007B/214